Ray,

Thank you for everything that you have done for me. You have cared for me when I have been sick, and cheered for me when I have made even the smallest triumphs. You have been a provider, nurturer, cheer leader, and fan. Most of all, you have loved me. For all of these things, I thank you and love you.

Ray

Elegy for Iris

Previous Works by John Bayley

The Red Hat: A Novel

Tolstoy and the Novel

Shakespeare and Tragedy

The Short Story: Henry James to Elizabeth Bowen

Elegy for Iris

John Bayley

St. Martin's Press
New York

Portions of this work have appeared,
in altered form, in *The New Yorker.*

ELEGY FOR IRIS. Copyright © 1999 by John Bayley. All
rights reserved. Printed in the United States of America. No
part of this book may be used or reproduced in any manner
whatsoever without written permission except in the case of
brief quotations embodied in critical articles or reviews. For
information, address St. Martin's Press, 175 Fifth Avenue,
New York, N.Y. 10010.

Book design by Ellen R. Sasahara

Library of Congress Cataloging-in-Publication Data

Bayley, John.
   Elegy for Iris / John Bayley.
      p.   cm.
   ISBN 0-312-19864-7
   1. Murdoch, Iris—Marriage. 2. Bayley, John—Marriage.
3. Women novelists, English—20th century—Biography.
4. Women philosophers—Great Britian—Biography.
5. College teachers—Great Britian—Biography. 6. Married
people—Great Britain—Biography. 7. Alzheimer's disease—
Patients—Biography. 8. Critics—Great Britain—Biography.
9. University of Oxford—Biography. I. Title.
PR6063.U7Z583   1999
823'.914—dc21
[b]   98-40895
                                                 CIP

First Edition: January 1999

10 9 8

The following have kindly given permission to print their
photographs in this book: UPI/Corbis-Bettman (p. ix),
Jill Krementz (p. 1), and Peter Conradi (p. 223).

For Peter Conradi and James O'Neill

Contents

Then

Photograph © 1999 by Jill Krementz

A hot day. Stagnant, humid. By normal English standards, really hot, insufferably hot. Not that England has standards about such things anymore. Global warming, no doubt. But it's a commonplace about growing old that there seem to be no standards anymore. The dog days. With everything gone to the dogs.

Cheerless thoughts to be having on a pleasure jaunt, or what used to be one. For years now, we've usually managed a treat for ourselves on really hot days, at home in the summer. We take the car along the bypass road from Oxford, for a mile or two, and twist abruptly off on to the verge—quite a tricky feat with fast-moving traffic just behind. Sometimes there are hoots and shouts from passing cars which have had to brake at speed, but by that time we have jolted to a stop on the tussocky grass, locked the car, and crept through a gap in the hedge.

I remember the first time we did it, nearly forty-five

years ago. We were on bicycles then, and there was little traffic on the unimproved road. Nor did we know where the river was exactly; we just thought it must be somewhere there. And with the ardour of comparative youth, we wormed our way through the rank grass and sedge until we almost fell into it. Crouching in the shelter of the reeds, we tore our clothes off and slipped in like water rats. A kingfisher flashed past our noses as we lay soundlessly in the dark, sluggish current. A moment after we had crawled out and were drying ourselves on Iris's half-slip, a big pleasure boat chugged past within a few feet of the bank. The steersman, wearing a white cap, gazed intently ahead. Tobacco smoke mingled with the watery smell at the roots of the tall reeds.

I still have the half-slip, I rediscovered it the other day, bunched up at the back of a drawer, stiff with powdery traces of dry mud. It is faded to a yellowish colour, with a wrinkled ribbon, once blue, decorating the hem. Could a woman of our own time, who became my wife, have actually worn such a garment? It looks like something preserved from the wardrobe of Marie Antoinette. I never gave it back to Iris after that occasion, and I think she forgot all about it.

In any case, we were having a busy day that day. We had a lunchtime engagement we could not miss. By the time we had cycled back into Oxford and down Woodstock Road, we were as hot as we had been earlier that morning, before we had crawled through the dense green undergrowth and discovered the river. Still dripping with sweat, and making vague efforts to tidy our hair and clothes, we rang the bell of a flat in Belsyre Court. As we waited, we looked at each other expressionlessly, then burst at the same moment into a soundless fit of giggles.

Our host, who had been getting lunch, was quite a time coming to the door. He was a brilliant green-eyed young doctor named Maurice Charlton. When even younger, he had been a classics don at Hertford College, and considered one of the best in the university. So good at it, indeed, that he gave it up after three years and turned to medicine. He now held a research appointment at the Radcliffe Hospital. He was supposedly rather in love with Iris. That was why he had asked her to lunch. She had told him she was spending the morning with me—we were going to cycle out together to see Cassington church—and so asked if I could come, too.

He took it like a man. He had prepared a delicious lunch. The flat was not his own, but belonged to a rich older don at Balliol, with whom he may or may not have had an ambiguous relationship. He seemed to be able to borrow the flat at any time, for his friend lived mostly at the college when he wasn't away in Italy or Greece.

Fifty or so years ago, life in the university seemed more constricted and formal, but at the same time more comfortable and relaxed. For us, in those days, there was no paradox involved. We maintained public standards and conventions almost without being conscious of them, while leading our own private lives. We worked very hard—at least Iris did; I was more naturally indolent.

Maurice Charlton probably worked harder than either of us, or than both of us put together, I should say. But he was totally relaxed, his green eyes sparkling, and had a delightful air—as soon as he saw us—of collusion in something or other: what he had been doing, what we had been doing. This intimate feel, as if we could become naughty children together any moment, was enhanced by the sombre dignity of the flat, which was full of rare books, good furniture, glass. I still remember the long-stemmed green and white wineglasses from which we drank a great deal of very cold hock. I think it was the white wine people usually drank in those days.

I feel admiration now for the way Charlton must have apprehended that Iris and I had been up to something together, and how he not only took it in his stride but encouraged us in some way to include him. We had never got to Cassington church, we said. It had been far too hot. We had cycled back in an exhausted state, and it was wonderful to be there in the cool, drinking the wine. We both said something like this without looking at each other. Iris jumped to her feet to go over and kiss Maurice, and it seemed just the right and spontaneous act, making all three of us laugh: we two men laughing both at and with Iris as she gazed delightedly round the dark and, as it seemed, rather mysteriously grand flat, as if she were

Alice in Wonderland on the threshold of a new series of adventures.

As we sat laughing and eating—I remember lobster and the delicious garlic mayonnaise our host had made—I was conscious of my soaking trouser pocket, where Iris's undergarment reposed, rolled up. I hoped the wet wouldn't get on the dining room chair, which was covered in some sort of damask. As lunch went hilariously on, we seemed more and more like a family. Through a bewitching miasma of hock, I was conscious of Iris as a kind sister, fond of both her brothers, equally close to them. Maurice had the air of a brother, but he also looked like a sort of patriarch as he sat grinning benignly at the head of the table.

Maurice Charlton died young, of cancer, I believe, more than twenty years ago. My impression is that he never married, but I may be wrong about that. He certainly looked at Iris with his green eyes as if he liked her very much. It was possible he had borrowed the flat and prepared the lunch with a purpose, and that my presence had thwarted his plans for the afternoon. In that case, I admire his behaviour all the more, at this distance in time. He carried off perfectly what might well have been a frustrating situation for him.

I mention the lunch with Maurice Charlton, and that enchanted Sunday morning when Iris and I had our first swim together, because I remember it all very vividly, not because it had any great importance in itself. Although I had met Charlton a few times, and admired him, that lunch was probably our only social occasion together. He continued to work in Oxford, but we lost touch which is why I don't know what happened to him later, except that he was a distinguished man when he died. It was typical of my relations with Iris at that time that I had very little idea of the other people in her life, or what they might mean to her. That was probably due to the ecstatic egoism of falling in love for the first time. For me, it was the first time, though I was not exactly young. Iris was thirty-four, Maurice Charlton about the same age. I was twenty-eight. Difference in age, which means a good deal at school and not much in later years, was only a part of the atmosphere of that lunch party, because we seemed for the moment like a family. And a family takes such differences in age for granted.

But, as I say, I still had very little idea of the other people in Iris's life, or what they meant to her. That was instinctive on her part, I think, rather than deliberate, as privacy pervaded all kinds of relationships. An "open" society is what we aim for now, or say we aim for, as an enhancement of our all being more classless and democratic. We were not consciously undemocratic, I think, in the fifties, but we took private life for granted. That was particularly true in Oxford, still an academic society, in which one could be on good terms with a large number of people, meeting them most days in college, at dinner in hall, or in lecture rooms and laboratories, without having any idea of how they were situated domestically, or socially, or sexually. Other people's lives might have seemed intriguing, which was part of the fun of privacy, but they remained what was on the whole an accepted and comfortable blank.

By some emotional paradox, being in love made me, at least at first, more incurious about this, not less. Iris existed for me as a wonderful and solitary being, first seen about six months before, bicycling slowly and rather laboriously past a window in St. Antony's College, where I was living. Trying to work, and gazing idly out at the passing scene on Woodstock Road, now intolerably full of traffic but a comparatively quiet thoroughfare then, I noted the lady on the bicycle (she seemed at once to me more of a lady than a girl) and wondered who she was and whether I would ever meet her. Perhaps I fell in love. Certainly it was in the innocence of love that I indulged the momentary fantasy that nothing had ever happened to her: that she was simply bicycling about, waiting for me to arrive. She was not a woman with a past or an unknown present.

For me she was a woman without a past, or a present.

She was looking both absent and displeased. Maybe because of the weather, which was damp and drizzly. Maybe because her bicycle was old and creaky and hard to propel. Maybe because she hadn't yet met me? Her head was down, as if she were driving on thoughtfully towards some goal, whether emotional or intellectual. I remember a friend saying playfully, perhaps a little maliciously, after she first met Iris, "She is like a little bull."

It's true in a way, although I have never seen it, because of course I have never seen her objectively. But if each of us resembles some sort of animal or bird, as our personalised bestiary emblem, then I can see that Iris could indeed be a small bull. Not unfriendly, but both resolute and unpredictable, looking reflectively out from under lowered brows as it walks with head down towards you.

In her first published novel, *Under the Net*, it is remarked of the leading female character that she never lets on to any one of her friends just how closely bound she is to all the rest of them. Few of them even know one another. That was true of Iris. Naturally enough, it made quite a difference to the heroine of the novel, but it has never made any difference to Iris. She always used to write back to fans who had written to her. Careful, long, intelligent letters, directed to a person, not just to a fan. They were real letters, even though she had never met, or probably would never meet, the person to whom she was writing. I have to try to write letters back to her fans now, and, naturally enough, I can't do it like that; although from their letters, and their attitude towards their adored author, I see why one of them at once replied, after Iris had written to him, that he felt now they had become "pals for life."

Like so much to do with our emotions, the egoism of

love has something absurd about it, though something touching, as well. It was certainly absurd that I should have taken for granted in those days that Iris was pure spirit, so to speak, devoted to philosophy and to her job, leading a nunlike existence in her little room in college, devoid of all the dissimulations and wonderings and plottings and plannings that I took for granted in myself. She was a superior being, and I knew that superior beings just did not have the kind of mind that I had.

Besides, there had been something almost supernatural about the way I had actually met her, after I had seen her riding past the window on her bicycle. The following day, I had encountered Miss Griffiths in the street, outside the Examination School, where university lectures were given. A diminutive figure, she was just taking off her billowing black gown, preparatory to mounting her own bicycle and cycling home to St. Anne's College. She had been lecturing on *Beowulf.* Miss Griffiths had had a soft spot for me ever since my viva—the face-to-face-oral exam—when she had congratulated me on my essay on Chaucer's *Knight's Tale,* even though she caught me out on a minor question of Anglo-Saxon syntax. After I had obtained my degree, she had followed my career, such as it was, with benevolent interest, and now she seized me by the arm as I walked past, enquiring how things were going. In fact, things were barely going at all, as I had no proper job and was staying on sufferance in the newly founded St. Antony's College, where I was supposed to act as a tutor and guide to a few ebullient Frenchmen and Americans who had come to study science or politics there.

St. Antony's at that time was a study in itself, but its principal interest for me now, and in memory, was its proximity to St. Anne's College, an institution designed at the time solely for women students, although, like most other colleges, it has since become co-educational. Out of the deference I felt for an older and senior member of the English faculty, I walked a few yards that morning beside Miss Griffiths, who showed no immediate disposition to mount her bicycle and be off. I think she wanted to enjoy reminiscing for a moment about the exam and the viva—like most dons, she was vain about her examination exploits and technique—and to recall with the pleasure of generosity her discernment about the good points of my Chaucer essay, as well as to remind me, with the pleasure of superior knowledge, about my errors in Old English grammar. Having done those things, she suddenly asked me if I would care to come to her college room for a drink that evening. I was happy to accept.

Although it was just across the road from St. Antony's, I had never been into St. Anne's, which I regarded as an all-female province, likely to be virtually out of bounds to males and male students. I wasn't wholly wrong about this. Incredible as it may seem today, there were then fairly strict rules governing the conduct of men who had the nerve and temerity to go visiting in these female strongholds. They had to remain in the public parts of the college, and the girls were not allowed to receive them in their rooms. The matter was, in any case, of little or no interest to me. Students like myself, who had been in the army at the end of the war, were older than the new generation of undergraduates, whom they were sometimes employed temporarily to in-struct, owing to the post-war shortage of teachers. Oxford at the time seemed to me like a school; apart from having to teach a few of its younger denizens, I took no account of them. The cinema was my resort for relaxation and refuge, and cinemas were cinemas in those days. In the afternoon, they were churchlike spaces dense with tobacco smoke, in-habited by couples, or by solitary worshippers motionless in the darkness, illuminated from time to time by the glowing tip of a cigarette.

The idea of a drink with funny, wizened little Miss Griffiths—I imagine she was only a year or two over forty, but if I thought of it at all, I thought of her past the boundaries of age—was a decidedly agreeable one. Drinks were drinks in those days, just as cinemas were cinemas, and I had heard that Miss Griffiths—Elaine, as I afterwards came to know her—liked a good strong drop of gin. Be-sides, it could only be a good thing to be on social terms with a senior member of the English faculty, to which I aspired in time to belong.

All such prudential considerations vanished when I presented myself at six o'clock that evening. Miss Griffiths was just finishing a tutorial, and as I knocked on the door, a young girl in a scholar's gown came out, dropping her eyes demurely at the sight of a man standing there. I barely glanced at her, for through the open doorway I had caught sight of the bicycle person—the woman? the girl? the lady?—standing and talking to some unseen character, with a well-filled glass in her hand.

She looked different from the bicycle lady, naturally enough. This was a social scene and she was not wearing an old macintosh. Her short fairish hair, unkempt and roughly fringed on the forehead, looked both healthy and greasy, as it still does. Later on, I was to cut and shampoo it for her now and then, but at that distant time, she hardly bothered. Indeed, I have the feeling that women then—certainly academic women—were nothing like so attentive to appearances as they are today, when girls may look like scarecrows, but only of set purpose. Slovenliness in those days was next to seriousness, at least in university circles. It was rare, however, for women in those circles to wear trousers. Iris had on a worn and grubby tweed skirt, rather overlong and ungainly. I noticed her legs were short and robust, clad in brown cotton stockings. Nylons were still uncommon in the early fifties.

This woman certainly had a serious look, and it dawned on me that my bicycle lady, who this clearly was, must be an academic of some sort. That gave me an immediate feeling of despondency. Just as my fantasy when I first saw her was that she had neither a past with others nor a future without me, so now I was reluctant to feel that she could be anything so commonplace as a university don. It placed her; and I disliked the idea that she should be placed, even by myself. At the same time, I was heartened by her general appearance, and its total absence of anything that for me in those days constituted sex appeal. There was nothing so conventional as that about this woman. She was not "a girl," and she had no girlish attractions. That made the fact that I was in love with her much more exciting; and it also seemed highly satisfactory, for what, as I instantly realised, was a rather ignoble reason. Since she had no obvious female charms, she was not likely to appeal to other men.

Why I was so convinced at first that there was nothing sexually attractive about Iris is a complete mystery. Other people, of both sexes, certainly didn't think so. It was my naïve and now inexplicable assumption that she could appeal only to me, and to no one else, that stopped me seeing how fearfully, how almost diabolically attractive everyone else found her. They knew more about such things, I suppose.

"Ah, there you are, John. I may call you John, mayn't I?" Miss Griffiths gave a characteristic small giggle. "Meet Miss Ady, and Miss Murdoch. Iris, this is one of the more promising young ones in the English school. Very good results in finals. I caught him out over Old English grammar, his weaker side, I fear, but he did a beautiful piece on the *Knight's Tale*."

That bloody *Knight's Tale*. Was I never going to hear

the end of it? Iris Murdoch gave me a kindly look, said "Hullo," and continued talking to Miss Ady. Miss Griffiths handed me a glass, from which I at once took a desperate swig. I coughed, and felt myself going scarlet in the face. It was a strong gin and French, the English equivalent of an American martini—no ice in those days, of course. Although I had become accustomed to strong drink in the army, I had barely touched it during my student days. I had lost the taste, and besides, it was too expensive. Iris and her friends drank a lot of it, and for me that was the first of many.

I resented Miss Griffiths referring to me as one of the "young ones" in the English school. I was not particularly young. Were these women so much older? For I now saw, and with a certain satisfaction in spite of my embarrassed state, that I was the only man in the room. There were four or five women at the party, and as a result of my confusion and fit of coughing, they were all looking at me in a kindly way. Obviously, they took it for granted that I was a clueless young creature, and that it behoved them, as sophisticated women of the university world, to be nice to me.

But they all seemed to want to talk to Iris. I was left with Miss Griffiths, who was herself looking at Iris with a wistful expression which even at that awkward moment surprised me.

What I had not the slightest idea of was that St.

Anne's, at that time, was a hotbed of emotion. The dons in general were not professional lesbians, so to speak. Many were, or had been, married; they led domestic as well as academic lives. They were nice, clever donnish women, hardworking and conscientious, but a lot of feelings ran beneath the surface, and I had the impression later on that they seemed to catch such emotional intensities from one another, like germs or fashions. Some time afterwards, I heard the novelist Elizabeth Bowen, who had become a great friend of Iris, describe an acquaintance as "an old-fashioned lesbian of the highest type." Elizabeth Bowen's inimitable stutter on the L made this sound both grand and comic. The ladies of St. Anne's were not grand exactly, but their type, I'm sure, was both high-minded and sound. Whatever they felt among themselves was never communicated to their pupils, nor were their pupils ever roped in. I had Iris's word for that, much later on. Any suggestion that one of their girl charges had been made advances to, or encouraged in a crush for one of them of her own, would have been universally frowned upon.

In any case, I had simplistic ideas about sex at that time, supposing that everybody must be either one thing or the other. When it dawned on me, a short time after the party, that they had all seemed to be in love with Iris, I had a sensation of despair. If they all felt like that about her, didn't it follow that she must feel the same about them? at least about one or two of them? Iris was, as I realised later, much too kind to discourage affection, even yearning affection, but she was apt to draw a line if a woman expressed it too physically.

Miss Griffiths seized her colleague in the English department, a lady with a resounding Polish surname, introduced me to her, and made thankfully off to join the little group around Iris. I saw the dashing Miss Ady, dark-haired and with beautiful eyes, tap Iris playfully on the wrist while emphasising some point to her, perhaps about their teaching, for Miss Ady, as I afterwards discovered, taught politics and economics, while Iris handled the philosophy. The Polish-sounding lady, who wore a black coat with a scarlet lining and seemed to me equally dashing, departed from the party's air of cheerful frivolity by asking in an intense and, as I thought, foreign tone a serious question about my "research." My reply failed to carry conviction to myself, or, it seemed, to her. Her gaze was forgiving but also a little reproachful, I felt.

Instead of talking to the person I had fallen in love with, or even meeting her properly, I seemed destined, as a result of Miss Griffith's heaven-sent invitation, only to make a decidedly mediocre impression on another of my senior faculty teachers. I discovered afterwards that Miss Griffith's colleague was well known for her air of severity among pupils and colleagues alike, but that she was in fact a kind as well as a devoted teacher, married to a Polish officer during the war. She was herself from Yorkshire and bore some sturdy name like Sidebotham, but she preferred to retain the more romantic surname she had acquired from a husband from whom she was now separated.

I never managed to talk to Iris at that party, although at a later stage, and after two or three other men had arrived, I hovered vainly near her, seeming to exchange words with every other person present. After a few of those gins and Frenches, I felt I could have made a good impression, but no opportunity arose, and Iris excused herself and departed well before the gathering dispersed, amid much conviviality.

The god of chance seemed, however, to be in a long-suffering mood. After seeing me fail to make anything of the unexpected coincidence he had arranged, he patiently set to work yet again. Asked to supper three weeks later by a couple who knew a friend I had not seen for years, I discovered that Iris was my sole fellow guest. But I soon felt that I was failing again. Although friendly and not at all shy, Iris was not a helpful conversationalist. I offered openings and raised points in what I hoped was an interesting way, but she smiled kindly and did not respond. Like many philosophers in Oxford, she had the habit of considering what was said in a silence that was judicious, almost sibylline. She turned my poor little point over as if asking, what exactly does this mean? and if she decided it indeed meant very little, she was too polite to say so. Mutual enthusiasm failed wholly to take fire. I was comforted to observe that our host, a lively law fellow who was clearly hoping to pump Iris about the fashions and topics of contemporary philosophy, fared no better than I did. At the same time, I resented his air of knowing her so well that he could often appeal to jokes or thoughts they had in common, or jolly times she had shared with him and his family. My solitary bicyclist, I felt, should not have been happy to go on holiday with these people. I became prey to the jealousy I was often to suffer from in the months to come. I began to see that there was a lot that Iris had done—must have done, during the long years I had not known her—which I could not approve of, which was not suited to the image my fancy had officiously formed of her.

Quite abruptly, and early, Iris said she must go home. Our hosts looked disappointed. For the first time, I managed to seize the moment, and I said regretfully that I must go, too. Our hosts looked more philosophical about that, for it was Iris they had wanted, almost greedily, to stay. I was surprised by this, because as a guest she had seemed to take very little trouble, if any, even though she had disseminated around her what seemed an involuntary aura of beneficence and goodwill. But she had not risen at all to the law fellow's blandishments, his attempts to interest her in his ideas and persuade her to set forth her own. To have observed this gave me some satisfaction.

Good nights having been said and the front door closed, we unlocked our bicycles and set out together into the damp, mild Oxfordshire night. My lights were in order; her front one dimmed and wavered, on the verge of final extinction, and I respectfully urged her to bicycle on the inside and to keep as close as possible to my own illumination. Then we rode in silence, and I assumed it was to break it that she asked me in her friendly way if I had ever thought of writing a novel. It was a wholly unexpected question, but for once I had an answer ready. Yes, I had. Indeed, I was writing one, or trying to write one, at that moment.

This was not strictly true. It was nearly true, and I determined on the spot and as we rode along to make it true that very night. The wife of my professor, a sweet, tremulous woman whose father had been a well-known critic, had asked me the same question about a month before. I had given her much the same disingenuous reply; and by way of encouragement, she had suggested with a gentle smile that we should both try to write one—she wouldn't mind having a go herself, she said. With some laughter, we had made a pact to see who could finish first. I had since attempted to gather a few ideas, and I had thought of an opening for the first chapter, but I had done nothing.

But why should Miss Murdoch ask me about novels? It must be to indulge me and get me to talk about myself, I thought, for clearly she, a philosopher, could have no interest in the matter. She probably never read them; far too busy with higher things. I made some deprecating comment to this effect, and the next moment could hardly believe my ears. Miss Murdoch said that she herself had written a novel, which was shortly to be published.

I felt overwhelmed with awe and admiration. So this extraordinary creature had thrown off a novel, as if negligently, in the intervals of a busy life of teaching and practising philosophy. What could it be about? I ventured to ask. "You mustn't tell anyone," she said, stopping her bicycle and putting a foot to the ground. She looked straight at me, speaking lightly but also very seriously. "I don't want anyone to know."

I gave a fervent promise. I would not reveal her secret to a soul. I was overwhelmed with joy that she could have confided this secret to me. She must for some extraordinary reason not only have complete trust and confidence in me, although we had scarcely met each other, but with swift and masterful decision have concluded that I was just the right person—the one who ought to know. Why? I could only marvel, and be aware that my heart was bounding with gratitude and joy. As well as with love, of course. I really felt as we stood there in the dark road, half on and half off our bicycles, that this wonderfully intuitive and perspicacious being had seen right down inside me, liked what she saw, judged it worthy of her fullest trust. Perhaps even loved what she saw? Could she have known that I had fallen in love with her, and have decided like a philosopher, on a ground of reason and good sense, that she was also in love with me?

As I came to know her, it soon occurred to me to wonder if she had not in fact revealed this secret of her novel to quite a number of people. Maurice Charlton seemed to know about it, so did the Johnsons—the law fellow and his wife. Most of her many friends in London must have known about it, too. What is more, some of them had even read it—in manuscript, in Iris's own hand-writing. The Johnsons had read it, as they took good care to let me know when they saw that I was becoming friendly with Iris and that I met her at places other than their own house. For, of course, there is something highly displeasing about one's friend getting to know one's other friends without telling one, as La Rochefoucauld might have said.

Iris's instinct here was essentially a kindly one. She wanted to have her friends, each of them, for themselves; she wanted them to know her in the same pristine way. No groups, no sets. No comparing of notes between two about a third. This desire that each of her relationships should be special and separate, as innocent as in the Garden of Eden, was of great significance to Iris. Since what she felt about each of them was totally genuine and with-out guile, it could have no relation to any other person. There was no graduation among her friendships, no com-parisons made. Each was whole in itself.

I had, in fact, misunderstood her. No doubt because I was in love with her. Like all lovers, I suppose, I wished to be a special case in quite the wrong sense. To be "the one." By telling me she didn't want anyone to know of the novel's existence, I felt she was singling me out. But it was a routine precaution, almost a formula. Her friends could know, should know. But she didn't want the matter talked about, either among them or in a wider context.

Naturally enough, the precaution functioned only on the higher level; as a practical measure, it was ineffective. That was brought home to me when I realised that many people who knew Iris were talking about her novel. I did not resent the fact, nor did I feel in the least disillusioned. I was so much in love (or so I told myself) that I saw clearly and without dismay that Iris was not in the least in love with me. She had told me about her novel as an act of kindness, seeing that I was interested in such matters. She had told me precisely because she was not in love with me; not because she was, or was beginning to be. We had become friends; that was all.

Friendship meant a great deal to her. It was a sign of how much she valued her friends that she kept them so separate. To me, it meant nothing, or at least very little. For me, friendship was a question of contextual bonding, as I believe psychologists call it. I had met people at school and in the army whose company was agreeable at that time and in that place; it did not occur to me to ask whether or how much I valued them as friends. When the situation changed, so did my acquaintance, so that I retained nobody who could be called "an old friend." The idea of Iris wishing, or at least being prepared, to regard me as one of her friends did not appeal to me in the least.

Nonetheless, that was the way it had to be. We met about once a fortnight. We both disliked the telephone—that was something about her I discovered early on—so communicated by note. Such notes were exchanged via the college messenger, by what was known as "pigeon post." I disliked pubs, but there was no alternative to suggesting we should meet in a pub. Iris liked them and had her favourites among them, as I soon found out. I also disliked eating out, which in Oxford at that time was expensive, at least in terms of my meagre income, and usually bad. We sometimes ate at cafés or in bars. I became a gloomy connoisseur of their shortcomings.

I suppose we got to know each other, and talked a good deal, but I don't remember what about. I know there was never anything so electrifying as the pause on our bicycles had been, when we confronted each other in the darkness and she told me not to mention the existence of her novel. After we had remounted, I enquired diffidently about the content of this work. What was it about? How had she come to write it? She made no direct reply, but, much more excitingly, she said with emphasis how important it was for any narration to have something for everybody, as she put it. This was a discovery she had made. I was surprised but also impressed by the simplicity of the idea, and the force with which she spoke of it, slowly and reflectively.

"A bit like Shakespeare," I suggested.

"Well, perhaps, yes."

I have often pondered that moment, wondering whether her words really meant anything very much, or were they, for me, part of the unwitting electricity of falling in love? Falling in love on my side, that is. For her, it was obvious, and still is: The words were grave, sober, and true. She wanted, through her novels, to reach all possible readers, in different ways and by different means: by the excitement of her story, its pace and its comedy, through its ideas and its philosophical implications, through the numinous atmosphere of her own original and created world—the world she must have glimpsed as she considered and planned her first steps in the art of fiction.

In the early summer, St. Antony's College gave a modest dance, a much simpler affair than the big college dances—"commem balls," as they are called—which are held after the end of the summer term and go on all night long. A double ticket for such an elaborate affair might then cost as much as thirty pounds, and nowadays it is of course far more expensive. The St. Antony's hop was not much more than a couple of guineas. Although I was not by training or by temperament a dancing man, I determined to go nonetheless, and to ask Iris if she would accompany me. I bought the tickets, with the idea that I could probably resell them if I had to. But to my astonishment, and not altogether to my delight, Iris accepted the invitation with alacrity. This caused a further range of complications in my heart. There were also practical problems which might well follow. Other people, my colleagues at St. Antony's, would ask her to dance, and suppose one of them were to fall in love with her, or she with him? (It did not then occur to me that she might equally well become attached to one of the girls who would be present.)

There were other and even more pressing practical considerations. Where would I take her to dine before the dance, which was a simple nine-to-midnight affair. I had no money to spare, but I felt it must be somewhere reasonably good, not just a pub or a café. In the end, I chose the Regency Restaurant, which advertised itself in the *Oxford Mail* as serving "probably the best food in Oxfordshire." This Delphic pronouncement could hardly be discredited, if one came to think about it, but, naturally enough, I did not think about it. At half past six, I went to collect Iris in her college room, waiting outside the door after I had knocked, and a voice from within had requested me to hang on a minute. While waiting, I speculated what she would look like, what she would be wearing. I assumed and rather hoped it would be something dark, preferably black, suited to the person of mature years and sober disposition whom I still assumed and hoped her to be. Was it not these imagined qualities in her which had attracted me so strongly when I first saw her on her bicycle?

The door opened. An apparition in what seemed a sort of flame-coloured brocade stood before me. I felt in some way scandalised: dazzled but appalled at the same time. All my daydreams, my illusions and preconceptions about the bicycle woman seemed to have torn away and vanished back into a past which I would still very much have preferred to be inhabiting, given the choice. But I had no choice. The person before me was exactly the same as the one riding the bicycle. I still thought her face homely and kindly, not in any conventional sense pretty or attractive, even if it was a strong face in its own blunt-featured, snub-nosed way; and for me, it was always mysterious, too. But now I was seeing it as other people saw it. Although her person was in no way conventional itself, its trappings, so to speak, were now conventional. They disappointed me sadly, for they seemed the sort of things that any girl would wear—a silly girl who had not the taste to choose her clothes carefully.

Well, there was nothing to be done about that. Iris seemed preoccupied. Perhaps about her face, which she now dabbed with powder, or her hair, or some hitch in her underwear. She wriggled and pulled her dress about uneasily, as if she were unfamiliar with whatever lay underneath it, and therefore uncomfortable. Or perhaps she was preoccupied with the thought of what she might be doing somewhere else, with some other friends. She seemed preoccupied with anything and everything except me, about whom she appeared as unconscious as she had been when she rode past under my window. She didn't look at me, but she did take my hand in an absent way as we went out to the entrance of the St. Anne's house where she lived; and that cheered me as much as the awkward movements she had made.

The restaurant was a disaster. I can't remember what we ate, but it was very nasty, and the waiter was both gloomy and supercilious. He seemed preoccupied with quite other things than us, just as Iris had seemed to be preoccupied with other things than with me when I met her at the door of her room. Even the bottle of red wine which we drank was tasteless and bad. But as the dreadful dinner went on—there were very few other people in the restaurant—our spirits for some reason appeared to rise amazingly. We began to giggle and to talk in whispers about the few other sepulchral-looking diners. At the end of the meal, Iris excused herself and went out to the ladies' room, leaving me to pay the bill. I did this and added an enormous tip, which the waiter paid no attention to when he came to collect the money. I felt discouraged by this, because I was hoping in some way for a friendly word, and perhaps a benevolent query about where we were going. The saturnine waiter simply took up the money and departed, as absent and intent on other matters as ever. Perhaps his wife had just left him. If the Regency Restaurant had "probably" the best food in Oxfordshire, it had certainly the worst service.

I was left to contemplate the green and white stripes of the wallpaper, a kind of wallpaper then very much in fashion and one which I have hated ever since. Iris was

29

away for an age. When she finally came out of the ladies' room, she was transformed again. Now she looked like a doll, a Watteau china doll with incongruously schoolgirl hair. She had lathered her mouth with lipstick, which she now proceeded in an amateurish way to kiss at with a scrap of paper taken from her bag. I noticed handwriting on this paper, and I wondered if it could be a love letter, an urgent note from some admirer. But at least she did not put it back in her bag; she just crumpled it up and left it on the table.

It was drizzling outside. By the time I had managed to find a taxi, it was well after half past nine. The dance was in full swing when we got to St. Antony's.

I felt, in a resigned way now, that I was taking some quite different girl to the dance: one with bright red lips, covered inexpertly with a substance which made them look thick and unattractive, not that I had ever noticed them particularly in the first place. This strange girl would no doubt appeal to my St. Antony colleagues and their friends. That would be something anyway, I thought, be-cause I had no wish myself to spend the evening dancing with her. My one wish now was that the whole thing should be over as soon as possible, and I was extremely glad that the dance was scheduled to end at midnight.

St. Antony's was a former Anglican convent, built around 1870. A steep flight of stone steps led down to the crypt below the nuns' chapel, now the library, in which the dance was to be held. As we went down, Iris trod on her long dress, slipped, and slid inelegantly down a few steps on her behind. People descending before and after us rushed to help me help her get up. I found myself entertaining the unworthy thought that she might have sprained her ankle—not badly, but enough to incapacitate her for the evening. She would not wish to stay on the sidelines, and I could take her home. Perhaps we could go on talking in her room.

But Iris was not hurt at all. She got up and smiled while the others brushed her down amid laughter and joking. The ice was already broken as far as fellow dancers were concerned. We moved onto the dance floor among a crowd of people all of whom seemed to be chatting to us and to one another. I made a few introductions. Iris seemed to have made new friends already. Her manner was no longer quiet and withdrawn. I made unconfident gestures indicative of asking her to dance, and we assumed the appropriate semi-embrace.

My dancing was indeed unconfident. I had sometimes enjoyed it at hops in the nightclubs or on weekends in the army, when already more than a little drunk. Now, when we moved, there seemed no correlation among the different parts of our bodies. Iris smiled at me encouragingly, then a few seconds later relinquished me and began to execute arm twirlings and arabesques on her own. She looked ungainly and rather affected, but touchingly naïve at the same time. It seemed clear that she knew no more about dancing à deux than I did; but when we brushed accidentally against a dancing couple a few seconds later and the man turned with a smile and seized hold of her, she melted into him at once and the pair swung off together in perfect unison. The girl whom the man had been with did not look a bit pleased, but she, too, had no choice but to smile at me as we began to revolve in some sort of way. I felt the dance was already going against me and that success, whatever it might have consisted of, had already gone beyond recall.

The band gave a flourish and then stopped. Iris came back to me at once, looking happy and relaxed. She asked about my room in the college, for she had not yet seen it. I asked if she would like to go up there for a minute, thinking of the bottle of champagne I had bought that morning and put in my cupboard along with two glasses. She said she would like to very much. I took her arm as we mounted the stone steps, in case she had another fall. My room was small and Spartan, containing only a bed, cupboard, table, and a wooden chair. But there was a gas fire, which I now turned on. I got the bottle and glasses out of the cupboard. As I put them down on the table, we fell into each other's arms.

It seemed as natural as it had been to take her arm when coming up the stairs, or for her to take my hand a minute when we had left her own room in St. Anne's. We never returned to the dance floor, but sat in my room until two in the morning. We talked without stopping. I had no idea I could talk like that, and I am sure she never knew she could, either. It was endless, childish chatter, and we put our faces together as we talked. I think Iris was accustomed only to talking properly, as it were: considering, pausing, modifying, weighing her words. To talk like a philosopher and a teacher. Now she babbled like a child. So did I. With arms around each other, kissing and rubbing noses (I said how much I loved her snub nose), we rambled on and on, seeming to invent on the spot, as we talked, a whole infantile language of our own. She put her head back and laughed at me incredulously from time to time, and I think we both felt incredulous. She seemed to be giving way to some deep need of which she had been wholly unconscious: the need to throw away not only the manoeuvres and rivalries of intellect but also the emotional fears and fascinations, the power struggles and surrenders of adult loving.

She asked me endlessly about my childhood, and she told me about her own. She had been a happy child, attached equally to both her parents. I saw that they had doted on her, but it seemed in a very sensible way. Her father, who came from Belfast, was a minor civil servant, now on the verge of retirement. His salary had always been extremely modest, and he could never have afforded to send her to a good school, even with a scholarship, if he hadn't borrowed money. A cautious and prudent man, he had been as brave as a lion about this, and tears came into her eyes as she told me about the sacrifices her parents had made. But our talk was too happy and silly to remain long on the actualities of childhood. It was the atmosphere of it that we suddenly seemed to be sharing together, having rediscovered it mutually and miraculously in each other's presence. The dance and the dancing, the dinner we had eaten and all that seemed like ludicrous adult activities which we had put behind us.

I had a wish to rub my nose and lips along her bare arms. She made me take off my dinner jacket so that she could do the same to me.

"If we were married, we could do this all the time," I said, rather absurdly.

"We shall be doing it nearly all the time," she answered.

"Yes, but if—"

She stopped that by starting to kiss me properly. We remained locked together for a long time. The bottle of champagne remained unopened on the table.

Long, long afterwards, I was having to look through her manuscripts and papers to find some material requested by the publisher. In the back of an exercise book containing notes for a novel were what seemed to be a few entries, some dated, others random observations, comments on books, philosophers, people she knew, denoted only by initial. Some notes on pupils, too, and on points that had struck her in their work. One entry, dated June 3, 1954, read: "St. Antony's Dance. Fell down the steps, and seem to have fallen in love with J. We didn't dance much."

$\mathcal{T}wo$

We trailed *slowly* over the long field towards the river. The heat seemed worse than ever, although the sun, overcast, did not beat down as fiercely as it had done earlier in the day. The hay had been carried some time before, and the brownish surface of the field was baked hard and covered incongruously with molehills. The earth in them was like grey powder, and I wondered how the moles ever managed to find any sustenance as they tunnelled within it. A pair of crows flapped lazily away as we approached the riverbank. Crows are said to live a long time, and I wondered idly if they were the same birds we had seen there on our bathing visits over the years.

I wished we had managed to come earlier this fall, before the hay was cut, and when wildflowers—scabious, white archangel, oxeye daisies—stretched among the grass over the entire field. It was not a lush river field, probably because a bed of gravel lay just below the surface. There were big gravel ponds not far away, by the main road, but this field was a protected area, a plant and bird sanctuary of some kind. Not a fish sanctuary, however: There were sometimes a few fishermen about, who kept to themselves and remained almost invisible among the reeds.

Our own little nook was seldom occupied, though, and it was empty today, as usual. Once, we would have got our clothes off as soon as possible and slid silently into the water, as we had done on that first occasion. Now I had quite a struggle getting Iris's clothes off: I had managed to put her bathing-suit on at home, before we started. Her instinct nowadays seems to be to take her clothes off as infrequently as possible. Even in this horribly hot weather, it is hard to persuade her to remove trousers and jersey before getting into bed.

She protested, gently though vigorously, as I tugged off the outer layers. In her shabby old one-piece swimsuit (actually two-piece, with a separate skirt and tunic top), she was an awkward and anxious figure, her socks trailing round her ankles. She was obstinate about not taking these off, and I gave up the struggle. A pleasure barge chugged slowly past, an elegant girl in a bikini sunning herself on the deck, a young man in white shorts at the steering wheel. Both turned to look at us with a slight air of incredulity. I should not have been surprised if they had burst into guffaws of ill-mannered laughter, for we must have presented a comic spectacle—an elderly man struggling to remove the garments from an old lady, still with white skin and incongruously fair hair.

Alzheimer's sufferers are not always gentle: I know that. But Iris remains her old self in many ways. The power of concentration has gone, along with the ability to form coherent sentences and to remember where she is, or has been. She does not know she has written twenty-six remarkable novels, as well as her books on philosophy; received honourary doctorates from the major universities; become a Dame of the British Empire.... If an admirer or friend asks her to sign a copy of one of her novels, she looks at it with pleasure and surprise before laboriously writing her name and, if she can, theirs. "For Georgina Smith. For Dear Reggie..." It takes her some time, but the letters are still formed with care, and resemble, in a surreal way, her old handwriting. She is always anxious to oblige. And the old gentleness remains.

Once in the water, Iris cheered up a bit. It was almost too warm, hardly refreshing. But its old brown slow-flowing deliciousness remained, and we smiled happily at each other as we paddled quietly to and fro. Water lily leaves, with an occasional fat yellow flower, rocked gently at the passage of a pleasure boat. Small bright blue dragonflies hovered motionless above them. The water was deep, and cooler as we moved out from the bank, but we did not go out far. Looking down, I could see her muddy feet, still in their socks, moving in the brown depths. Tiny fish were inquisitively investigating her, and I could see and feel them round me, too, gently palpating the bare skin.

Once, if there had been little river traffic about, we would have swum at once the hundred yards or so across the river and back. Now it was too much trouble, and a possible producer of that omnipresent anxiety typical of Alzheimer's patients, which spreads to the one who looks after the sufferer. Not that it would have been dangerous; Iris still swims as naturally as a fish. Since we first entered the water here together, forty-four years ago now, we have swum in the sea, in lakes and rivers, pools and ponds, whenever we could and wherever we happened to be.

I recalled now a moment in Perth, Australia, when we managed to get into the Swan River, scrambling down a tiered concrete slope from a busy arterial road. The famous Swan brewery was just up at the broad river's next bend, and the water flowing past us was peculiar, to say the least, but we enjoyed our swim. We saw the faces of motorists going past up above, staring at us with surprise and, presumably, disapproval. In fact, there was a swimming pool at the hotel the university had put us into, but that would not have been the same thing. It was always fringed with strapping Australian girls sunning themselves. We never used it: I think we felt too shy.

Iris was never keen on swimming as such. She never swam fast and noisily or did fancy strokes. What she loved was being in the water. Twice she came quite close to drowning. I thought of that, with the anxiety that had now invaded both our lives, as we approached the riverbank again to scramble out. This had always been a more difficult and inelegant operation than slipping into the river, but it had never bothered us in the past. The river was as deep near the bank as in midstream, the bank itself undercut by the water's flow. It shelved a little in our own corner, the soft clay occasionally imprinted by the hooves of drinking cattle. I pulled myself out first and turned to help Iris. As she took my hands, her face contracted into that look of child-like dread which so often comes over it now, filling me, too, with worry and fear. Suppose her arm muscles failed her, and she slipped back into deep water, forgetting how to swim and letting water pour into her mouth as she opened it in a soundless appeal to me? I knew on the spot that we must never come to bathe here again.

The panic moment passed, but it had never existed for either of us at the time when, ten or fifteen years before, we had swum with a friend, the artist Reynolds Stone, off the Chesil Bank in Dorset. The Stones lived a few miles inland, and in summer we used to go down to the sea, to the great inshore curve that sweeps all the way from Portland Bill to Bridport and Lyme Regis. The tides have left a massive embankment of grey shingle there, graduated as if by hand from huge smooth pebbles at the Portland end to fine gravel twelve miles farther west. When a sea is running, it is a dangerous place, and even in calm weather, the swell and the suction of the undertow make it a tricky beach to go in from. Fearlessly gentle and absent-minded,

Reynolds Stone never mentioned any danger nor, apparently, was he aware of it. In we always went together, laughing and talking, and on one occasion Iris missed the pulse of the wave that carried us back onto the shingle and was sucked out again as it ebbed. Speaking of Piero or Cézanne, two of the artists he most admired, Reynolds noticed nothing; nor did I. Listening to him as we trod gingerly over the stones to where our clothes lay, I turned back to include Iris in what he was saying. She was not there. But in a moment, she was, and I helped her over the shingle while Reynolds stood gently and imperturbably conversing.

Only afterwards did she tell me of her moment of incredulous surprise and terror as she felt herself drawn back under the smooth sea. It was deep over her head, but she kept her mouth tightly shut by instinct, and in another moment, the next wave had brought her ashore. Had she panicked and swallowed water, the insidious undertow might well have carried her farther out and down; and then, easy swimmer that she was, she could have drowned in a few seconds.

She said nothing until we were in bed that night, and then she was not frightened, but full of curiosity and an excitement she wanted to share with me. "I'll put it in my next novel," she said. And she did.

After she had become well known, she never mentioned the novel she was working on in public; nor, I think, to her friends; scarcely to me, either. She would say something about it if I asked, but I soon had no habit of asking. One of the truest pleasures of marriage is solitude. Also the most deeply reassuring. I continued to do my own job, teaching English at the university, writing the odd critical study. Iris soon gave up St. Anne's—the emotional pressures in that community may have had something to do with it—and entered her own marvellous world of creation and intellectual drama, penetrating reflection, sheer literary excitement. Something for everybody, in fact—just as she had said as we first stood there that late evening beside our bicycles.

Occasionally, she used to ask me about some technical detail she wanted to include in a novel. Once, she enquired about automatic pistols—old army training made it easy to answer that one—sometimes about cars, or wine, or what would be a suitable thing for a certain character to eat. The hero of *The Sea, the Sea* required, so to speak, a very special diet, and I had fun suggesting all sorts of unlikely combinations to which he might be partial: oat bran and boiled onions, fried garlic and sardines, tinned mango and Stilton cheese. Some of these found their way into the novel; and when it won the coveted Booker Prize, one of the judges, who happened to be the distinguished philosopher A. J. Ayer, remarked in his prize-giving speech that he had much enjoyed everything in the novel except for the food.

Only to one of Iris's novels, and that was a long time ago, did I contribute a small section myself. It was in her fourth published novel, *The Bell*. For a reason I now forget, she asked me to read the first chapter, which has one of her most sibylline epigrammatic openings. She never used a typewriter, and in her first handwritten version, it read:

"Dora Greenfield left her husband because she was afraid of him. A year later she returned to him for the same reason." I was thrilled by this instant concision, as many a subsequent reader must have been, for the sentence remained substantially as quoted here. But as I read on, I began to feel an immediate inquisitiveness about young Dora Greenfield and her husband, Paul, which the early pages did not satisfy. So arresting were they, as characters, that I wanted to know a little more about them at once, to be given a hint by which to glimpse their potential. I said something of the sort to Iris, who said, "Okay, then, you write something for me." I think she may already have felt herself something of what I, as reader, was now feeling: our sympathy and intuition automatically intermingled.

At the time, I was trying to write a critical study, later titled *The Characters of Love*. I was bewitched by Henry James, who observed to a friend about one of the ladies in the novel he was writing that he could already take "a stiff examination" about her. Concerning such a personality, he had remarked, the author needs to supply a forewarning, "an early intimation of perspective." With this in mind, and highly flattered by Iris's suggestion, I set out to produce some idea of what *might* have happened to Dora and her husband, even if it was to have no part in the book, whose story I did not know as yet.

My idea was that, as a husband, he deeply needed and wanted children, even if he was not necessarily conscious of the fact, while she—much younger than her husband—

did not. I suggested that she had it in her to become "a prompt and opinionated mother" nonetheless, and that in their marriage this would be her only means of standing up to Paul. As it was, she was highly alarmed at the prospect of "becoming two people," though in her passive manner she had done nothing to inhibit conception. Indeed, she had come back to her husband like an apprehensive sleepwalker, still unconsciously depending on the ability of her fears to "whisk her instantly away, like a small animal." At the same time, she wanted him because she feared him, and because she knew he had it in him to allay her fears.

I produced something to this effect, and the results are on page ten of the novel as first printed, in a longish paragraph. It reads a bit too much in the Jamesian style, rather than merging into Iris's own inimitable originality, but nonetheless perhaps it does serve the function of suggesting alternatives and open spaces, which the scope and intent of the novel will not necessarily want to occupy. The novel's theme is the desire and pursuit, whether in true or false ways, of the spiritual life; and I had nothing to contribute to Iris's own marvellous feeling for what some people hunger for, and how, consequently, they behave. Indeed, I have very little understanding of the spiritual life, but that has never stopped me having a passionate appetite for Iris's novels, which I have usually read only after publication. *The Bell*, or at least the first piece of it, was an exception.

This sympathy for what was or might be going on in

Iris's mind, together with my inability to understand or enter into it, must have developed quite early on. The sympathy alone was what was needed in the case of our communing together over the beginning of *The Bell*, and I remember vividly my then-unexpected sense of it. Normally, it was something which by then I took for granted in our marriage, like air or water. Already we were beginning that strange and beneficent process in marriage by which a couple can, in the words of A. D. Hope, the Australian poet, "move closer and closer apart." The apartness is a part of the closeness, perhaps a recognition of it; certainly a pledge of complete understanding. There is nothing threatening or supervisory about such an understanding, nothing of what couples really mean when they say (or are alleged to say) to confidants or counsellors that their partner doesn't understand them. This usually means that one partner understands the other all too well, or that both do, and doesn't rejoice in the experience.

Still less is such apartness at all like what the French call *solitude à deux*, the inward self-isolation of a couple from anything outside their marriage. The solitude I have enjoyed in marriage, and, I think, Iris, too, is a little like having a walk by oneself and knowing that tomorrow, or soon, one will be sharing it with the other, or, equally perhaps, again having it alone. It is also a solitude that precludes nothing outside the marriage, and sharpens the sense of possible intimacy with things or people in the outside world.

Such sympathy in apartness takes time to grow, however, as well as being quite different by nature from that intoxicating sense of the strangeness of another being which accompanies the excitements of falling in love. The more I got to know Iris during the early days of our relationship, the less I understood her. Indeed, I soon began not to want to understand her. I was far too preoccupied at the time to think of such parallels, but it was like living in a fairy story—the kind with sinister overtones and not always a happy ending—in which a young man loves a beautiful maiden who returns his love but is always disappearing into some unknown and mysterious world, about which she will reveal nothing. Eventually, he makes some dire mistake, and she disappears for good. At this distance in time, that comparison seems more or less true, if a bit fanciful. Iris *was* always disappearing, to "see" her friends (I began to wonder and to dread, early on, what the word *see* might involve), about whom, unlike the girl in the fairy tale, she was always quite open. I knew their names; I imagined them; I never met them.

And there seemed to be so many of them. Persons who were, in a sense, in my own position. Iris seemed deeply and privately attached to them all. No doubt in all sorts of different ways. I could only hope that she did not talk to any of the others in quite the way that she talked to me, chattered childishly with me, kissed me. This Iris was so different from the grave being I had seen on the bicycle, or at a party in the public domain, that I sometimes wondered what had become of the woman I had fallen in love with, as I then supposed. Absurdly, I had imagined our future together as somehow equally grave, a wonderfully serious matter, and only the pair of us, of course, for no one else in the world was or would be in the least interested in either of us. We would simply be made for each other, and exist on that basis.

The happy childlike woman she had now turned into when she was with me was delightful, but also—as I sometimes could not stop myself wistfully thinking—fundamentally unreal, like the girl in the fairy story. This could not be the real Iris. But with the hindsight that also saw a parallel with the fairy story, I can now feel that I was giving Iris without knowing it the alternative being that she required: the irresponsible, even escapist persona (*escapist* was a word often used in those days, accompanied by a disapproving head shake) which she had no idea that she wanted or needed. Neither did I have any idea that I was supplying it. I felt I was in love; indeed, I was sure of it; and I was innocently sure, too, that it must be the most important thing for both of us, although Iris never gave any indication that she thought so, too. The Iris with whom I talked nonsense and gambolled about, the woman who entered with such joy into those frolics, was delightful; and yet I could not but feel that she was not the same woman I had first seen and marked out. Nor was she the "real" Iris Murdoch, the serious, hardworking, responsible being observed and admired by other people.

After our relationship itself became more serious, and

as we became aware that we were travelling inevitably towards a separation or a solution we couldn't anticipate or foresee, Iris once or twice mentioned the myth of Proteus. It was in reply to my despairing comment that I couldn't understand her, or the different person she became for the many others with whom she seemed, in my view, helplessly entangled. "Remember Proteus," she used to say. "Just keep tight hold of me and it will be all right." Proteus had the power of changing himself into any shape he wished—lion, serpent, monster, fish—but when Hercules held tightly on to him throughout all these transformations, he was compelled in the end to surrender, and to resume his proper shape as the man he was.

I used to reply gloomily that I was not Hercules, lacking that hero's resources of muscle power and concentration. Then we would laugh and become our old secret and childish selves again for the moment. As we did when we first crawled through the undergrowth and slipped secretly into the river.

That occasion for me marked a turning point in our relations, although it was one I didn't grasp at the time, nor could I have defined it until much later. The fact was that on that day she had let me for the first time into another of her friendships, by asking Maurice Charlton if I might be included in the lunch he had planned for the pair of them. I had no idea of this, nor, as I said, of the admirable good nature which Charlton himself must have displayed. If he was disappointed, he gave no hint of it at all. Because I was there with them both, I was not conscious of him as a rival, nor did I mind at all the way in which he seemed spontaneously included in the relations between Iris and myself. All fitted in and seemed beautifully natural.

I never asked Iris how I had come to be included in that party. It would not have occurred to me to ask. Now, of course, it is too late. Iris does not remember the lunch party, or the bicycle ride, or the morning swim, or Maurice Charlton himself. I have sometimes mentioned that occasion, without evoking any response beyond a usual and touchingly anxious interest in what I am talking about. And yet I think she would recognise Maurice Charlton, or other friends from those days, were they to appear suddenly before her in the flesh. Memory may have wholly lost its mind function, but it retains some hidden principle of identification, even after the Alzheimer's has long taken hold.

A woman I sometimes meet, whose husband is also an Alzheimer's sufferer, once invited me to share in a brisk exchange of experiences. "Like being chained to a corpse, isn't it?" she remarked cheerfully. I hastened to agree with her in the same jocular spirit, feeling reluctant nonetheless to pursue that particular metaphor. "Oh, a much-loved corpse, naturally," she amended, giving me a slightly roguish glance, as if suggesting I might be thankful to abandon in her presence the usual proprieties that went with our situation.

But I was not at all thankful. I was repelled—I couldn't

help it—by the suggestion that Iris's affliction could have anything in common with that of this jolly woman's husband. She was a heroine no doubt, but let her be a heroine in her own style. How could our cases be compared? Iris was Iris.

Troubles do not necessarily bring people together. I felt no togetherness at all. This lady wanted—needed—to dramatise her situation and claim me as a fellow actor. I felt I could not cooperate in the spirit, though out of politeness I made a show of doing so. My own situation, I felt, was quite different from hers. It's not an uncommon reaction, as I've come to realise, among Alzheimer's partners. One needs very much to feel that the unique individuality of one's spouse has not been lost in the common symptoms of a clinical condition.

But the woman's figure of speech did not lose its power to haunt me. Her image of the corpse and the chain still lingered. There is a story by Thomas Hardy called "On the Western Circuit," one of those soberly ironic tales the author obviously enjoyed writing, in which a young barrister meets a country girl while accompanying a circuit judge on his rounds. They fall in love, and she becomes pregnant by him. She implores the sympathetic married lady in whose house she works as a maid to write letters for her to the young man, she being illiterate. Her mistress does so, and as a result of their correspondence, she begins to fall for the young man herself, while he, instead of escaping from his predicament, as he had first intended, is so charmed by the girl's sensible and loving little letters that he determines to marry her. The outcome, though predictable and characteristic of Hardy, is nonetheless moving for that. The marriage takes place in London, and the sole meeting between the young man and the girl's employer, before she returns to her own lonely and barren married life in Wessex, reveals to him how their involuntary intimacy has taken place. The love letters she has written have made him love her, not the girl. The poor girl is distracted by her husband's discovery of the deceit—he had asked her to write a little note of thanks to one of the guests—and he is left to face the future fettered to an unchosen partner, like two slaves chained in a galley. Hardy's grim metaphor no doubt seemed wholly appropriate both to him and to his young hero.

I remembered the story while the woman was speaking. Our own situations were not the same, it was to be presumed, as those of the young man and girl. Fate had not deceived us. We had known our partners as equals over many years, told and listened and communed together, until communication had dwindled and faltered and all but ceased. No more letters, no more words. An Alzheimer's sufferer begins many sentences, usually with an anxious, repetitive query, but they remain unfinished, the want unexpressed. Usually, it is predictable and easily satisfied, but Iris produces every day many such queries, involving "you know, that person," or simply "that," which take time and effort to unravel. Often they remain totally enigmatic, related to some unidentifiable man or woman in the past who has swum up to the surface of her mind as if encountered yesterday. At such times, I feel my own mind and memory faltering, as if required to perform a function too far outside their own beat and practice.

The continuity of joking can very often rescue such moments. Humour seems to survive anything. A burst of laughter, snatches of doggerel, song, teasing nonsense rituals once lovingly exchanged awake an abruptly happy response, and a sudden beaming smile that must resemble those moments in the past between explorers and savages, when some sort of clowning pantomime on the part of the former seems often to have evoked instant comprehension and amusement. At cheerful moments, over drinks or in the car, Iris sometimes twitters away incomprehensibly but self-confidently, happily convinced that an animated exchange is taking place. At such moments, I find myself producing my own stream of consciousness, silly sentences or mashed-up quotations. "'The tyrant of the Chersonese was freedom's best and bravest friend,'" I assure her, giving her a solemnly meaningful look. At which, she nods her head gravely and seems to act a conspiring smile, as if the ringing confidence of Byron's line in "The Isles of Greece" meant a lot to her, too.

Our mode of communication seems like underwater sonar, each bouncing pulsations off the other, then listening for an echo. The baffling moments at which I cannot understand what Iris is saying, or about whom or what—

moments which can produce tears and anxieties, though never, thank goodness, the raging frustration typical of many Alzheimer's sufferers—can sometimes be dispelled by embarking on a joky parody of helplessness, and trying to make it mutual, both of us at a loss for words.

At happy moments, she seems to find words more easily than I do. Like the swallows when we lived in the country. Sitting on the telephone wire outside our bedroom window, a row of swallows would converse animatedly with one another, always, it seemed, signing off each burst of twittering speech with a word that sounded like "Weatherby," a common call sign delivered on a rising note. We used to call them "Weatherby." Now I tease her by saying, "You're just like a Weatherby, chattering away." She loves to be teased, but when I make the tease a tender one by adding, "I love listening to you," her face clouds over. She can always tell the difference between the irresponsibility of a joke, or a straight tease, and the note of caring or of loving care, which however earnest and true always sounds inauthentic.

All this sounds quite merry, but in fact, most days are for her a sort of despair, although despair suggests a conscious and positive state, and this is a vacancy which frightens her by its lack of dimension. She mutters, "I'm a fool," or "Why didn't I..." or "I must..." and I try to explain the trouble while rapidly suggesting we must post a letter, walk round the block, go shopping in the car. Something urgent, practical, giving the illusion of sense and routine. The Reverend Sidney Smith, a benevolent clergyman of Jane Austen's time, used to urge parishioners in the grip of depression who appealed to him for help to "take short views of human life—never further than dinner or tea." I used to quote this to Iris when troubles began, as if I were recommending a real policy which could intelligibly be followed. Now I repeat it sometimes as an incantation or joke, which can raise a laugh if it is accompanied by some horsing around, a live pantomime of "short views" being taken. It is not now intended to be rationally received, but it gets a smile anyway.

That is something to be tried for all the time. It transforms her face, bringing it back to what it was, and with an added glow that can seem almost supernatural. The face of an Alzheimer's patient has been clinically described as the "lion face." An apparently odd comparison, but in fact a very apt one. The features settle into a leonine impassivity which does remind one of the king of beasts, and the way his broad expressionless mask is represented in painting and sculpture. The face of some suffering from this disease is neither tragic nor comic, as a face can appear in other forms of dementia, one that would suggest humanity and emotion in their most distorted guise. The face of the Alzheimer's sufferer indicates only an absence: It is a mask in the most literal sense.

That is why the sudden appearance of a smile is so extraordinary. The lion face becomes the face of the Virgin Mary, tranquil in sculpture and painting, with a gravity that gives such a smile its deepest meaning. Only a joke survives, the last thing that finds its way into consciousness when the brain is atrophied. And the Virgin Mary, after all, presides over the greatest joke of the lot, the wonderful fable made up, elaborated, repeated all over the world. No wonder she is smiling.

The latest smile on Iris's face seems to come from association with another Mary. Trying to cheer her up one day, I thought of an inane childhood rhyme, forgotten for years.

> *Mary had a little bear*
> *So loving and so kind*
> *And everywhere that Mary went*
> *You saw her bear behind.*

Iris not only smiled; her face looked cunning and concentrated. Somewhere in the deserted areas of the brain, old contacts and impulses became activated, wires joined up. A significance had revealed itself, and this seems only to work with jokes, particularly bad jokes, which in the days of sanity would have been received with smiling but slightly embarrassed forbearance. Iris always mildly disliked and avoided what used to be called vulgar or risqué jokes. Maybe the innocence of the bear rhyme pleased her—who can say what subtle feelings and distinctions from the past can be summoned back to her mind by something as silly—but perhaps as touching, too—as the bear rhyme? My own memory had retained it despite my conscious wishes, which is something that often happens. I could recall now the small boy at school—I secretly thought him rather repulsive but was too polite to say so— who told me the rhyme with a knowing air of complacency, sure that it would be a hit with me. I resolved on the spot to forget it at once, but here it was, back again.

When I quoted Byron's certainly very memorable line about the old Greek hero Miltiades, tyrant of the Chersonese and victor at the Battle of Marathon, I thought involuntarily again of Maurice Charlton and the enchanted lunch on that hot summer day. He had been this fabulous young Greek scholar, before he had become a medical doctor. No doubt Iris had admired him, as she had admired all great skill and learning. And had he been going to attempt seduction that warm afternoon, a project thwarted by his own courtesy in acceding to her suggestion that I should come along, too? I had no idea, and still have none. Clueless as I still was, I did know then that Iris had several lovers, whom she was apparently juggling at the same time. I also intuited—quite how, I don't know, but it turned out to be correct enough—that she usually gave her favours out of admiration and respect: for, so to speak, the godlike rather than the conventionally attractive or sexual attributes in the men who pursued her. Men who were like gods for her she also found erotic, but sex was something she regarded as rather marginal, not an end in itself.

$\mathcal{T}hree$

had no illusions about being godlike. I realised that she loved to be with me as if we were children again, and she was tender when she saw with what childlike eagerness I had come to desire her. She sensed I had next to no knowledge of lovemaking (how absurdly old-fashioned it all seems today). A little while before our own swimming expedition on that hot morning, she had remarked with brisk indulgence, "Perhaps it's time we made love," and she had shown me how, although as I had no condom with me (they were known as "French letters" in those days, and a good deal of guilt and secrecy hung about their supply and use), she did not permit me to get very far. We had done better once or twice after that, but in a genial and wholly unserious way that did not in the least mar for me the unfamiliar magic of the proceedings: doing this odd and comical thing with someone whom one really loved. The paradox was itself comical, though not at all depressing.

What was a trifle depressing was the growing knowledge that I was far from being the only one with whom she was making love—probably in all our cases only on occasion. She was much too busy and interested in other things to make a habit of it, so to speak. But to me in those days, she seemed at the negligent disposition of these unknown and godlike older men, whom she went humbly to "see" at times when it suited them. Here, I began dimly to perceive, was where her creative imagination lay, and it was in order to feed it—almost, it seemed, to propitiate it—that she would make what appeared to me these masochistic journeys to London, and chiefly to Hampstead, for me the abode and headquarters of the evil gods.

As my own feelings deepened, I saw all such matters in an absurdly lurid light. In reality, the people Iris went to see were not gods or demons, but intellectuals, writers, artists, civil servants, mostly Jewish, mainly refugees, who knew one another and formed a loose-knit circle, with its own rivalries, jealousies, and power struggles. They loved Iris and accepted her as one of their own, although she remained inevitably an outsider, living and teaching as she did in humdrum academic circles, away from their focus of attention. In time, I met most of them and got on with them well, surprised and, in later days, amused when I looked back at the storm of fears and emotions they had once aroused in me. It was Iris's own imagination which had in a sense created them, and continued to create and nurture them as the strange and unique characters of her wonderful novels. It was the second of these, *The Flight from the Enchanter*, in 1956, which first showed me how the genius of Iris's imagination did its own work, in its own way. And all the teeming complex variety of her later novels continued in its own mysterious fashion to be distilled from the alembic of those original obsessions and enchantments.

But Maurice Charlton was quite different: a sunlit character whose spiritual home was that hot but never oppressive Oxford summer, even though he lived for the moment, as if himself the beneficiary of some enchantment, in that gloomy, exotic flat, surrounded, as it seemed to me, by heavy, glittering cutlery and tall green Venetian wine-glasses. When first in love, one feels attended on all sides, almost jostled, by such unexpected and incongruous symbols of romance. That first day we visited Charlton marked a turning point, however little I realised it at the time, in the way in which Iris behaved towards me. The lunch party and the river made me too bemused and delighted to see it, but she was not only including me in another part of her social life; she was also indicating to a third person that I played a role in that life, a role which had begun to possess a public continuity and thus was not something to be privately taken up between us and discarded from moment to moment. I was far from becoming her official "swain," in the quaint old sense, but in the eyes of the world, I had come to have some kind of status beyond the sphere of mere acquaintanceship.

With the perception that made him an excellent doctor as well as a brilliant classical scholar, Maurice Charlton may well have been aware of all this in some sense as his green eyes went on surveying us in their merrily convivial but impassive way. He reminded me in some way of the great Professor Fraenkel, whom I had seen once or twice at the time, a venerable, almost gnomelike figure, shuffling up High Street after giving some class or lecture, surveying the world with a disconcertingly bright and youthful eye. A Jewish refugee from Germany, Fraenkel arrived in Oxford at the time Iris was a student, and such was his reputation that he soon obtained a chair, even though Oxford had a glut of distinguished refugees. He had given Iris tutorials, and she attended his famous *Agamemnon* class. I had been a mere schoolboy then, and so, for that matter, had Maurice Charlton himself, though an older one. But Maurice's green glance had much the same light in it as Fraenkel's black twinkle. Perhaps that resemblance was what had attracted Iris to him.

She had already told me how fond she had been of Fraenkel, both fond and reverential. In those days, there had seemed to her nothing odd or alarming when he caressed her affectionately as they sat side by side over a text, sometimes for half an hour over the exact interpretation of a word, sounding its associations in the Greek world as he explored them, as lovingly keen on them as he seemed to be on her. She had been pleased it was so, and she revelled in the sense of intellectual comradeship she felt. That there was anything dangerous or degrading in his behaviour, which would nowadays constitute a shocking example of sexual harassment, never occurred to her. In fact, her tutor at Somerville College, Isobel Henderson, had said with a smile when she sent Iris along to the professor, "I expect he'll paw you about a bit," as if no sensible girl, aware of the honour of being taught personally by the great man, would be silly enough to object to that.

Nobody did, so far as Iris knew. She sometimes spoke to me of the excitement of the textual world Fraenkel revealed to her, and she mentioned in an amused way how he had stroked her arms and held her hand. Few female students had any sexual experience at that time, and Iris was, in any case, unusually virginal. We sometimes laughed together over her memories of the one "bad" girl in Somerville, a dark-haired beauty who used to climb back into the college late at night, assisted by her boyfriend. Iris didn't disapprove, but as a student she felt no urge to compete in the sex game. Incidentally, Professor Fraenkel was devoted to his wife, and he had told a close friend that when she died, he would follow her. He did, taking an overdose the same night.

My ancient Greek is virtually nonexistent, and Iris's, once extensive, has gone completely, of course. I used to try reading *Agamemnon* and other Greek plays to her in a translation, but it was not a success. Nor was any other attempt at reading aloud. It all seemed and felt unnatural. I read several chapters of the *Lord of the Rings* and *The Tale of Genji*, two of Iris's old favourites, before I realised this. For someone who had been accustomed not so much to read books as to slip into their world as effortlessly as she slipped into a river or the sea, this laborious procession of words clumping into her consciousness must have seemed a tedious irrelevance, although she recognised and reacted to them, even knowing, as they appeared before her, the people and events described. But the relation of such recognition to true memory is clearly a painful one. Tolkien and Lady Murasaki had been inhabitants of her mind, denizens as native to its world as were the events and people who so mysteriously came to her in her own process of creation. To meet them again in this way, and awkwardly to recognise them, was an embarrassment.

On the other hand, she was always roused to the point of animation if I managed to turn some matter from reading into our own sort of joke. Then we would stop at once and I would embroider the idea into a mini-fantasy, as I did when attempting to interest her again in a translation of the *Odyssey*. The Lestrygonian giants had just sunk eleven of Odysseus' twelve ships and devoured their crews. I imagined him calling an office meeting in the surviving flagship next morning and starting the proceedings by saying, "Gentlemen, we shall have to do better than this." She thought that quite funny, and she always seemed to remember it if I said to her when she had arranged dead leaves and bits of rubbish from the street in patterns round the house, "Come, gentlemen, we shall have to do better than this." I was unconsciously copying the phrase from some other context half-remembered—possibly the moment in *Pride and Prejudice* when Mr. Bennet remarks to his younger daughter, who has been playing her instrument before the company, "Come, Mary, you have delighted us long enough." (The unfortunate Mary is the only one among Jane Austen's characters who never gets a fair deal from the author at all, any more than she does from her father.)

I think this attempt at reading and being read to is also a reminder of the loss of identity; although reminder is hardly the word, for an Alzheimer's patient is not usually conscious in any definable way of what has happened. If it were otherwise, the process, however irreversible it becomes in the end, would have developed along different lines, in a different form. Some sufferers do remain conscious of their state, paradoxical as this seems. The torment of knowing that you cannot speak or think what you want must be intolerable, and I have met patients in whom such a torment is clearly visible. But when Iris talks to me, the result seems normal to her and to me surprisingly fluent, provided I do not listen to what is being said but apprehend it in a matrimonial way, as the voice of familiarity, and thus of recognition.

Time constitutes an anxiety because its conventional shape and progression have gone, leaving only a perpetual query. There are some days when the question "When are we leaving?" never stops, though it is repeated without agitation. Indeed, there can seem something quite peaceful about it, as if it hardly matters when we go, or where, and to stay at home might be preferable in any case. In Faulkner's novel *Soldiers' Pay*, the blinded airman keeps saying to his friend, "When are they going to let me out?" That makes one flinch: the writer has contrived unerringly to put the reader in the blind man's place. Iris's query does not in itself suggest desire for change or release into a former state of being; nor does she want to know when we are getting in the car and going out to lunch. The journey on which we are leaving may for her mean the final one; or, if that sounds too portentous, simply some sort of disappearance from the daily life which, without her work, must itself have lost all sense and identity.

Iris once told me that the question of identity had always puzzled her. She thought she herself hardly possessed such a thing, whatever it was. I said that she must know what it was like to be oneself, even to revel in the consciousness of oneself, as a secret and separate person—a person unknown to any other. She smiled, was amused, looked uncomprehending. It was not something she bothered about. "Then you live in your work? Like Keats and Shakespeare and all that?" I asked. She disclaimed any such comparison; and she did not seem particularly interested when I went on to speak (I was, after all, in the English Lit business) of the well-known Romantic distinction, fascinating to Coleridge, between the great egocentric writers, Wordsworth or Milton, whose sense of self was so overpowering that it included everything else, and these identity-free spirits for whom being is not what they are, but what they live in and reveal. I suspect that as a philosopher she found all such distinctions very crude ones. Perhaps one has to be very much aware of oneself as a person in order to find them at all meaningful or interesting. Nobody less narcissistic than Iris can well be imagined.

Conceivably, it is the persons who hug their identity most closely to themselves for whom the condition of Alzheimer's is most dreadful. Iris's own lack of a sense of identity seemed to float her more gently into its world of preoccupied emptiness. Placidly, every night, she insists on laying out quantities of her clothing on my side of the bed, and when I quietly remove them, back they come again. She wants to look after me? Is that it? It may be a simpler sort of confusion, for when we go to bed, she often asks me which side she should be on. Or is it something deeper and fuller, less conscious and less "caring" than that far too self-conscious adjective suggests? She had never wanted to look after me in the past, thank goodness; indeed, one of the pleasures of living with Iris was her serenely benevolent unawareness of one's daily welfare. So restful. Having a busy personality, I made it a point to look after her, she never needed to tell herself to look after me. But when I broke my leg once in the snow at Christmas and had to lie up for a few days in Banbury hospital, a dozen miles off, she came and stayed in a bed-and-breakfast hotel outside the hospital gate. I besought her to remain at home and work, instead of wasting her time. There was nothing she could do. But no, she stayed there until I was fit enough to return home with her.

Philosophers once used to argue the question of whether you could have a pain in your foot that someone else experienced. Iris certainly could not. Presumably, the point of the argument, if it has any, is to investigate the possibilities of physical sympathy. "She may not understand you, but she always feels with you," remarked Coleridge fondly of his ideal woman. One doesn't need to be a feminist to find this to be nonsense. Either sex may or may not be able to feel the pleasure or pain of other persons, just as either sex can possess or lack a sense of smell. Iris, as it happens, has no sense of smell, and her awareness of others is transcendental rather than physical. She communes with their higher being, as an angel might, and is unconcerned with their physical existence, their sweaty selves. I have often been struck by the brilliant accuracy with which she can notice details about the lives of the characters in her novels, their faces and bodies, without any instinctive sense of how those characters function in themselves, on the humbler level.

But of course she was instantly aware of emotion, and quick to respond to it. She intuited misery or mere sadness in her friends at once, and she was always able to help, often by letting such feelings assume for her some dramatic appearance, gently encouraging them to take some form gratifying or reassuring to their owner. She never participated in the drama of themselves put on by others, but she could feel intensely herself emotions of love, jealousy, adoration, even rage. I never saw these emotions myself, but I knew they were there. In my case, she could always take jealousy away simply by being with me. In early days, I always thought it would be vulgar—as well as not my place—to give any indications of jealousy, but she knew when it was there, and she soothed it just by being the self she always was with me, which I soon knew to be wholly and entirely different from any way that she was with other people.

In those early days, as I now think of them, about a year or eighteen months after we first met, she was engaged every Saturday evening with a Jewish Italian professor, another wartime refugee, from London University. He loved her deeply, an affection she sweetly and reverently returned. He was a gentle little man, neat and elderly, and they did not go to bed together (I believed that), but sat talking all evening about the ancient world while he kissed her sometimes and held her hand. He had a wife and grown-up daughter in London, both of whom Iris knew well and was greatly attached to. His wife accepted their relationship with complete understanding. Punctually at half past eleven, the professor would leave her room—she was then living not in college but on a top floor in Beaumont Street, close to the centre of Oxford—and walk to his small hotel in Banbury Road. I knew this, because I was usually there. Sometimes I would follow him back—he never guessed my presence: he did not know about me—or sometimes I continued to stand in the street, looking up at her lighted window.

There was nothing obviously godlike about this quiet little professor of ancient history, although he was probably the most distinguished man in his field at the time. In a respectful way, I felt quite fond of him, even proud of him. With the other master figure in Iris's life, a *Dichter* of legendary reputation among people who knew, it was another matter. This man held court, as I thought of it, secretly and almost modestly in Hampstead, and Iris was very much under his sway. He had several mistresses whom Iris knew, and she seemed to revere them almost as much as the great man himself. His wife, too, she revered. Sometimes Iris spoke to me of this woman, her sweet face and air of patient, welcoming reserve, who was sometimes present in the flat when the *Dichter* made love to Iris, possessing her as if he were a god. This she told me later, before we got married, when her close relationship with the man had come to an end and he had given us his blessing, as she put it. She continued to see him from time to time and her creative imagination continued to be enthralled by him, even though, as she told me, by writing about him in her own way she got him out of her system, and finally in a sense out of her novels, too.

The *Dichter* was a *Dichter* in the German sense, not actually a poet, but a master spirit of literature. He had been a friend of another German Jewish writer, a real poet, with whom Iris had been very much in love. She would possibly have married him had he lived, but he had a serious heart ailment and knew that he could not live long. He died a year before I met her. She grieved for him deeply. He sounded a delightful man, gentle (like all Iris's close friends, as opposed to her "gods") and humorous. The gods were not funny, I suspect; perhaps it was beneath the dignity of godship. The poet was in the anthropology department at Oxford, although he was never strong enough to go "into the field," as it's called. At the time he gave his weekly lecture, he told Iris, he invariably found himself confronting a blank page on which he had written, "As I was saying in my last lecture…" During the week, he had never managed to get any further, and on the morning of the lecture, he always found himself confronting the page. It had been a joke between them, and it became a joke between Iris and me. It still is. She always understands it, and when it comes up, I always speak of her dead poet by name, though I am never sure if she remembers him. Only the joke remains alive.

Iris's seriousness—a friend once seriously annoyed her, she told me, by implying that her air of gravity was too great for her ever to be imagined as having fun—could, it was true, take disconcerting forms. Greatly to my anguish, there was never an actual moment when she told me she had decided to marry me—the matter remained still un-settled a few weeks before it occurred—but there was one occasion when she sat me down in her room and said she had better tell me something of the people in her past. I was reminded of her originally remarking that perhaps it was time to make love. I was startled by her almost por-tentous air. Had I not heard all about them, the people of her past and present, at one time or another during the period of our own intimacy?

It appeared that I had not. Unknown figures arose be-fore me like the procession of kings in *Macbeth*, seeming to regard me with grave curiosity as they passed by. There was so-and-so with whom she had first been to bed, and so-and-so and so-and-so who had wanted to marry her. There was a friend and fellow student whose advances she had resisted in her virginal days (she did not of course put it quite like that). At the beginning of the war, he had joined the army and asked her half-jokingly to marry him, pointing out that he was sure to be killed before the war was over and she would be able to draw a widow's pen-sion. Iris's seriousness broke down in smiles at this point, and also in tears.

She had said she still did not want to marry him but that she would go to bed with him before he went overseas. He was killed in action later in the war, when she was working at an office in Whitehall.

Incongruous as the memory was at that moment, I found myself back for a moment at my first school, when the headmaster gave us each a few moments alone in his study, to tell us about "the facts of life"; and here were the "facts" of Iris's life, in grave procession. Suppressing the impulse to recall this for Iris's amusement, I found myself telling her instead that even an officer's widow received only a very small annual sum. I knew this because some of my own contemporaries and fellow soldiers had been killed before the war was over. It was a feeble attempt to assert myself, and my own meagre experience in the face of what seemed a rich and stately litany of other days, joys, faces, which I would never share. It felt graceless, too, as I said it, but I could not think of anything else to say.

It broke the mood anyway. Iris laughed and kissed me. "After all that, isn't it time for me to have a kind word?" I said, and then we both laughed. Getting "a kind word" had become a regular plea on my part, and a part of our amative speech. It still is, and the phrase continues always to mean something to her. To me at that time, of course, it was wholly different from what I had guessed of her behaviour with others. No doubt it really was different. I could not imagine the god in Hampstead getting a kind word, or giving one. Not even the quiet professor of ancient history, whom I had followed in a doglike manner back to his hotel. Kind words, in Iris's style to me, were not for them. That was a kind of consolation. Yet I divined already how good she was at the real business of cheering other people's troubles. She had present and former pupils, some of whom—often the sad-faced ones—I had seen gazing at her with looks of heartfelt gratitude as well as adoration. But that again was quite different from anything she said or did with me in response to my plea for a kind word.

Nonetheless, I was really very cast down by everything she had just been telling me. There seemed so many of them, these fortunate persons, and to my amazement, I had just learned that some quite ordinary people, as I thought of them, acquaintances and even colleagues of my own, had at some time or other in the past been recipients of Iris's kindness. They had desired her, and not been rejected. However different that "kindness" was, and however unimaginable in terms of what I asked and received, it had nevertheless been given.

Looking back from the standpoint of today, it seems all very unreal, and so old-fashioned. But a woman with a past was different in those days, just as the past itself is always different, and always a foreign country. Today, even caring about the past seems an emotion or indulgence that belongs to the past itself, not to the present or future, to the place where we live today. That talk we once had— the way Iris delivered it, and the way in which deep inside me I received it—now seems to me almost medieval.

Could we really have thought and behaved like that?

It seems that we did. And now, nearly fifty years later, we remain for ourselves the same couple, even though a sort of incredulity comes over me in remembering what we seem to have been like, the ways in which we behaved. Looking back, I separate us with difficulty. We seem always to have been together. But memory draws a sharp divide nonetheless. The person I was at that age now seems odd to me—could I have *really* been in love? Could I have felt, at least some of the time, all that jealousy, ecstasy, misery, longing, unhopefulness, mingled with a fever of possibility and joy? I can hardly believe it. But where Iris is concerned, my own memory, like a snug-fitting garment, seems to have zipped itself up to the present second. As I work in bed early in the morning, typing on my old portable with Iris quietly asleep beside me, her presence as she now is seems as it always was, and as it always should be. I know she must once have been different, but I have no true memory of a different person.

Waking up for a peaceful second or two, she looks vaguely at the "Tropical Olivetti" lying on my knees, cushioned by one of her jerseys. Not long ago, when I asked if it disturbed her, she said she liked to hear that funny noise in the morning. She must be used to it, although a couple of years ago she would have been getting up herself at this time—seven o'clock—and preparing to start her own day. Nowadays she lies quietly asleep, sometimes giving a little grunt or murmur, often sleeping well past nine, when I rouse and dress her. This ability to sleep like a cat, at all

hours of the day and night, must be one of the great bless-
ings that sometimes go with Alzheimer's, converse of the
anxiety state that comes on in wakefulness and finds worried questions such as "When are we leaving?"

Dressing most days is a reasonably happy and comic
business. I myself am still far from sure which way round
her underpants are supposed to go: We usually decide
between us that it doesn't matter. Trousers are simpler:
Hers have a grubby white label on the inside at the back.
I ought to give her a bath, or, rather, a wash of some sort,
since baths are tricky, but I tend to postpone it from day
to day. For some reason, it is easier to do the job in cold
blood, as it were, at an idle moment later in the day. Iris
never objects to this; she seems in a curious way to accept
it as both quite normal and wholly exceptional, as if the
two concepts had become identified for her. Perhaps that
is why she seems to accept her daily state as if none other
had ever existed; assuming, too, that no one else would
find her changed in any way; just as my own memory only
works with her now as she is, and so, as my memory seems
to assume, must always have been.

It seems normal that the old routines of washing and
dressing have vanished, as if they too had never existed.
If she remembered them, which she doesn't, I can imagine
her saying to herself, Did one really go through every day
all those unnecessary rituals? My own memory, after all,
can hardly believe that I once went through all those other

rituals of falling in love and becoming agitated, ecstatic, distracted....

At the same time, Iris's social reflexes are in a weird way still very much in place. If someone comes to the door—the postman, the man to read the gas meter—and I am for the moment occupied elsewhere, she receives him with her social smile, then calls for me in those unhurried, slightly "gracious" tones which married couples automatically use with each other in the presence of a stranger. "Oh, I think it is the man who has come to read the meter, darling." In the same way, she deals instinctively with more complex social situations, seeming to follow the conversation and smiling, prepared to bridge a silence by asking a question. Usually, the same question: "Where do you come from?" or "What are you doing now?"—questions that get repeated many times in the course of a social event. Other people, visitors or friends, adjust themselves well to these repetitions as soon as they grasp what is happening and what motivates them: They usually manage to adopt the same social part that she is playing.

I find myself making use of the behavioral instincts that survive. In the old days, I would sometimes produce what in childhood used to be called "a tantrum," if something had gone wrong or not been done properly, something for which, rightly or wrongly, I held Iris responsible. She would then become calm, reassuring, almost maternal, not as if deliberately, but with some deep, unconscious female response that normally had no need to come to the surface, as it would have had to do on an almost daily basis with a young family. Iris in general was never "female" at all, a fact for which I sometimes remembered to be grateful. Nowadays I have learnt to make on occasions a deliberate use of this buried reflex. If she has been following me all day, like Mary's bear, interrupting tiresome business or letter writing (very often letters to her own fans), I erupt in what can seem even to me an uncontrolled fit of exasperation, stamping on the floor and throwing the papers and letters on it, waving my hands in the air. It always works. Iris says, "Sorry…sorry…" and pats me before going quietly away. She will be back soon, but that doesn't matter. My tantrum has reassured her as no amount of my own caring, or my calming efforts to reply to her rationally, could have done.

The lady who told me in her own deliberately jolly way that living with an Alzheimer's victim was like being chained to a corpse went on to an even greater access of desperate facetiousness, saying, "And, as you and I know, it's a corpse that complains all the time."

I don't know it. In spite of her anxious and perpetual queries, Iris seems not to know how to complain. She never has. Alzheimer's, which can accentuate personality traits to the point of demonic parody, has only been able to exaggerate a natural goodness in her.

On a good day, her need for a loving presence, mutual pattings and murmurs, has something angelic about it; she seems herself the presence found in an ikon. It is more important for her still on days of silent tears, a grief seemingly unaware of that mysterious world of creation she has lost, and yet aware that something is missing. The "little bull" aspect of her, putting her head down, and herself moving determinedly ahead, used once to be emphasised when she got up in the morning and headed for the bathroom. Dressed, she would visit me, still working in bed, and then go down to open the garden door and see what was going on. The weather and the birds, the look and sound of things, were sometimes jotted in her diary as she settled down to work. She never had breakfast then, although if I was at home, I brought her coffee and a chocolate biscuit later in the morning.

Now that once-good morning time has become the worst time. Like "stand to" in the trenches for soldiers in the two world wars. Trench humour is the natural response, even if one can only crack the dark joke inside oneself; it would be heartless at that once-hopeful hour to try to share it with the victim. While trying to think of ways of getting through the day, I feel all the more comradely at this time with the woman who had found some relief—at least I hoped so—in being facetious about herself and her Alzheimer's husband. Although I hadn't felt inclined to join very heartily in the joke, it was better, far better, than having to sympathise, in a caring po-faced, prissy way, from a similar position. In any case, those in the same boat have a natural desire to compare notes. A spruce grey-haired man whom I had once known, when we were both eighteen-year-olds and in the army, wrote to me to commiserate. Aside from his job as a stockbroker, his chief interests had been girls and vintage cars. When his wife, younger than he, developed Alzheimer's and deteriorated rapidly, he looked after her with exemplary devotion. He liked reporting progress, or the reverse, in terms of effective notes. Once, he wrote, "I used to view the female form divine in a rather different light. Now I just find myself hosing it down every morning."

I do it much less often. But I giggle internally if that jest comes into my head when washing between her legs and working over the contours of Iris's "female form divine." From where had my old army acquaintance obtained that unexpected specimen of Edwardian archness, a comic but also rather lyrical cliché that had also appealed once to James Joyce? No use trying to share this joke with Iris. Not that she would object, but the bounderish absurdity of the idiom has passed beyond her critical faculty. I recently came across a collection of palindromes somebody sent us years ago—ingenious and surreal sentences, appropriately illustrated. One of them, which had amused us as much by the illustration as by the telegraphic simplicity of the palindrome, was "Sex at noon taxes." Recently, I showed this and other onetime favourites to Iris, and she laughed and smiled a bit, out of the wish to share them with me, but I knew that they were not getting through. On the other hand, she will watch the animated cartoons on a children's TV programme with something approaching glee. They can be great standby at ten or so—the trickiest time—till eleven in the morning. I usually watch the Teletubbies with her, and I become absorbed myself in their odd little sunlit world, peopled with real rabbits, real sky, real grass. Or so it seems. Is some human agency inside the creatures, some actual and cunning little mannikin? It certainly looks like it, and the illusion, if such it is, continues to hold both our attentions.

We have only had television a few months—it never occurred to us before. Now I listen for its noise from the kitchen and hope it will remain switched on. If there is silence, I know that Iris has switched it off and is sitting there without moving. Attention span does not seem to be the trouble. She will watch with absorption a football game, cricket, bowling, or tennis without knowing the play or the scores, but immersed in the feel of the thing. My woman friend chained to the corpse told her husband every evening, "There's a snooker programme on." Then she played an old one on the video. It was always a new one for him, she said.

Unfortunately, not having a handy six-year-old child about, I have never managed to programme the video. In any case, Iris turns the thing off not because she is bored with it—boredom doesn't seem with her a possible state of mind—but out of an instinct to get away, the one that makes her say, "When are we leaving?" or "Must do go." She leaves offered and attempted occupations—all now tacitly given up—for the same reason. When are they going to let us out?

Neither of us ever attempted, from our earliest married days, to do much about the house. A routine of chores never existed. Neither of us felt any need to keep the house clean, and we were bothered by the notion of some-body coming in to do it for us. Now I suppose the house has reached what seems a comfortable point of no return. Once nothing seemed to need to be done, or so we took it all for granted, and now nothing can be done. If friends notice the state the place is in—a perfectly cosy one really—they don't say anything. Nonetheless, I feel from time to time that if we had ever developed a habit of working together on the chores, we might be able to continue with it now. Self-discipline. And a way of passing the time. But somehow, as the tramp more or less says in *Waiting for Godot*, the time seems to pass anyway.

We don't exactly keep a dust museum, like Dickens's Miss Havisham. If undisturbed, it seems to fade easily into the general background. Like the clothes, books, old news-papers, letters, and cardboard boxes. Some of them might be useful sometime. In any case, Iris has never been able to bear throwing anything away. She has always felt a tenderness for the feelings of torn-open envelopes, or cap-less plastic bottles, which has now become obsessive. Old leaves are rescued, sticks, even cigarette ends smoked not very furtively in the street by the girls at the high school near by. Smoking in our time has become an outdoor activity. Quite a wholesome one, I sometimes think.

It is wonderfully peaceful to sit in bed with Iris reassuringly asleep and gently snoring. Half-asleep again myself, I have a feeling of floating down the river, and watching all the rubbish from the house and from our lives—the good as well as the bad—sinking slowly down through the dark water until it is lost in the depths. Iris is floating or swimming quietly beside me. Weeds and larger leaves sway and stretch themselves beneath the surface. Blue dragonflies dart and hover to and fro by the riverbank. And suddenly, a kingfisher flashes past.

Four

Rivers featured on our honeymoon.

We were married in 1956, nearly three years after we first met. I once worked out the number of days that had gone by since the morning I had seen Iris bicycling slowly past the window; but I have forgotten the number now, and it would take me too long to work it out again. We were married at the registrar's office in St. Giles, a broad street which runs between the Martyrs' Memorial at its south end and the War Memorial at the north end, at the junction of Woodstock and Banbury roads. Opposite the registrar's office, now disappeared or moved elsewhere, is the judge's house, a fine Palladian building which is supposed to have given Henry James his idea for the house in his novel *The Spoils of Poynton*.

I talk like a guidebook, because in a way I felt like

one that morning of our marriage. I gazed at these familiar landmarks as if I had never seen them before. In a sense, I never *had* seen them before, because I had always hurried along, going somewhere, late for something, preoccupied with my own affairs, taking no notice. Now I found myself looking round as I waited on a corner near the office, seeing everything very clearly and as if for the first or the last time. I remember that the painter David, who sketched Marie Antoinette in the tumbril on her way to execution, noticed that she kept glancing all round her with vacant curiosity, as if she had never seen those streets and squares of Paris before. I felt rather like that, I think. I was also preoccupied, as every bridegroom is supposed to be, with the question of the ring, which I had amongst various other things in my right-hand trouser pocket. It was obviously an unsatisfactory place to keep it, but I could not think of a better one. I was wearing a dark suit, which I had been issued on demobilisation from the army nine years previously. It had no waistcoat, or perhaps the waistcoat, a necessary attribute of gents' suiting in those days, had become mislaid. I had selected the suit from among others lighter in colour, and it had been quite a good choice, because I had scarcely ever worn it, except on rare occasions of this kind—weddings, christenings, funerals.

I had bought the ring the day before at a pawnbroker's. It was a solid job, plain and old-fashioned, possibly disposed of by a widower in needy circumstances. It had been my idea. Iris had never mentioned it. She never wore rings, and I had never thought of giving her one, since we had never been engaged. I had no idea whether this ring would fit, and I was anxious about that. Fortunately, it was a beautiful fit, and still is, though it has now worn down from its old robust self into the slimmest of gold bands.

After the operation—one could hardly call it a ceremony—which lasted about three minutes, the wife of my senior colleague—they were a very nice couple—said in her rather fussy way, "I must go and look after Mrs. Bayley." She meant my mother, but her husband said to her with what Iris later described as "a grim laugh," "Every woman here is called Mrs. Bayley, except you." It was true. My mother and sister-in-law, also a Mrs. Bayley, were present, but no other ladies. Iris said that this was the ghastliest moment of what was for her an extremely gruesome occasion. She was now lumped among a lot of Mrs. Bayleys. Her own mother, incidentally, had managed to miss the train from Paddington to Oxford. After the business was over, we went down to the station to meet the next train, found her, and cheered up a good deal over a drink at a nearby pub.

This was not a very good start, but it was not exactly a start, in any case. It seemed more of an anticlimax, the world we knew ending not with a bang but a whimper. At the same time, this feeling of *détente* was very welcome. All tensions, queries, and uncertainties, all the things that for months and years seemed to have made up the drama of living, were now over. That was a real source of satisfaction for both of us. At least I knew it was for me; and when Iris squeezed my hand at the station and said how nice and settled and yet unfamiliar it felt now to be together, it reassured me that all was well. Reassurance was probably what was wanted.

In another sense, it seemed to be there already, in the mere fact of marriage. In his memoirs, the novelist Anthony Powell observes that marriage does not resemble in the smallest degree any other comparable human experience. You can live with someone for years and not feel in the least married. Alternatively, you could finally take the step, as Iris and I had done, and at once feel you had moved into a wholly different sphere of sensation and behaviour. As Powell puts it, in order to know what it is like, you have to experience the thing itself. "Nothing else will do."

The meeting with Iris's mother was also reassuring. She was a quite exceptionally nice woman, who looked rather younger than her daughter. She had been only nineteen when Iris was born. She was a Dublin girl, and a young man from Belfast, recently joined up in the army, had fallen in love with her. This was in 1917. Iris was proud of the fact that her father, who had been brought up on a farm, was in a yeomanry cavalry regiment, King Edward's Horse. That probably saved his life, as the cavalry was rarely able to get into action during trench warfare. Iris's mother, who had been an amateur soprano of considerable promise, gave up her singing when she got married. Iris inherited her singing voice to some degree, and she was always sorry that her mother had never gone on with a serious musical career.

Instead, she had had Iris, a difficult birth, following which she had made a silent decision to have no more children. Iris told me later that she knew this by instinct, although her mother had never said anything about it. I had pointed out that if more children had been born, a son among them, her own life would have been drastically different. As it was, she had lived on the happiest terms of equality with her mother and father, who had adored her. After the Irish Troubles, the small family had moved to England, where her father had obtained a modest job in a branch of the civil service. Iris's childhood was spent in a small semidetached house in Chiswick. She went first to a Froebel Fay School in the same district. Then she was sent to Badminton, an excellent private boarding school for girls, near Bristol. Her father's sacrifices for her education, including the borrowing of money, was something altogether against the instincts of a frugal and godly Belfast upbringing, although by that time neither parent had any interest in religion, or affiliations with any church. Iris's childhood was happily godless.

Her appetite for the spiritual developed during her Oxford days, nurtured by Plato and by her studies in philosophy. It was part of the inner world of her imagination and never appeared on the surface. The way she fell in love when young, and the people she fell in love with, resembled in some degree the search for wisdom, authority, belief, which a lot of people feel the need to embark on at some point, whether young or old. At the same time, I suspect there was always something both tough and elusive about Iris, perhaps the circumspectness of her Northern Irish ancestors. Falling in love with people who represented for her spiritual authority, wisdom, beneficence, even a force that might seem darkly ambiguous and enigmatic was an adventure in the soul's progress and experience; she craved it, needed it, but she was far too sensible ever to become enslaved. Like silly young Dora Greenfield in her novel *The Bell*, she could always whisk away when she wanted: Common sense was the final arbiter of her emotional impulses.

Her sunny adolescence, happiness at school, and happy relationship with her parents may well have played their part in giving her this need, as she grew up, for strongly contrasting kinds of experience. But with her parents, she always seemed to return, as I felt she did with me, to the cheerful and enterprising innocence which seemed to have been her natural character when young. She behaved with her mother with complete naturalness, as if they were sisters, herself the elder. Her father at that time, newly retired, was already an invalid, and he died of cancer the next year. (He had always smoked his sixty a day, but so had her mother.) Iris was deeply attached to him, and she grieved for and missed him greatly, while instinctively taking over the role he had played in her mother's life. I still wish there had been time for me to know him better.

When the three of us got back from the station that day, my mother had a moment's hesitation when introduced to Mrs. Murdoch and her daughter. Which of them had her son just married? The instant of confusion was pardonable; and I attempted, perhaps not very wisely, to make a joke of it. How this went down, I don't know, because we were immediately plunged into the business of the party, modest as was the number attending it. It was given in a small reception room in my college; and the college butler, a genial patriarch, had suggested to me that he serve from the college cellars some champagne which was already many years past its prime. He wanted to use it up. "I don't mind telling you, sir, that it's not entirely reliable," he warned me, "but I can let you have it cheap."

In the event, every bottle proved delicious, deep gold in colour and without much fizz, but giving just the right amount of conviviality to the few guests, and valuable support to the wedding couple. I can still remember the romantic name of the marque: it was called Duc de Marne. The duke still seemed to be giving us his benevolent support as we got through the other trials of the day, culminating in a debacle at the posh hotel, The Compleat Angler at Marlowe, where we had been going to spend the night. The name had seemed propitious; and when we had been in to book a room, we saw the River Thames pouring itself over a weir outside the windows. The sound of that weir at night would have been a delightful epithalamium.

When we turned up there, however, the members of the hotel staff were polite but puzzled. The hotel was full up. Had we booked a room? Yes, we had—I had been there in person a week before. (In those days, the telephone seemed, at least to me, a not entirely trustworthy instrument to make so vital a reservation.) The young women at the reception desk exchanged a swift look. "That must have been when Camilla was on," murmured one. I gathered at once and despairingly that Camilla was a delinquent girl, since sacked no doubt, who had forgotten to record the booking. In those days, fashionable country hotels prided themselves on the attractive amateur debutantes they employed as part-time staff. Camilla had no doubt been attractive, but not, it appeared, reliable. Profuse in their apologies, the hotel booked us by phone into a solid old-world establishment in the main square of neighbouring Henley. It was called The Catherine Wheel.

Our mothers had hit it off pretty well at the wedding party, and they continued doing so on the basis of not seeing much of each other until both were old, when they became closer friends. Iris's mother seemed to take it for granted that we would not want to have children. Although she apparently had not wanted them herself, Iris as she grew up had become her pride and joy. How such a conclusion could have been reached by one as an outside party is difficult to say, but Mrs. Murdoch certainly seems to have assumed from the start that the three of us would form a harmoniously self-sufficient triangle, similar to the one she had shared with her daughter and husband. Nor was she wrong, although her own presence in the relationship was happy but hardly noticeable. She continued to live in London; she never bothered us.

Although no more intrusive concerning the affairs of her son and daughter-in-law, my own mother would, I knew, have liked grandchildren. She had three sons, and only one produced an heir. But she had too much sense and tact to voice this hope. After some initial uneasiness— she had barely met Iris before the wedding—my mother became very deeply attached to her increasingly famous daughter-in-law, and she continued to be so until she died, not so very long ago, in her late eighties. By then, Iris's mother, herself a victim of Alzheimer's, had died.

It had never for a moment occurred to either of us that the disease, or the gene for it, could be hereditary. Indeed, apart from the blanket term *senile dementia*, the condition had then no specific name, nor did the specialists we consulted about her mother's case prove in the least helpful, beyond suggesting various physiological explanations and attempting to treat them. Mrs. Murdoch's own doctor, a hard-bitten London GP, merely hinted at a fondness for the gin bottle, a suggestion that upset Iris very much, although it was obvious to me that her mother had for some time been putting away a good deal. Why not? She was never lonely, because we had subsidised an old friend of hers, a sterling character, to live with and look after her, but age and its problems are surely entitled to any aids they can find. Alcohol undoubtedly exacerbates the symptoms of Alzheimer's in many of those who suffer from it, but where would they have been without the stuff? Iris drinks wine nowadays, as she has always done, but in diminished quantity, which for her seems natural. Other bottles of various kinds lie about the house, but she ignores them.

As regards children, more than forty years ago, her attitude seemed equally natural. We hardly spoke of the question, because I suppose we knew we both understood her viewpoint. Iris's attitude about procreation, as about sex, was not dismissive; it was detachedly and benevolently indifferent. She herself had other things to do. How many women feel the same but also feel that it is unnatural to do so, as if motherhood were an achievement they could not let themselves do without? Stevie Smith, the poet, whom Iris knew and liked, used to say in her rather deliberately elfin way, "My poems are my kiddo." Iris would never have spoken of her novels as her children: she would never have said anything about the matter at all. Her reserve was deep, and as natural to her as it was deep.

D. H. Lawrence worship was getting into its stride in the mid-fifties, reaching a sort of climax in 1963, the year in which the failure of an Old Bailey court case against

Penguin books licensed *Lady Chatterley's Lover* for unlimited printing; the year in which, according to a sardonic poem by Philip Larkin, "sexual intercourse began." There was a sense in which this was true for England, where the matter had not previously been much discussed, or thought suitable for discussion. And so to the postwar generation, Lawrence appealed less as a writer than as a cult figure, like the newly famous Beatles, a symbol of enlightenment and modernity. For Iris, it was only as a writer that he mattered. I remember hearing a philosophical colleague complaining to her about Lawrence's "half-baked religiosity" in matters of sex. Iris mildly demurred, saying she thought he was such a marvellous writer, it didn't matter what he wrote about, or how. But sex certainly did become one of the new religions of the sixties and seventies; and when disillusionment set in, it was succeeded by a crudely Faustian view: sex as a performance sport, forever striving after new records, new achievements in the state of the art. All this passed by us, and our own cosy and quietistic approach to the matter.

There have been moments when I found myself wondering how Iris got on in bed with lovers whose approach was more ambitious or more demanding than my own; and on one occasion, I accidentally received an unexpected hint from an acquaintance who had, as I knew, been for a brief period a successful admirer. I did not greatly care for this character, a highly distinguished figure in his own sphere, with a weakness for keeping his friends a trifle overinformed about a current love affair, and how painful or ecstatic or both it was turning out to be. On this occasion, he made some remark about how important it was to get the girl proficient at what you wanted to do yourself, indicating that if she was gone on you enough, she would do whatever it was. "Nothing more discouraging than a partner who won't enter into the spirit of the thing," he observed sagely, and then gave me a sudden guilty look, as if he might have given something away. It was unlikely that he knew I was aware of his onetime dalliance with Iris, but that brief hangdog look gave me a strong suggestion that he was thinking of her and her shortcomings in bed, thoughts which he realised were now not best communicated to the husband.

Certainly our bedroom habits (the deep, deep peace of the double bed after the hurly-burly on the chaise longue, as Mrs. Pat Campbell noted) were always peaceful and unbothered by considerations of better, or more. The lady in Iris's novel A Severed Head who complained that her marriage "wasn't getting anywhere" would probably have made the same observation about her sex life. We expected neither sex nor marriage to get anywhere: we were happy for them to jog on just as they were.

Although Iris remained quite untroubled by any wish to have a family life of her own, she had a touching desire to join in any family activities that might be going on around her. As an only child, she greatly welcomed the prospect of having two brothers-in-law, although neither of them showed much interest in her. She bore this patiently, being rewarded in the course of time by the increasing regard, almost devotion, given her by my middle brother Michael, a bachelor and brigadier in the army, now retired. He had a distinguished military record, but his occupation since retirement has been the repair of monuments in churches derelict and no longer in use—some of them magnificent buildings, mainly in East Anglia. Nothing seemed to give him more pleasure than to take us on tour and to show Iris round any work he had been doing, commenting on the finer points of alabaster restoration—his speciality—and proudly showing off any neglected statue or cherub's head he had unearthed in the course of his work.

The now-restored church of St. Mary the Virgin, in Lydiard Tregoze, Wiltshire, was a special showpiece of his. A frugal person and careful with his pension—he made almost nothing out from his restoration work—he used to sleep in his camp bed in the churches where he worked, however remote or desolate they might be. I once asked him if this wasn't a shade spooky at times. He pooh-poohed the idea, then added, after a pause for reflection, that he had once felt a little uneasy on waking up in the night in a private chapel on the Harewood estate in Yorkshire. We enquired whether any explanation for this had manifested itself. Not exactly, he said, and yet he had been beset with the sense that something flat and dark, of considerable size, was in motion on the floor in the half-light, slowly coming closer to his bed. Rather tactlessly, I mentioned M. R. James's ghost story "The Treasure of Abbot Thomas," in which a creature resembling a damp leather bag has been set in mediaeval times by some satanic cleric to guard a treasure concealed under a church's nave. He had not read it, he said shortly. In fact, as he occasionally remarked, almost the only book he had read since his schooldays was *A Month in the Country*, not Turgenev's play but a brief romance by J. R. Carr about a young man engaged, like himself, in the work of church restoration. About this book, my brother was prepared to be enthusiastic.

I don't think he ever read any of Iris's novels, but in his own way he greatly respected her achievement. Perhaps because he saw her in a sense as a dedicated fellow soldier: one who had been prepared, as a good commander should be, to devote herself single-mindedly to the job of winning the battle. Certainly there was an unspoken accord between them, notwithstanding his extreme reserve, which was perhaps in secret sympathy with her own. Undoubtedly, they felt close to each other, although only meeting on rare occasions, family Christmases and the like. Since Iris developed Alzheimer's, he has expressed, most uncharacteristically for him, a wish to come and see us at fairly frequent intervals, driving down from London on Sundays for lunch. Although she doesn't remember him beforehand, or grasp who it is that is coming, these visits always have a cheering effect on her.

My own feelings are more mixed, as I have to produce

something in the way of lunch, instead of our vague little everyday picnic. When at home or on a job, my brother lives on sardines and tomatoes, a healthy diet, although he's not concerned with that. But he unconsciously expects his younger brother to take trouble for him. There is something I enjoy in this fraternal manifestation—essentially one of kindness, unspoken protectiveness—even though it is a bit irksome, practically speaking, to go along with it. He is punctilious about not drinking when he drives, bringing his own bottle of alcohol-free beer with some military name like Caliber.

I sometimes used to tease Iris by telling her that she possessed, in mild form, a "Lawrence of Arabia" complex. She smiled, but did not deny it. I have always held the opinion that T. E. Lawrence was a bogus figure. *The Seven Pillars of Wisdom*, once worshipped as a cult book among upper-class homosexuals and academics pining for action, seemed to me so turgidly written as to be almost unreadable. I still think this is true, but Iris always remained quietly loyal to her affection for the book and its author. She had read it at school, "soon after my Rafael Sabatini period," as she once told me. (Sabatini, author of *Captain Blood* and *The Black Swan*, was a prolific swashbuckling performer of popular literature.) This willingness to be uncritical about *The Seven Pillars* went along with its much deeper and more serious romantic influence, strongly discernible in many of her own novels. Transmuted as they are, and as is the world she gives them to inhabit, her characters frequently have for the addicted reader the same sort of powerful fascination that the Lawrence legend and personality once exerted. My brother himself has a shadowy presence in some of her novels, appearing in *An Unofficial Rose* as a character named Felix. I doubt if he would be recognised in the role, by himself or by anybody else, and I never commented on the point to Iris. She always hated to think her characters were in any sense identifiable, least of all by her own family. She had made them up: They were completely her own and belonged to her own world, which in its own way was certainly true.

At the time we got married, she had written three successful novels and had begun her fourth. An unforgettable scene in her third, *The Sandcastle*, has a green Riley car undergoing a complex underwater adventure. I was proud of knowing where the original of the Riley, as a fixture in the book, had come from, because I had found the car for Iris after a diligent study of the advertisements in the *Oxford Mail*. This had itself followed a mildly unfortunate incident involving a car—her car. It was a pale blue Hillman Minx, and it had been bought out of the proceeds of the preceding novel, *The Flight from the Enchanter*. During the fine summer of 1955, I had acted as driving instructor. I had an old Morris car I had bought cheaply from my parents when they had acquired a more respectable vehicle, and Iris quickly learnt to drive, and to drive very well. It would be presumptuous to say I taught her, but I sat beside her and made suggestions. My old car was known to us by its number EKL, which, as I pointed out, indicated the German word *ekelhaft*—meaning "disgusting"—but we were fond of it nonetheless. Iris took her test in it and passed the first time. I was hovering in the background when she met the test official—in those days, even driving tests were more informal than they are now—and I was relieved to see her make a conspicuous point of adjusting the rearview mirror before moving off, as I had advised her.

After this sage display of advice and instruction on my part, it was I who managed to crash the poor Minx on an icy road in December. I had borrowed the car to go to a party outside Oxford. No one has ever taken a piece of bad news better than Iris did when I broke it to her. She loved her Minx, and its life had been a sadly short one. But looking back, I think that was the moment at which our life together really began, even though there was still nothing said about marriage, and I had long since given up even hinting at it. But on its own minor scale, this was the kind of domestic disaster which tests a relationship, and shows whether or not it is going to work. Iris was so relieved I wasn't hurt that she didn't mind too much about the Minx. The accident had shown my importance to her more effectively than any loving deeds on my part could have done. Moreover, the insurance company paid up, and the green Riley, though impractical in many ways, was a far more romantic and beautiful car. It was a 1947 model, nearly ten years old, and its dark green chassis, recently and rather amateurishly repainted, was set off by elegant black wings and the graceful curl of the marque's radiator, with the name enamelled in blue. No one could have been less fickle than Iris, but in her excitement over the Riley, the Minx was soon out of mind, if not forgotten.

Not forgotten until now, that is. That memory has passed beyond her mind, but when I mention the Riley and describe it to her, there is still a very faint flicker of recognition. She even smiles when I go on to remind her of its bad habits and its bad brakes. It would be a valuable car today if it still exists. We kept it in honoured retire-ment for more than twenty years, until we could no longer afford garage space and so let it go for a few pounds.

Rivers, as I said, featured in our honeymoon, although not by intention. Our idea had been to take a cultural tour in a leisurely manner, down through France and over the Alps into northern Italy, keeping clear of famous places like Florence and Venice, which we would leave for an-other time, staying instead at Urbino, San Gimignano, and Arezzo, places earnestly recommended to Iris by a couple whom I thought of as her "art friends"—Brigid Brophy and her husband, Michael, who was later to become director of the National Gallery. Brigid had chided Iris for allowing herself to do anything so banal as to get married, but her sarcasm was weakened by the fact that she had, however reluctantly, taken the same step herself. She wanted the experience of having a child, and single mothers in those days had not yet acquired the glamour they would achieve later on.

Wisely, we were not going in the Riley, but in a very small Austin van, which I had recently bought new for a modest sum. It was all the cheaper because being a "commercial vehicle," it was exempt from what was then known as purchase tax. The same Elaine Griffiths who had asked me to the party at St. Anne's where I met Iris had recently acquired one of these, and, being a crafty lady, she had had a garage remove the metal side panels at the back, substituting neat glass windows. The vehicle now became officially a saloon car, and as such, it was not subject to the thirty-mile-an-hour speed limit imposed in those days on all trucks and vans. She recommended this method, but after consideration, we rejected it, unwisely as it turned out, because I was soon stopped and fined by an unsporting policeman for doing nearly forty miles an hour.

Notwithstanding this setback, I clung to my idea that it would be better for the van to remain as it was, because then we should be able to sleep in it, at a pinch, when on our travels. In fact, we did this only once, and that was a few years later, in the west of Ireland. We had been to see the famous black granite cliffs of Moher, and a large farmer, whom we christened the "Moher Giant," had conscripted us and the van to help him get in the hay from a field almost on the edge of the abyss. He even offered to buy the van, enquiring with interest "what price would it be now" in England. Escaping at last in a state of exhaustion, we found a fishing hotel which could give us a high tea of grilled trout but which had no room for the night. So we drove to a quiet beach, fried a further supper of bacon and eggs in a rugged iron frying pan bought in a Belfast market, and settled down for the night. We slept soundly, roused early by the scream of the gulls meeting the scallop boats as they chugged into the next cove. We then returned to the hotel and had bacon and scallops for breakfast, the favourite morning dish, as I recalled, of good Queen Elizabeth I, who used to wash it down with a pint of lager. We had Irish coffee instead.

It was on this trip, during which we explored the rocky coast of County Clare and the strange stony waste of "the Burren," that Iris conceived the idea of her haunting novel set in Ireland, The Unicorn, and found the landscape that embodied the feel of it. With its fantasy of a woman immersed in a kind of sexual cloister near the wild coast, The Unicorn has always been for me the most purely Irish of all her novels, more so even than The Red and the Green, her novel featuring the Easter Rebellion of 1916.

During this trip, I made the discovery of how to swim comfortably in cold water. Or rather, not to swim but to hang suspended in a narrow bay, observing the flora of the seabed with a snorkel and mask. The underwater scene off a rocky northern shore is far more magical than anything in the tropics. Fronds of seaweed, dark red and amethyst, undulate quietly over vast smooth stones, polished by the storms of the winter. Green crabs as big as dinner plates limp away sideways. Fish are rare, but a plaice looking like a freckled partridge lay half-hidden on the white sand and looked up at me obliquely. Enthralled, I was unaware of the cold, but when I came out, I shook and shivered uncontrollably. Iris rubbed some feeling into me, clucking like a disapproving parent, but when I handed her the snorkel and mask, she became as enraptured as I had been, nor did she feel the cold. She remained in the water for what seemed hours while with trembling hands I lit a driftwood fire and crouched beside it, taking swigs from our whisky bottle. Later I tried going into the sea in all my clothes, and a macintosh, and that worked well, although removing the saturated garments that clung like an icy shirt of Nessus was far from easy. Hercules had been set on fire by his fatal shirt, and at those moments, I quite envied him.

Having acquired the habit, I usually kept a vest on when swimming, even in warm water. Once in Pisa harbour, in a drizzle of rain, I was examining the fishes, numerous and even colourful, which congregated by the side of the harbour breakwater, where one or two anglers were fishing. Iris, who had decided not to follow me into the water, was standing there under an umbrella; and she later reported seeing one of the fishermen give a start of surprise and peer down intently into the harbour. The reason for this was not clear until I reappeared under my snorkel, clad in an ancient vest. "I saw the fishermen peering down and trying to read the label on your neck," chortled Iris. "I really did." The episode much amused her, particularly the moment—sometimes mimed by her in later years—when the incredulous Italian fishermen had craned their heads sideways, so as to keep in view the apparition slowly progressing below them in the harbour.

Half a century ago, the roads of France were empty. Long, straight poplar-bordered roads, still full of *déformations* as a result of wartime neglect, but wonderfully relaxing to buzz happily down in a reverie *à deux*. No trouble going through towns. A helpful sign promised TOUTES DIRECTIONS; a bored gendarme blew his whistle unnecessarily; small restaurants advertised their *repas* with a sign on the pavement. France existed not for the tourist nor for its own people (Where were they? Who were they?) but for honeymoon couples like us, without much money, listening together to each poplar saying *hush* as we drove past, as regularly as the telegraph wires of those days used to rise and fall beside the train. Then we would stop at one of the little restaurants, three-quarters empty, and have charcuterie and entrecôte aux endives, with unlimited quantities of red wine, which never had to be uncorked or bought by the bottle. Cramped little hotels (de la Poste or du Gare) had scrubbed floors that smelt of garlic and Gauloise cigarettes. Natives were taciturn, speech formalised and distant; but I noticed that the severest French person (and to me all their faces looked austere, like those of monks and nuns) responded to Iris's smile.

Of course she knew France already—another France, inhabited entirely, in my eyes, by writers and intellectuals who sat in cafés and wrote books between drinks. It was not so long since Iris had been under the spell of Sartre's novel *La Nausée* and Raymond Queneau's *Pierrot Mon Ami*. She had met Queneau in Brussels cafés at the end of the war, and through him had heard of Samuel Beckett's pre-war novel *Murphy*. *La Nausée* had interested her philosophically, and *Murphy* had bequeathed to her own first novel, *Under the Net*, a notional spirit of bohemia. Along with existentialism, and perhaps partly in response to it, there went at that time with Iris something less engagé and more irresponsible, something that made me think of the young person in Boswell's Johnson who wished to study philosophy, but "cheerfulness kept breaking in."

Our own cheerfulness found a perfect foil in quiet, empty, unresponsive France, which fed us so deliciously and so cheaply, and sent us on our way down endless roads on which one seemed to cover hundreds, if not thousands, of kilometres without any effort at all.

Our first swim was in a river of the Pas-de-Calais, a deep, placid tributary of the Somme. Perhaps the place in the poem by Wilfred Owen where hospital barges had been moored during those futile offensives of World War I. The next was much farther south, in a steep and wildwooded valley, with pine and chestnut growing up the mountains. The water was warm, and the stream so secluded that we slipped in with nothing on. Usually cautious, Iris may have felt that now we were in France, Anglo-Saxon inhibition could be discarded. It was in this remote spot that my feet encountered a smooth round object in the shallows. It was half-buried in the ooze, but I fished it up without difficulty and found an object resembling a Greek or Roman amphora, earth-coloured and cracked in one or two places. It was clearly not ancient—we found a trade name stamped on the base—and I was about to let it sink back into its underwater home when Iris, treading water beside me, vigorously demurred. Even at that date she wanted to keep everything she found. Wrapped in French newspapers, it reposed in the bottom of the little van and lived on for years in a corner of our garden back home, until its cracks were found out by the frost and it came to pieces.

After setting it down on the bank, we slipped in again for another swim. Iris seemed dreamy and absent. "Suppose we had found a great old bell," she said as we dried ourselves. I pointed out that this would hardly be likely in such a wild spot, far from any town or village. But her imagination was equal to that one.

"It could have been stolen from a belfry and buried in the river until they could dispose of it. People at home are stealing lead from country churches all the time, aren't they? Then the thieves here never came back."

"Quite a recent event? Nothing legendary about it?"

"No, wait.... The church was desecrated at the time of the Reformation by those—what did they call them in France?" she asked as she stood beside me, an earnest figure streaked all over with river mud, which she was vaguely spreading over herself with the towel.

"Huguenots?"

"That's it. The Huguenots got down the bell and wanted to break it up or melt it or something, but some devoted worshippers of the old church managed to steal it away and bring it here for safekeeping."

Although she had done ancient history in her exams, Iris was a scholar who had done her best papers in philosophy. So she had often told me; and her sense of the historical was certainly rather sketchy. But as her novels show, her imagination possessed its own brand of sometimes almost pedantic accuracy.

The most striking episode in her next novel, *The Bell*, certainly came out of that river. A great bell is found in an old abbey, now the centre of a modern religious community. The symbol of the bell is enigmatic, but not so the penetrating and perceptive account of characters who wish to try to lead the religious life.

Next day we were in a mountain region, nearing the frontier. In order to make an early start for crossing the Alps, we decided to stop for the night at a small town with a railway junction. In the dead of night, our bedroom door was suddenly flung open and a voice proclaimed in dramatic tones, "*Georges! C'est l'heure.*" The unshaded light over the bed dazzled us, and when he saw how things were, the young railway worker who had come to rouse his comrade hastened to switch it off again, muttering in a more subdued way, "*Ah, Madame, mille pardons.*"

As we negotiated the hairpin turns next day, I could talk of nothing but Hannibal. I remembered the story told by Livy. Confronted in the pass with a wall of solid rock, perhaps the result of a landslide, Hannibal had great fires lit and attempted to crack open the obstacle by pouring vinegar on it as the stone cooled. "But where could he have got enough vinegar," demanded Iris, "and in any case, would it work? Has anyone tried it?" Her scepticism was an instance of the meticulous way she always planned the more outlandish episodes in her fiction, testing them in her mind with careful common sense to make sure they really worked. *The Bell* itself was an example. I always felt there was something wonderfully literal about the discovery of the great bell, which reminded me of *Alice in Wonderland*, one of Iris's own favourite books.

We continued to debate the logistics of Hannibal's campaign, and the difficulties his quartermasters must have had with the vinegar supply. As we drove higher, we came into mist, and there was a sound of cowbells. We had a bottle of sparkling Burgundy with us in the van, bought with this ceremony in mind. At the top of the pass, we drank it, then laid the bottle to rest under a stone beside the road. I marked the place carefully, or so I thought, for our idea was to retrieve the bottle on our return journey. When it came to the point, Iris did not like to think of the bottle we had shared being left there. On our return, we repeated the ceremony with a bottle of Asti Spumanti, from its home town, but try as I might, and I was sure I had the right place, I could not find the other bottle. So we put the Italian one in a similar place, Iris hoping they would keep each other company.

The life of inanimate things was always important to her. I used to tease her about Wordsworth's flower, which the poet was confident must "enjoy the air it breathes." Iris would say, impatiently and somewhat mysteriously, "Never mind about flowers. There are other things that matter much more." Though good about it at the time, she also felt real sadness for the abandoned bottles, and I think of it now when she stoops like an old tramp to pick up scraps of candy paper or cigarette butts from the pavement. She feels at one with them, and will find them a home if she can.

Intellectuals, I have noticed, are apt to dislike in her novels what they regard as such signs of whimsy, even of sentimentality. They misunderstand, or do not bother to be aware of, the unobtrusive seriousness with which she treats such things, and the way she feels about them. I think of it as her Buddhist side. She has always had a strong regard for that religion, which, as its enlightened practitioners will tell you, is not really a religion at all. One of the most enlightened is our friend, Professor Peter

Conradi, who is writing a biography of Iris, and whose devotion to her novels is certainly connected with his practice of Buddhism. One does not of course "believe" in Buddhism, or even in the sacredness of the Buddha. "If you meet the Buddha on the road, kill him." Peter sometimes repeats to us the ancient proverb, with a smile that is far from being whimsical. There seems no doubt that Iris's own private devotion to things finds a response in some of the tenets of Buddhism.

Safe down the Alps, in Susa, we ate our first Italian spaghetti. It was sunny now, after the grey Alps, and hot, even though we were still high up. As we left Susa, full of spaghetti and red wine, a stout grocer who had been standing at the door of his shop stepped out in the road and held up his hand. Did we perhaps require any supplies? Wine? he could let us have jars of very good wine— his own. Lowering his voice, he said we could have it all free in exchange for a few petrol coupons—*coupone*. Petrol was scarce in Italy and extremely expensive. Supplied by the travel agent at home with these coupons for the journey, the tourist motoring on the Continent found himself a popular figure.

We would have liked to oblige, but we would be needing the coupons ourselves—how many, we could not yet say. The friendly grocer appreciated the dilemma. If there were coupons left over when we returned, then we would do business. A fortnight or so later, we did so.

Massive salamis a yard long were pressed upon us, and huge bottles of wine. When we stopped again on the way over the Alpine pass, Iris unearthed a vast smooth stone— perhaps it had been dislodged by Hannibal's experiment with the vinegar? She longed to take it home, so I heaved it on top of all the other rubbish that by now cluttered the floor of the van. It must have landed on top of one of the big wine bottles. Unknowingly, we descended into France with a gallon or so of red wine trickling through onto the road. Much remained behind. I still have an old vest, marbled, despite occasional washings over the years, in a delicate patterning of pink and Tuscan red.

Our appetite for *spaghetti pomodoro* was insatiable. We seemed to eat or want to eat nothing else on that honeymoon. And we ate it very often in the open air, under what Shelley called "the roof of blue Italian weather." In the afternoons, we slept deeply after several lunchtime carafes of cold white wine, and Chianti, too. The white wine came in carafes beaded with condensation and with a little leaden seal on one side, certifying a *mezzolitro*. We persuaded the friendly maternal waitress of a trattoria to sell us one of them.

Our search for rivers continued, and the afternoon we left Susa for the south, we found another one. As I later discovered from the map, it was the Tanaro, a branch of the Ticino, where Hannibal's Numidians had soundly beaten the Roman cavalry. In contrast to our last swim, this now-idyllic stream ran through the open sun-filled plain, reached after bumping for a mile along on a sandy track which instinct told me must lead to a river. No one was about: We had the whole landscape and the hot afternoon to ourselves. Or so we thought. We were about to come out of the water, when Iris gave a warning cry. The bank was lined with people—Italian farmers, a uniformed policeman. Some child must have spotted us and called his elders to come and see what these strange foreigners were up to. Conversing animatedly, they gazed on us with friendly smiles, teeth flashing in their brown faces and under the policeman's fine black moustache. It was a frieze from a painting, perhaps the *Baptism of Christ*. But there we were in the water, with nothing on, and somehow we had to get out and get to our clothes. And without shocking any local sensibilities.

Suddenly, the policeman seemed to appreciate the problem. How did he do so? It may have been the look on our faces. With authoritative gestures, he drove the farmers and children—there were no women present—along the riverbank and back to the road. When they were gone, he remained where he was, beside our belongings and bedraggled towel, and seemed to smile invitingly. There was nothing else for it. We emerged with what dignity we could, bowing our thanks and smiling graciously, as if we were fully clad.

A day or so later, we were in Volterra, the "lordly Volterra" of Macaulay's *Lays*:

Where scowls the far-famed hold,
Piled by the hands of giants
For god-like kings of old.

The mountains were full of marble quarries and there were shops selling alabaster. We used to sit in the square at a café where the waiter looked exactly like photographs of the young Kafka. Iris took a great interest in him. Unlike most Italian waiters, he moved with diffidence, as if uncertain of what he was carrying or where to put it. He seemed to like us, but his smile was *distrait*, a little tormented, as if he were planning some work he knew he would never finish. His head was always surrounded by wasps, which he made no attempt to brush away, as if they were visible embodiments of the angst within him. "Perhaps he will put us both in one of his stories," said Iris.

It was while asking poor Kafka and his attendant wasps for Punt è Mes, the delicious slightly bitter Italian vermouth we had both taken a fancy to, that I realised a difference, suddenly seeming to me very important, between our sense of him and his interior troubles and our growing sense of each other. If Kafka were really a troubled soul, and not just worried about the football results, there was nothing we could do about it, no way we could establish contact with him. His sadness, if it existed, was that of an unknown life, a part of life we were familiar with back home and took for granted but which here had no existence we could enter into. Sitting at the sunlit table, the desolation of things, the tears of things of which Virgil's Aeneas was reminded in passing, seemed all around us, but in an inaccessible, almost surreal form, that of young Kafka wandering in and out of the café carrying glasses of Punt è Mes and the tiny cups of espresso.

Iris seemed to be in a reverie, too. I took her hand and it pressed mine. What was she thinking? I had no idea, any more than I had in the case of Kafka, and I knew very well there was no way to find out. But this realisation reassured me deeply: it made me as happy as the hypothetical woes of Kafka had made me feel sad. Such ignorance, such solitude! They suddenly seemed the best part of love and marriage. We were together because we were comforted and reassured by the solitariness each saw and was aware of in the other.

The hotel we found in a back street was old and shabby; our room, with its furniture and its dusty red velvet hangings, might have been in a decaying palazzo. It provided no meals, and in the morning we returned to the square, where Kafka brought us coffee and buns. It was in Volterra, I think, that we began to feel really married, as if something in the old, grand, forbidding little town had reminded us of both good and bad fortune, of the brevity of time, and the long wearisomeness of history. It was in Volterra, too, that Iris's life of secret creation became a reality for me. I felt her at work, with no idea of what she was doing or how, and that gave me the same feel of safe and yet distant closeness. I think she realised then how much I was beginning to enjoy this, and would come to depend on it.

At a comically lower level, both of us realised then that we daydreamed about the people we encountered together—in my case, girls and women; in hers, men. It was another aspect of our closeness, another safe and reassuring one, and in this case, an amused one, too. And we did then, in fact still do, sometimes show our amusement about it to each other. I think Iris may have dreamed a little about Kafka and what it would be like to mother him, to encourage him, perhaps have an affair with him.

I don't know whether she dreamed about the police-man by the riverbank, but that, too, seems quite possible, for he had been in his own way a memorable figure. We had done our best to ignore him when we came out of the river. Iris seized the towel and wrapped it round her-self. But our policeman, I noticed, had turned away and, with his hands behind him, was gazing into the distance. He combined boldness with delicacy. When we were dressed, he had turned with his friendly smile and en-quired if we had enjoyed our swim. "*Non troppo fresco?*" Iris had spent one or two holidays by herself in Rome and Florence and her Italian was considerably better than mine. She engaged him in conversation, and it soon turned out that he would like a lift to the neighbouring town. He had come to see relatives on the farm near the river; this farm, like most buildings in such an Italian landscape, blended in so well that it was hardly visible. I was rather relieved to find that despite his grey uniform and military cap, he was not on duty and was not going to accuse us of violating the civic code of public decency. As he talked, his face ceased to look like that of a modern functionary and took on that withdrawn, dignified air which portraits and faces possess in Quattrocento painting.

Were we going to stay in Orbessano? If so, he could recommend a hotel kept by friends of his aunt. By this time, we were bumping back towards the road, with Iris sitting on the policeman's lap. The van had only its two front seats and the back of it was thoroughly encumbered. We parted on the best of terms. I thought of the policeman on the way back home, when on a very hot afternoon in Padua we were trying vainly to find somewhere to stay. There were a lot of young conscripts in uniform about, and Iris asked one of them, a scholarly-looking weedy boy wearing spectacles, if he knew of any hotel. He seemed surprised but politely beckoned her to follow him, I trailing behind with the bags. An officer was passing, and he appeared to ask the young soldier rather severely what he thought he was doing. Iris later reported that the young soldier replied with dignity, "Sir, I am taking this lady to a hotel." The officer smiled, unbent, and uttered what was presumably the Italian equivalent of "Vive le sport!"

The policeman by the riverbank entered, I know, into Iris's imagination. In some of her novels, he, or someone very like him, is a ghostly presence, transmuted into a flux of different types and personalities. Such persons are surrounded by water, as if it were their native environment: The story of their spirits seems to arise from sea or river and return to them. Iris never cared for the novels of George Eliot, but her own wholly different plots and beings sometimes remind me of Maggie Tulliver in *The Mill on the Floss* saying, "I am in love with moistness." Maggie lives by the river, and in rather contrived circumstances— much more contrived than any comparable scenario in Iris's work—eventually drowns in it.

A few years ago, a writer named Charles Sprawson sent Iris his remarkable book with the odd title *Haunts of the Black Masseur*, a title inspired by a story the author had read when young about such a Negro massage expert. The tale mingled in his mind with a film he had thought marvellous, *The Creature from the Black Lagoon*, and it became for him a symbol of the whole swimming mystique. Iris had no such mystique, only one about water, but we both liked the book very much and I reviewed it under her name.

Black masseurs and lagoons were a far cry from sun-filled Italian landscape and the green rivers full of rushes and golden sandbars that meandered past hills resembling those in the background of Bellini's pictures, or Perugino's. The sea in Italy was, by contrast, the greatest possible disappointment to us. In most cases, the surrounding area was divided off into holiday camps by barbed wire, and the sea was impossible to get at. When we once managed to do so, near Pesaro, we had hardly got into the water before an immense caterpillar of holidaying toddlers came crawling over the beach, engulfing our possessions and undulating onwards as we rushed out to rescue them. By contrast with France, Italy and the Italian seaside were distinctly overcrowded.

Rivers and pictures were our holiday ideals. We have never been greatly drawn to spectacular or picturesque tourist attractions, but picture galleries are another matter. We visited Borgo San Sepolcro, a small place in those days and quite difficult to get to, situated, as I recall, in Tuscany, near the border with Umbria. In a bleak room of its town hall, one was suddenly face-to-face with the *Resurrection*, the masterpiece of Piero della Francesca. Aldous Huxley refers to it quite simply as "the greatest painting in the world!" What awed and amazed us, and what must indeed be the first impression the picture makes on the ordinary viewer, is the immense difference between the figure of Christ that Piero represents and that found in any other religious painting. It is a fresco, and was for years concealed under a layer of whitewash, conceivably even because of this startling and almost alarming singularity. When finally brought back to light, it was in excellent condition, looking as it must have when first painted.

Huxley's essay, entitled "The Greatest Painting in the World," is by far the best thing ever written about it. He does not emphasise unduly the originality of Piero's statuesque figures, a product of the painter's interest in geometry and linear mathematics. Art historians dwell on this unusual interest, and it might well be that Piero's impassive geometry was what suddenly brought him into such outstanding favour with the modernists, for whom romanticism meant emotional indulgence and, as T. E. Hulme put it, "spilt religion." No religion is being spilt in Piero's painting, no human impulses emotionally indulged. We can see why the painter was disregarded in the nineteenth century, as in the late Renaissance. The figure in the great fresco that seems to hoist itself effortlessly out of the tomb, one muscular leg poised on its stone coping, is not the Christ of mediaeval or Catholic Christianity, nor the liberal humanitarian Christ who took over a new human role at the end of the age of faith. He is, as Huxley says, a masterful, even an insolent figure, his expressionless eyes fixed on no goal that religion would recognise or aspire to. Huxley calls him the embodiment of the classical ideal, the superb image of man as self-sufficient, immortalised by his own sense of art and form.

However that may be, the picture is not only supremely satisfying but also electrifying. It inspires awe. We ate our spaghetti that day with a sense of high achievement, for who can see a great picture or read a great book without taking some of the credit for it himself, albeit in a sober mood. The restaurant was almost empty; there seemed to be no other tourists in the sleepy little town. Things are different today: There are phalanxes of buses bearing German and Japanese tourists. The section of the town hall housing the picture has been turned into an arty art gallery; the picture itself lit up, set off, protected. I am glad we saw it before these transformations took place. The picture would have been even more inaccessible when Huxley first saw it, arriving at Borgo San Sepolcro after a laborious train journey. Piero has now become a major tourist attraction.

The picture fascinated Iris. We talked of it a lot, but however much we talked of it, I knew the real impression it had made on her lay below the level of speech, like the iceberg below the water. The god whose own physical strength and dark force of being seemed to be impelling him out of the tomb would inspire in the future many visions and creations of her own. She once said to me when I commented on the importance of the role, visible and invisible, that pictures played in her novels, "You're right. They're all just pictures really."

"Well, I wouldn't say 'just pictures.' But I've often thought that what some of your readers find spiritual and uplifting in your novels is, unknown to them, a silent fellowship with great art of other kinds. You are the only novelist I know who can make the whole world of art come into your novels without being laborious about it, or making it seem fancy."

Iris smiled. "Well, thanks very much. I don't like to think about what happens when I do it. You're the critic, not me."

Almost any picture could inspire her in these invisible ways. Once we were in Lille, the big bustling industrial town in the north of France, a sort of Pittsburgh or Manchester, one would think, where the fine arts are concerned. We were going to do our usual thing, a joint discussion and a question-and-answer session. The occasion was a festival, boosting the cultural life of the university and town. We always enjoyed such outings. Iris loved meeting new people; and although she never wanted to give a proper lecture, she was always immensely popular as a speaker because of her candidly unofficial approach and the warmth with which she talked to everyone she encountered. Lille was no exception, but what was surprising in those days was the unexpectedly magnificent bookshop, called "Le Furet"—The Ferret—and the equally grand and well-filled art gallery. We had trouble in finding it—a long walk—but there was a small picture by a lesser Dutch master which absorbed Iris's silent attention while I wandered on among enormous nineteenth-century canvases by Bouguereau and his contemporaries—ample naked ladies expanding like balloons into a sky full of sickly tinted flowers. No doubt they had once been popular with the burghers of Lille, but Iris had found a small gem (I still cannot recall the name of the painter) which showed no more than a narrow white road ascending through broom bushes over a hill, then disappearing. As with the Italian policeman, and Piero's mysterious and saturnine Christ, that picture has a ghostly presence among the landscapes and characters of many of her later novels.

There were other pictures. The one by Balthus of the girl with the slyly indulgent smile playing cards with a flamboyant opponent who holds a card or two behind his back. Perhaps a retarded youth from the locality, to whom in her own self-possessed way she is being kind? Perhaps a younger brother? Having seen it in the catalogue, Iris and I searched for that painting through the many galleries and corridors of the Museo Thyssen-Bornemiza in Madrid. This emanation, as the poet Blake would have said, is there transmogrified in her next novels, as are the Beckmanns we were to see in the St. Louis Art Museum.

But the painting which had the deepest and at the same time the most visible effect on her work was the very late Titian, the faun Marsyas flayed by Apollo, which is located in a remote monastery in Moravia and was lent a few years ago to a Royal Academy exhibition in London. Iris went to see it countless times but never said a word. To be mute about pictures was her way of paying them homage. Once when we were in the gallery together, and almost to tease her, I remarked that the martyred faun was like Piero's Christ in reverse, and that the terrible smile—of agony? of ecstasy?—on his upside-down features reminded me in some way of the terrifying detachment of Christ's face as it rises indifferently above what is happening lower down in Piero's painting. She looked at me, thought, and smiled to herself, but she said nothing. The Titian became her most "public" picture, however, the one whose effect on her was most apparent and acknowledged. It features as a background ikon, dusky but unmistakable, in the portrait of her done by the London artist Tom Phillips, which hangs in the National Portrait Gallery.

So married life began. And the joys of solitude. No contradiction was involved. The one went perfectly with the other. To feel oneself held and cherished and accompanied, and yet to be alone. To be closely and physically entwined, and yet feel solitude's friendly presence, as warm and undesolating as contiguity itself.

$\mathcal{F}ive$

$\mathcal{I}$ never missed Iris, and I don't think in that sense she ever missed me. Separation, when it happened, was itself a kind of closeness. In those early days, when televisions were all black-and-white ones and we never possessed or wanted one, there was an advertisement we saw on the flickering screen sometimes when we visited her mother. It showed a young man on a genteel urban street corner with an English drizzle gently falling. He is turning up his hat brim against the rain (hats were still quite normal then) and lighting a cigarette. Along the road, some young people have emerged laughing from a well-lit house and are getting into a car. Our young man surveys them with a self-satisfied and slightly pitying amusement and puffs on his cigarette. The caption was "You're never alone with a Strand."

We had often seen the Strand advertisement together

on her mother's TV and had laughed about it. And so TV advertisements as well as great painting entered the emerging world of her novels. More important for me, the advertisement symbolised the satisfactions of our own kind of solitude in closeness.

The Strand was one of the most unsuccessful brands of cigarette ever marketed. I remember later hearing from a young man, an ex-pupil who worked in advertising, that in those circles it was mentioned in the same breath as Craven A. Craven A, though it continued to be a popular brand, once nearly ruined itself with the advertisement: "Craven A—does not affect your throat." Smokers had at once put their hand to their throats and thought, God, I'd better cut them out. The young man in the Strand advertisement had the same effect on the smoking public. He was so clearly going to be alone for a long, long time. But I took the same satisfaction in the advertisement that I did in our new way of life.

It was very different from the life we live today. It was like being alone, and yet we were not alone. I never travelled in spirit with Iris when she was away for a brief period—in London or teaching—or once when she had a half semester's fellowship at Yale—and I don't think she ever needed or wanted to rush back to me. We were separate but never separated. I never looked at a photograph of her, either. It seemed to have no connection with her, as she was.

Now we are together for the first time. We have actually become, as is often said of a happy married couple, inseparable—in a way, like Ovid's Baucis and Philemon, whom the gods gave the gift of growing old together as trees. It is a way of life that is unfamiliar. The closeness of apartness has necessarily become the closeness of closeness. And we know nothing of it; we have never had any practice.

Not that we ever practised the opposite: the way of life, not uncommon in academe, which a philosophical friend of Iris defined by coining the word *telegamy*. Telegamy, marriage at a distance, works well for some people, who prefer to remain an independent part of an entity. It may sharpen their satisfaction in time spent together, as well as being of practical convenience if careers are to be pursued in places far apart. But it is not, as noted by Anthony Powell, the same thing as being married. Apartness in marriage is a state of love, and not a function of distance, or preference, or practicality.

A goose which cannot find other geese will attach itself to some object—another animal, even a stone or a post—and never lose sight of it. This terror of being alone, of being cut off for even a few seconds from the familiar object, is a feature of Alzheimer's. If Iris could climb inside my skin now, or enter me as if I had a pouch like a kangaroo, she would do so. She has no awareness of what I am doing, only an awareness of what I am. The words and gestures of love still come naturally, but they cannot be accompanied by that wordless communication which depends on the ability to use words. In any case, she has forgotten public language, although not our private one, which cannot now get us far.

I sit at the kitchen table and make desperate efforts to keep it as my own preserve, as it has always been. Iris seems to understand this, and when prompted, she goes obediently into the sitting room, where the TV is switched on. In less than a minute, she is back again.

Before we got married, we had found a house to live in. Visiting houses round Oxford, in the Riley, armed by the real estate agent with a sheaf of particulars and prices, was more like a game than the real thing. (Perhaps we were never the real thing, in that serious sense, the sense intended by Iris's character in *A Severed Head* who complained that her marriage was not going anywhere.) We looked at these houses in an atmosphere of frivolity. One, at Bampton, fascinated Iris because it had a powder-closet next to one of the bedrooms. It was an old house. In the eighteenth century, a valet would have groomed the master or mistress's wigs there. Another had a sizable pond in the garden, perhaps big enough to swim in. A third, rather far out, possessed a real swimming pool, even though a small one and obviously neglected. But man-made pools had little appeal for us. In those days, there was a rich variety of country houses for sale, mostly old ones, going cheaply. We got as far as saying to one another, "This could be your workroom," or "The kitchen fireplace would be nice to sit in front of," but we had no idea about heating, cooking, drains, bathrooms (though we admired one all-tiled number done in peacock blue).

Iris fell in love with a house in the village of Taynton, near Burford. The place itself, near the River Windrush, was very beautiful. This was the house she must have. Even though she was still not at all sure she wanted to get married. She could always live there on her own, I said craftily and as if in the most rational way. I would come to visit her. "But what about the badgers?" she said, smiling. The badger joke had already become well established. How would she cope with them when they broke in if I didn't return home from work every evening? "But you would be working in Oxford, too. The badgers would have to look after themselves." We laughed, and never decided anything, except about this house.

It was June 1956. Iris was going over to Ireland to stay with the novelist Elizabeth Bowen, with whom she had recently become very friendly. I was left in charge of making a bid for the house, arranging a down payment, all that sort of thing. I did so, and everything seemed satisfactory. Then the agent rang to say the owner had changed his mind. He would sell the house not to the buyer who offered the asking price, but to anyone who made an offer, unspecified, above it. No doubt he had heard that several potential buyers were interested. I knew how much Iris wanted the place, wanted to marry it more than she wanted to marry me. Perhaps I was jealous. I was certainly innocent about property selling and its techniques, and I felt cross with the owner, whom I felt had deceived us, although the agent seemed to regard his procedure as perfectly normal. I told the agent we would stand on the offer we had made. Next day, he rang to tell me we had lost the bid; the house had gone to another prospective purchaser.

The day after that, Iris arrived back from Ireland. On the phone, she was unusually expansive and confiding, telling me of the great time she had at Bowen's Court, the gaunt house in County Cork, where she and the owner had sat chatting and drinking Guinness and brandy. Iris disliked telephoning, using it only for the briefest of practical messages, and I was both touched and disturbed by her ebullience about the Irish visit. I dreaded having to tell her she had lost the Taynton house. But when I steeled myself to do so, she was as calm and understanding as she had been on the occasion when I had crashed the Hillman Minx. She was generously philosophical: She told me not to worry—it couldn't be helped. I have sometimes wondered at odd moments whether those two accidents did more to make her feel she would like to be married than any amount of faithful and supportive attention on my part could have done. Misfortunes suffered together, even before the normal misfortunes of married life, can no doubt have such an effect.

There might have been something else, as well. She told me a good deal later, after we were married and when we were going to see Elizabeth Bowen, who was by then living in Oxford, that Elizabeth had shown a good deal of quizzical Irish curiosity about her younger guest's emotional life. Perhaps under the influence of the Guinness, or the brandy, Iris had most uncharacteristically confided in her hostess. Alone together in the big house, apart from the gardener and a young girl who cooked, the pair had several heart-to-hearts together. Elizabeth told Iris of the happiness of her own marriage, which many of her intellectual friends had regarded as incongruous, even incomprehensible: her husband having been a worthy man but painfully dull. She and her husband had agreed together not to have children. She had wanted above all things to write; her husband had been through the war on the Western Front and sincerely felt the modern world too awful to justify bringing a new life into it. Unlike Iris, Elizabeth had some regrets in later life about this decision, as her last novels touchingly, though fleetingly, reveal. Her husband's death must have increased her sense of loneliness and lack of family life, for her own mother and father died before she was twelve.

I find it touching myself to think of the two women, normally of an almost masculine reserve, confiding in each other during those quiet damp days in an Irish country house. In the mornings, they had remained apart and got on with their own work—each was writing a novel. After lunch, they walked or went out in the car, then more work after tea. Claret flowed freely at both meals, but for Elizabeth, the high point of the day, well documented in her late novel *The Little Girls*, was the drinking time at six, the "happy hour," as she used sardonically to refer to it, for she loved America and the Americans. For the fellowship of this hour, she had always depended on what she called a "boon companion," and it so happened that Iris filled a gap between the departure from Doneraile of two of Elizabeth's old friends and her own sudden decision to sell the family house and leave Ireland. This, too, she had confided to Iris, and insensibly they had got on to the question of how one decided things in life. For Elizabeth, the business of leaving Ireland, with no husband to support her and to confer with, was going to be agonising. "I couldn't buy a pair of shoes without Alan," she told Iris, and the most terrible moment in her life had come when she woke up in the night at Bowen's Court and found him dead beside her.

I think Iris was much moved by the helplessness revealed to her by this strong, sardonic, reserved woman, whose work she admired without being at all familiar with it, and whose friendship at that moment she so greatly valued. No doubt she had been unusually confiding in her own turn, and she told me later that Elizabeth had impressed upon her almost with urgency the advantages of the married state. Before she left, Iris had said something about me, and about her idea of a house in the country. Elizabeth, whom I had not met at that time, sent her best wishes to me, and for the house.

And now I had to tell Iris that the house had fallen through. I did not tell her that it had been through my own caution, or lack of enterprise and financial spirit. The truth was that, apart from possible feelings of jealousy, I had never believed in that house. There was something fishy about it. Iris, carried away by its undoubted charm and the beauty of village and countryside, perhaps also its proximity to the River Windrush, had been indifferent to all else. As it happened, the house agent rang me again a few weeks later to report that the other sale had not come off and that we could have the house on the old terms. This information, too, I suppressed, for by that time, fortunately for me, another house had turned up, and it engaged all of Iris's attention.

I had never met Elizabeth, but I had read everything she had written and had lived in the world of her novels and stories with immense pleasure, almost with passion. *The Death of the Heart* was my favourite. I once made the mistake of telling Elizabeth that, and she looked displeased. She had never cared for *The Death of the Heart*, or its success; she preferred her fans to find whatever was her latest book her most intriguing, challenging, unexpected. Those things were certainly true of her later novels *The Little Girls* and *Eva Trout*, but what I had specially liked about them was her return to the magic place she had made her own, the seaside country of Romney Marsh and the little town of Hythe. She had lived there as a girl before her mother died, and after trying Oxford, she bought a little house on the hill in Hythe. No doubt she knew well that it is usually a mistake to return to live in a place in which one has been happy, and about which she had incidentally created so vivid a comedy world. Or perhaps she didn't know it: She was very simple and uncalculating in some ways. She never spoke of it, but I had the feeling on our visits to her that the experiment of living in Hythe had not been entirely a success, although she had no trouble there in finding "boon companions" and being at home in a wholly unliterary and unintellectual world, rather like that of *The Little Girls* and of the Heccomb family in *The Death of the Heart*.

She was far from well when she decided to return to Oxford, to settle in a couple of rooms in an annex of the Bear Hotel at Woodstock. She had throat cancer—always a sixty-a-day smoker, she liked to puff on a cigarette between mouthfuls at lunch and dinner—but she made a good recovery after the operation and often came to visit us. I was once teaching a class on Jane Austen, and to my great concern, she asked if she could come along. I felt overwhelmed at first by her powerful presence, but she could not have been nicer or more quietly helpful, silent most of the time, but now and again injecting a shrewd query or making some encouraging comment on a point raised by one of the young students. Quite unacademic by nature, she was of course well read, a sharp and droll natural critic. About this time, she had great success as a visiting professor on an American campus, where the students viewed her queenly presence with delight and awe.

There could indeed be something peremptory, almost

alarming, about her. Lord David Cecil, who was a very old friend, told me that he had once asked her to a small dinner party, with carefully chosen and congenial company, which he was sure she would enjoy. But the party was not a success. Elizabeth could never be silent, but she remained uncommunicative and reserved all evening. Afterwards, she said to her host severely, "David, I think you should know me well enough by now to realise that I want to see you either on your own or at a large party." There was no answer to that one. She could be jealously possessive of her close friends, and hostile to their wives or husbands; and she could be fiercely loyal to an institution or person, even if she disapproved of what they stood for.

Her own family was Protestant—"Ascendancy," as it used to be called in Ireland—and she would have attended the Church of Ireland service as a part of her position and lifestyle, but she never forgave her fellow novelist Honor Tracy for investigating a financial scandal which had occurred among the local Roman Catholic clergy and then denouncing it in an article which appeared in the *Sunday Times*. Honor was a Roman Catholic herself, but that was neither here nor there. The point was the indecency, as Elizabeth saw it—and here all her Irish and local instincts were atavistically at work—of being disloyal to neighbours. By seeking to uncover its scandals, Honor Tracy as journalist was guilty of treachery to a hallowed Irish institution, the Roman Catholic church.

Elizabeth knew very well that the clergyman involved

was a crook, as she privately put it, and she also greatly disliked the role played by the Catholic church in Irish society, but she would never have said so in public, nor would she have been disloyal to a man of the district which she loved and lived in.

Honor Tracy was also a great friend of Iris. She was a fearlessly independent woman with flaming red hair, flamboyant in manner, unrestrained in the expression of her opinions and prejudices. She came from an older family than Elizabeth, the Norman De Tracys, who helped to conquer England, then took part in the conquest of southern Ireland in the twelfth century. The Bowens arrived much later: Colonel Bowen had been one of Cromwell's trusted officers, presented with the estate and land on which he had begun to build Bowen's Court. Irish history counted for a good deal in the background of both ladies, and each was redoubtable in her own style. Nonetheless, Honor Tracy, as she once told Iris, shook in her shoes at the thought of Elizabeth Bowen's displeasure.

Elizabeth, oddly enough, was not really at her best as a novelist when writing about Ireland. Perhaps its sorrows, and her own responsibilities there, inhibited her sense of fun. Her own best novels, including the one she was working on at the time of her death and which survives only as a fascinating fragment, were comedies—sometimes tragicomedies—of English life and manners. She had been most at home in wartime London. Hitler's blitz on the city helped produce one of her finest novels, *The Heat of the*

Day, as well as some brilliant short stories. The unearthly light of what was called a "bomber's moon" transfigures "Mysterious Kor," a story about bombed-out wartime London, which a girl working there sees as the ghost city of a poem she had once read.

> *Not in the waste beyond the swamps and sand*
> *The fever-haunted forest and lagoon,*
> *Mysterious Kor, thy walls forsaken stand,*
> *Thy lonely towers beneath a lonely moon.*

I always meant to ask Elizabeth where she had read the poem, but I never got around to it. Years after her death, her story was our subject at a class I was teaching, and when one of the students asked who had written the lines, I had to admit I had no idea. Bowen had perhaps written them herself? My curious student—now a doctor and don at Glasgow University—did not leave the matter there, but investigated in the Bodleian Library until he found the answer. The poem turned out to be the work of a minor Edwardian poet and man of letters named Andrew Lang, who had written it to his friend Rider Haggard, explorer and author of many best-selling romantic tales, including *King Solomon's Mines*. Most of the poem is poor stuff, but Elizabeth, when a young girl, had no doubt come across it in some long-forgotten anthology of the period, and it had returned to haunt her imagination in maturity, and help to create her story.

Iris's own creative mind worked the same way. Her novels are full of buried quotations remembered from childhood, or once quoted and discussed between us. (One of them is "the ouzel cock so black of hue" from *A Midsummer Night's Dream*, which surfaces in *A Severed Head* and refers obliquely to a cuckolding which takes place in the novel. We used to chant it, together with other catches, when driving in the car.)

Both Honor and Elizabeth sometimes stayed with us at Steeple Aston after we had settled in the house there. Honor liked to rest between quite gruelling bouts of investigative reporting, and she usually left us to stay at the Bell Inn at Aston Clinton, where she knew the landlord and where she used to stand us marvellously alcoholic lunches and dinners. After giving up journalism, she lived in a small cottage on Achill Island in the west of Ireland, where she wrote her lively comedies of Irish life. The best of these, *The Straight and Narrow Path*, concerns an Irish priest who once exhorted his flock "always to follow the straight and narrow path between virtue and wrongdoing." It was a true tale: Honor had heard the sermon herself; but though the Irish can be totally irreverent in private and among themselves, they do not care to be publicly teased. Honor's delightful novels were not read on her native soil, nor were they obtainable. It is a shame, too, that they never seem to have been reprinted, either in England or the United States. The peculiar powers of Irish censorship, once paramount on the island itself, are still to be reckoned with elsewhere.

It turned out to be a blessing that we viewed the house at Steeple Aston, because it at once drove all longings for poetical and rivery Taynton out of Iris's head. Neither house nor village were as pretty as those she had first fallen in love with, but both were old and solid and friendly. A farmhouse had been built onto in the early nineteenth century and turned into a gentleman's residence not far from the church. The grounds were large, almost two acres, and sloped sharply downhill to a stream that ran through the valley. On our side of this were ancient ponds, possibly mediaeval fish ponds. These appealed to Iris at once. So did the sheer impracticality of the place, from the point of view of two teachers working in Oxford, fifteen miles away. That did not daunt her at all: She did not even consider disadvantages. The equal impracticality of Bowen's Court may have influenced her. Cedar Lodge, as the house was rather primly called, was cheap to buy—startlingly cheap—but we discovered later that it was in bad condition, however solid it looked. Mr. Palmer, a veteran builder with very bright blue eyes, was soon in constant attendance. He used to gaze wonderingly at Iris as she sat and wrote in an upstairs room, through the ceiling of which water from an undiscoverable source was apt to drip.

Apart from Mr. Palmer, who constituted no sort of social burden, we had the place to ourselves. The previous owner was going to live on the island of Guernsey, in a small modern bungalow her son had bought for her. She was an old lady who had lived long in the village, and she recommended various persons who might come to help or "do" for us. We both felt disinclined to be done for. For the thirty years and more we lived at Cedar Lodge, we had no help in the house or garden, and both were presently in a state in which help of any kind would have come too late. That seemed to suit us, or at least to suit Iris: I was less sure of the benefits of what the novelist Rose Macaulay—Iris met her once or twice—used to call "letting things go to the devil and seeing what happens when they have gone there."

At first, I made strenuous efforts to assert will—my will—over the place. I cleaned, mowed, chopped, painted, and tried to repair the electricity. But I soon gave up. Iris always helped me, and she seemed to enjoy the idea of doing all the things women do in houses, but it was a dream occupation, a part of her imagined world, of the worlds she was creating in her novels as she sat in her dusty sunlit room upstairs, submerged by old letters, papers, broken ornaments, and stones she had picked up, or which had been given her by friends. It grieved me then, and still does, that these stones, once so naturally clean and beautiful from continual lustration in a stream, or by the tides of the seashore, should have become as dusty and dead-looking as everything else in the house. But this never seemed to bother Iris in the slightest. The stones for her were Platonic objects, living in some absolute world of forms, untouched by their contingent existence as a part of the actual and very grubby still life that surrounded us.

Stones were not the only Platonic objects in our daily life, or—so close that it came to the same thing—in Iris's imagination. Cooking pots, never properly cleaned in practise, had the same status. So, I felt, did those imaginary badgers which she had invoked once when I had tried to suggest to her what the rewards of married life might be like. "Yes," she had replied with a sort of wistfulness which gave me a sudden hope that she might be prepared to take the idea of marriage seriously. "I do like to imagine your coming home, and me meeting you and saying, 'Darling, the badgers have broken in.'" Her ancient badger fantasy, with its image of a cosy domestic drama, has probably been forgotten, but she sometimes used to say with a smile to friends, or even to interviewers, that she originally had every intention of doing the cooking after we got married. "But after a few days, John suggested it might go better if he took over." The image of herself as cook and apron-wearer stayed in her mind less long than the delightful and hopeful one—to me at least—of rushing down to greet her husband with a kiss and with the news, announced with mock horror, that the badgers had broken in.

And yet her intention of becoming the cook was no idle boast. Iris could cook—could have cooked—magnificently, just as she could have done all sorts of other practical things. While working during the war years at the treasury, the most prestigious branch of the civil service, she had made herself an expert on a tricky concept known as "notional promotion *in absentia*," which involved assessing pay raises and promotions that would have accrued, had they remained in their old jobs, to functionaries called up at that time into the armed forces. Senior colleagues consulted her on this question and accepted without demur what she told them. Had she concentrated on any of those careers, she could have become a doctor, an archaeologist, a motor mechanic. It used to be thought at one time that Shakespeare might have started off as a horse-holder outside the theatre. A nineteenth-century scholar had observed that, if so, one could be sure that the Bard had held his horses better than anyone else. A really great artist can concentrate and succeed at almost anything, and Iris would have been no exception. If she had borne a child, she would have looked after it better and more conscientiously than most mothers, and no doubt would have brought it up better, too. But in that case, she would not have written the books that she did write.

I can't recall myself saying that I would be the cook. As far as I am concerned, it just happened, and in any case, it was not really cooking. The point was that Iris was working—properly working—and I was determined she should not be distracted from this. Getting something to eat was easy, and we often used to go to a pub on the main road, where a good plain dinner could be had cheaply. That was long before the present situation in England, when cooking has at last become an art to be treated seriously—overseriously. There was no fiddly *nouvelle cuisine* forty years ago.

Yet there was one occasion when Iris took as many pains as any acolyte in the media-haunted kitchens of to-day. Well before we were married, and when I really thought she never would marry me, she decided to enter-tain for supper the same pair—the academic lawyer and his wife—at whose table we had eaten our first meal to-gether. She had another guest, too, and made no apology for not including me in the party. She was living in her Beaumont Street flat at the time, on the top floor. There was no dining-room and her attic kitchen was barely a room at all. I had been a little hurt, nonetheless, and had suggested that if she must entertain the Johnsons, couldn't she take them to a restaurant? She'd said pacifically she didn't want to do that: They'd asked her to supper so many times, and she felt the least she could do was to make a special effort of her own. Iris, as I saw then a little gloomily, could be very conscientious about such things.

She took immense trouble. First of all, she bought her-self at great expense a red enamel casserole, a boat-shaped one with a close-fitting lid. It weighed about a ton. I think it was the first time either of us had seen such a thing. I gazed at it in awe, and Iris regarded it with all the pride of new possession. A culinary-minded friend of hers who was partly Greek had told her this was what she needed to prepare a very special Attic dish, *stifaclo*. He had told her that if properly done, which only very rarely happened, it was the most delicious dish in the world. He was a philosopher, a follower of Plato, but his real interest was in cooking and telephones. Since he was the inspiration for the dish Iris proposed to prepare, it was natural that he should be one of the three guests invited.

Iris took two days to prepare that dish. I cannot recall exactly what was in it, as neither she nor I ever attempted to prepare it again, but there was a lot of high-quality beef from the market, as well as olive oil, aubergines, spices and herbs, and tomato puree. It was, of course, a colossal success. She allowed me to finish it with her, cold, the following day, and I honestly don't think I have ever eaten anything more delicious in my life.

So Iris could cook, and to perfection, just as she might have done all sorts of other things superlatively well. But as I sat eating it with her the following day—and to my great satisfaction, she admitted it was even better cold than hot—I had not been able to avoid a feeling of disappointment. Somehow it was not like Iris to have done such a thing, to have pulled off a culinary *coup* that must have staggered the Johnsons, accustomed as they were to thinking Iris an odd but lovable and unworldly person, a philosopher, a hopeful writer of novels, whom they had got the measure of, whom they could patronise in their own fashion. Was that why she had done it? If so, I could not escape a fellow-feeling with the Johnsons. Friends, who fill their own allotted place in your life, should not behave wholly uncharacteristically. Still less so if you are in love with such a friend, as I was.

Perhaps Iris knew this, too. Perhaps that is why it was such a singular occasion. It surprised me nonetheless, and continues to do so, trivial as the occasion might now seem. My memory of it could arise from the difficulty I now feel in writing about Iris as she was. Is it that I can think of her only as she now is, which is for me the same as she has always been? In any case, no description of anybody, however loving, can seem to do anything but veer away from the person concerned, not because it distorts his or her "reality," whatever that may be, but because the describer himself begins to lose all confidence in the picture of the person he is creating. The Iris of my words cannot, I know, be any Iris who existed. In writing about the *stifaclo* episode, I can no longer believe in my own account of the Iris who willed it, who so uncharacteristically made it happen.

As for the expensive red casserole boat, it was never used again, or hardly ever. Maybe it was cooked in by me once or twice, without conviction and without much success. I may have made a few stews eaten without comment by our guests, or perhaps with some kindly routine commendation by one of the women present. Like so many other things in the house, it is lost now, undiscoverable, although I remember that the last time I saw it, covered with cobwebs at the bottom of a cupboard, it looked as if worn-out, terribly old and tired, with rust patches coming through the red enamel from the iron underneath. But when new, it once housed the most perfect dish in the world, made by the person who then seemed, and in a sense was, the least likely person to make it.

I can record one other cooking experience in Iris's life, and one I still find quite upsetting to remember. It must have taken place about the time I first met her, or perhaps before I met her. Two friends of hers, the strong-minded female philosopher who practised "telegamy" and a mathematical logician of international standing who was a bachelor, had asked to borrow her room for a day while she was absent. The room she then lived in had a gas ring and washbasin but not much else, and they required it not for secret sexual congress but because the mathematician wanted to indulge himself in a culinary experiment. Why they should have required Iris's room for this purpose, I still cannot fathom, except that the room was handy and they knew they could presume on her discretion and her unbounded good nature. (They were right of course, but I still grind my teeth when I think of it, even though they are not my own teeth any more, but false ones.) The experiment was in the manufacture of herring soup, which the mathematician, Viennese but possibly with Baltic origins, swore he was on the verge of perfecting. The philosopher affected not to believe him, and swore in her turn—she was a lady with a strong streak of puckish humour—that she could never be induced under any circumstances to partake of such a dish, however exquisitely prepared. The very idea of it was repellent to her. So they made what amounted to a bet.

The mathematician won the bet. The soup was a triumph, and the philosopher capitulated and said that it was so. Indeed, she consumed it with relish. When Iris returned a few days later, it was to find her room in the most gruesome possible disorder, smelling strongly of fish, and her landlady furious. Other tenants had complained of the noise and the smell. Miss Murdoch's reputation, once immaculate, was now in ruins. In the eyes of the landlady, she was, and remained, a fallen woman: one who allowed the most unspeakable orgies to take place in her room, and no doubt participated in them herself. Iris left the house not long after, although its position and amenities had suited her very well. But that was not what upset me when Iris told me the tale, which she did in a tolerant, amused way, without a trace of resentment.

Indeed, she remained, and still does, on the best possible terms with both parties, even though neither attempted an apology for what had taken place, or even seemed to think one might be appropriate. It annoys me intensely that she should still revere them, nonetheless. But what upset me even more, and for some reason can still go through me like a spear, was that Iris found one of her most treasured possessions lying on the floor of the room, hideously violated. It was a blue silk chiffon scarf which her mother had given her as a special birthday present. Its

147

state when discovered was so repulsive that Iris had no choice but to take it straight out to the dustbin, holding her nose while she did so. The logician had required the finest possible sieve to strain the end product of his masterpiece, and the philosopher, casually opening a drawer, had handed him the scarf.

I can still see and imagine the pair, wringing out the last drop. I have only met either of them a few times, but when I do, I find it difficult to be more than barely civil.

It is too late to remind Iris of the story now, but if I were able to do so, I am sure that she would reveal the same Christ-like qualities of tolerance, amusement, and good nature—forgiveness would not even be in question—which she must have felt as she gazed on that fearful scene. Or perhaps it only became fearful in the telling—more specifically, in the way she told it to me. All my instincts, or so I still feel, would have led me into some wild counterexcess. I would have gone after the pair, murdered one or both of them, or, at the every least, cut as many of their possessions as I could find into ribbons with a sharp knife. And yet here I was, when Iris told me the story, longing to share my life with a woman who could behave as angelically as she seemed to have done.

I think that was what really upset me most of all. It seemed so unnatural. And it still does. If I am not careful, I can upset myself still more by wondering whether Iris really behaved so angelically after all. Did something in her secretly long to be violated in this way by the pair?

Did she in some sense invite this wanton exercise of power over her? Was she submitting to these gods of logic and philosophy as she submitted to the god-monster of Hampstead? Was she, almost as if in one of her own novels, the absent victim of a sacrifice in which she would have participated as a willing victim had she been present?

The idea still makes me shiver a bit. Have I really been sharing my life with someone like that? But if I have, it has never seemed to matter much, even though the idea of having behaved in a way so unlike myself can give me the occasional shock of incredulity. One thing remains certain: Iris has always disliked fish, and particularly abominated the whole herring tribe. That may well have been true before the episode; it has certainly been the case ever since.

Why should someone who loves water so much have so little desire for the creatures that live in it? Or is it that she feels in unconscious fellowship, and so would not dream of eating them? As a strict matter of fact, however, she *will* eat my sardine pâté, heavily flavoured with curry powder. Perhaps she doesn't recognise it as fish at all. But there must have been no doubt about what caused the appalling smell that came from her scarf when she picked up the poor bedraggled thing. My instinct, nonetheless, would have been to try to wash it out, to rescue and cherish it. But Iris was not like that. She sacrificed the scarf cheerfully, and seemingly, at least, on the wholesome altar of friendship.

$\mathcal{T}$he house and premises known as Cedar Lodge," as the old deeds described them, were neither warm nor dry. There were the remains of a huge cedar near the front gate, just a vast plate of rotten wood nearly flush with the earth. Perhaps they had chopped this great tree down and burnt it indoors in a vain attempt to keep warm. We ourselves tried various ways of doing the same thing. An old Rayburn stove my mother gave us, night storage heaters, electric fires, an expensive affair in the front hall with a beautifully fluted stainless-steel front, which burned anthracite nuggets as expensive as itself—nothing seemed to do any good. After one of Iris's novels had been turned into a film, we at last installed some partial central heating, which also failed to work properly. Something about gravity, the position of the oil tank, the installation of pipes...Our dear Mr. Palmer was dead by then, and his son put it in.

But we never seemed to have minded the cold and the damp; indeed, I think we rather enjoyed them. We were always warm in bed, and in retrospect, I seem to spend most of my time in bed. I very soon developed the habit of working there. I remember coming home on a snowy evening and uttering wild cries as we rushed about the garden together hand in hand, watching our feet make holes in the printless snow. It often snowed at Steeple Aston, which was several hundred feet higher than Oxford, where it seldom or never does snow. Our bed, too, was the one place from which the house felt safe and natural to me. The bed was home, even if unknown people might be living at the other end of the long house, perhaps unaware of our existence.

It was when Iris was away for a day or two that I realised that the existence of these other creatures was not just fantasy. We had never heard anything, but as I came from the garden and went up the dark, rather narrow staircase, I saw something going up ahead of me. It was a large rat. It reached the top, looked around unhurriedly, and dived with a plop into a wide crack between the oak boards. It had come home.

Those rats were gentlemen. Until that moment, we had no idea of their existence. Nor did their presence, once defined, cause us at first any bother. They led their lives and we led ours. But since we knew they were there, and they knew we knew they were there, our relations could never feel quite the same. For one thing, their behaviour ceased to be so considerate. Now we often heard them moving about in their own solid subterranean world beneath the floorboards. Although the house was in bad condition, it had been built in the solid style of its period, and there must have been plenty of room in that other world, and plenty of massive woodwork to gnaw upon. Those rats took to gnawing it as a nighttime occupation, and sometimes out of sheer *joie de vivre*, or so it seemed, they charged up and down those long invisible corridors at one or two in the morning. They must have been in residence for many generations, and the arrangements they had made must by now have suited them perfectly.

Clearly, it appeared that something had to be done. From the rural chemist, I obtained large quantities of a substance alleged not only to destroy rats without pain, but also to be positively enjoyed by them in the process. We spooned it lavishly through the cracks. Soon we could hear the rats enjoying it. Now there were not only cavorting noises in the night but squeals of ecstasy, as well. Iris began to look worried—anguished, in fact. Didn't I think we ought to stop, while there might still be time? I began to waver, but fortunately the rats solved the problem for us. The sounds ceased quite abruptly, as if the animals had decided that if we would not play the game, neither would they—they would rather leave home. Iris looked more anguished than ever. I was concerned about the probable smell of unburied rat bodies. But the cold old house remained odour-free. It really looked as if they had staged a final feast and moved out.

And indeed, something like that may have happened. I think mutual awareness of one another's presence may have unsettled them, inclined them to change their habits. Previously, they had seemed to accommodate us by leaving to work in the outside world by night and sleeping in the house by day. That had caused no problems, and I daresay the previous owner, the kindly old widow Blanche Tankerville-Chamberlayne (her real and fabulous name), had never bothered them, nor they her. Perhaps she never knew they were there.

And now, of course, we missed them. Iris ceased to look so agonised, and we never mentioned the rats, but I think we sometimes listened for them, perhaps a little wistfully, if we woke up in the night. I can feel and hear their almost sympathetic company in some of Iris's novels, written at her table just above their heads; for after we first became aware of their presence, she would say she was aware of it in the daytime as well as at night and found it congenial, even stimulating. In summertime, it blended with sounds from the garden, the song of black-birds and the twittering of the swallows—"the Weather-bys"—on the telephone wire outside the window.

After she had given up her teaching post at St. Anne's, Iris used to write every morning, from about nine to one o'clock. If I was away in Oxford, she listened to the news, had something to eat, and then went into the garden. She didn't actually do much gardening, if any, but she liked to find places to put things. It was the time when the new fashion for the old shrub roses was coming in. They had wonderful names: Duc de Guise, Captain John Ingram, Cuisse de Nymphe, and Cuisse de Nymphe Emue. They had tissuelike petals and smelt of wine. The white petals looked as transparent as ice, with a vivid green centre ("muddled centres," as the book called them, became a favourite phrase with Iris). The deep mauve ones, such as Captain Ingram, faded almost into black.

We bought them at a rose garden at the weekends and I put them in inexpertly. Iris soon had her rose walk, and in a sense they were all "Unofficial Roses," of the sort her heroine Fanny Peronet would have approved. (The title *An Unofficial Rose* comes from a poem by Rupert Brooke which Iris had always been fond of.) But we had no idea how to look after them, and roses need a lot of looking after. Quite soon, they began to look sickly, and the leaves became covered with black spots. When a friend saw them, he teased Iris by remarking that she seemed to be keeping a concentration camp for flowers. The pleasantry was not in good taste, nor was it taken in good part. For a short while at least, Iris's behaviour towards the friend cooled distinctly. She could be quite touchy, but never for long, and the friend was soon received back into favour. I don't think he put her off the roses, but somehow they had their day—most of them—

and ceased to be, without either of us getting distressed about it. One only, I remember, continued to survive and flourish without appearing to need care or attention at all. It had thick, luxurious foliage deeply furrowed and indented like a tropic plant, and its crimson hips were as big and glossy as a tropical fruit. It was called, I think, the Queen of Denmark.

Possibly as a result of all the effort that I felt I should—and indeed wanted—to put into the place, I fell ill with the glandular fever after we had been there less than a year. Like a Victorian illness, it makes the patient weak, as if fading painlessly away. It also keeps recurring at intervals. After the first recovery, I used to totter down beside Iris through the tall grass to the pond, where she swam—or, rather, paddled—about, stirring up the dark mud. I felt I should be there, but had she got into difficulties, I should have been far too weak to do anything about it. Of course she didn't, and in my enfeebled state I was greatly cheered by the sight of her face smiling blissfully up at me from under the willow shadows. Then I climbed thankfully and laboriously back into bed.

It was the sort of bed you do have to climb into, or onto—a wide, high Victorian bed with a carved oak frame and a great soft, almost soggy, mattress. We had attended an auction in Oxford at the time we moved, and we got the bed for a pound. No one else seemed to want it, and when I got up the courage and offered a bid, the auctioneer gave me a pained look. "That's a bad bid, sir," he remarked, "a very bad bid, but in the absence of another offer, I shall have to accept it." That summer, the bed became my home, as the house itself never seemed to do. I read in it, ate and drank in it, wrote reviews in it, for I was still reviewing novels for the *Spectator*, and the bed was always covered with them.

Up inside the bed, secure and, as it seemed, protected from the world, I could feel that this was marriage, the true nirvana of the wedded state. One of the books I reviewed in that dreamy time was by Pamela Hanford Johnson, a very capable novelist of the fifties, wife of the scientist and PR man C. P. Snow, who also wrote novels. Power was his chief interest: *The Masters*, concerning the power struggle among the heads of a college, was an early and original specimen of the campus novel.

Snow's wife had what for me were more subtle interests, and I enjoyed her novel, the last of a trilogy. An earlier one, advertised on the jacket and which I had not read, had its title borrowed from a poem of Donne's: *This Bed Thy Centre*. I felt that was a good omen, though I discovered later that the author had intended it satirically. The novel was an early feminist outcry against the sexual and domestic subordination of women. For me, domestication on and in the bed was sheer bliss.

Certainly, Iris did not at all regard the great bed as her centre, and the knowledge of that seemed perfectly harmonious to me, too. Our marriage was shared, but the bed was mine. Iris would sit beside it, after bringing me barley water and orange jelly, the only things that the ulcerated glands in my throat would tolerate. As I got better, we seemed to live mostly on poached eggs. Iris developed a skill in doing these which I have since envied. I have never been able to master it as she did: I regard skill in poaching an egg as the ultimate cooking test.

What I appreciated, too, was Iris's complete indifference to the womanly image of a helpmate. She was not in the least a Florence Nightingale. She just looked after me, and as she did so, I could see from her face that her mind was far away, pursuing the plot of the story she was engaged on. She found no bother at all in getting on with it while I was ill, and indeed told me later that she owed the genesis of that particular tale to the quiet time my illness had brought us both. That gave me such satisfaction that I at once fell ill again.

The second bout was worse than the first, and our doctor, an elderly dapper little man who always wore a rose in his buttonhole, looked a little worried, I thought, under his professionally jovial manner, just as one of his Victorian predecessors might have done. I was gratified by this, and also because Iris paid no attention. She knew in some way that there was nothing to worry about, although she politely shared the doctor's pleasure when he looked in later after making a blood test to announce that it had shown "the Paul Bunnell effect," which meant that the trouble was indeed glandular fever and not something worse. A charming and probably an extremely competent doctor, he used to look from one to the other of us with his bright old eyes, as if incredulous that two such absurd, if engaging, creatures could be living in this house, pretending to be husband and wife. While I was ill, he came over every day from Bladon, a good many miles distant. It was in the early days of the National Health Service, and Dr. Bevan—his name coincidentally the same as that of the minister who had just done the most to plan the NHS— took no private patients, but he always behaved as if we were the only people he had to look after, and that it was never any trouble to do so.

The comfortable feel of space, distance, and separation which seemed to me to confirm the pleasures of the married state, in spite of Dr. Bevan's incredulous and amused glances at what he appeared to regard as two quaint children rather than a married couple, was greatly enhanced by that summer of illness. When the term began, I had to get sick leave. I luxuriated in the business of Iris working and me being ill. She was working away at her novel, now nearly finished. Bed had inspired me, too, after a fashion. I had the idea for a book that became *The Characters of Love*, a study in detail of three texts—a poem, a play, and a novel—which seemed to me to exemplify in one way or another the understanding about love which I had picked up in the course of my relationship with Iris. It was a very naïve idea, although some of the comments that I made about Chaucer's long narrative poem *Troilus and Criseyde*, Shakespeare's *Othello*, and Henry James's *The Golden Bowl* still seem to me quite sophisticated if I reread them. Critical books of that sort were in fashion at the time, and *The Characters of Love* did quite well, although I can't now imagine anyone trained on literary theory in the new schools of English literature wanting to read it, or indeed being able to do so. Its vocabulary of appreciation and technique of appraisal are too different from anything currently in vogue.

The real satisfaction I got from it at the time was Iris's wish to read it as it slowly proceeded, and what was for me the unexpected warmth of her reaction. This was not just automatic loyalty and a simulated interest in what hubby was up to, any more than her care of me when I was ill had been an imitation of wifely behaviour. She was really interested. We talked about it a lot, although, as always, without any attempt to have rational and serious discussion of the kind she would have engaged in with her pupils, or with friends and colleagues. We had already got to the stage of a relationship which Tolstoy writes about in *War and Peace*, where Pierre and Natasha, as husband and wife, understand each other and grasp each other's viewpoint without having to make sense or needing to be coherent. I was fascinated in my turn when I found later how much of what we had felt and spoken together had gone into Iris's landmark seminal essays. *Against Dryness* and *The Sovereignty of Good* are not in the least incoherent. They are not "muddled centres," but lucid dewdrops, pearls of distilled wisdom, and yet I recognise in them the things we used to talk about in our own way, of which we had become conscious together by our own private and collective means.

Iris is without question the most genuinely modest person I have ever met, or, if it comes to that, could ever imagine. Modesty is apt to be something acted, by each individual in his or her own way, part of the armoury with which people half-consciously build up the persona they wish others to become aware of, and with which they intend to confront the world. Iris has no pride in being modest: I don't think she even knows she is. The normal anxieties and preoccupations of a successful writer about status and the future—whether, to put it crudely, they can keep it up—were completely absent with her. Now that she has forgotten all about it anyway, I am struck by the almost eerie resemblance between the amnesia of the present and the tranquil indifference of the past. She went on then secretly, quietly doing her work, never wishing to talk about it, never needing to compare or discuss or contrast, never reading reviews or wanting to hear about them, never needing the continual reassurance from friends or public or the media which most writers require in order to go on being sure that they are writers.

This normal need for status and reassurance, for feeling, at however humble a level "a published writer," can have its endearing side. It often goes with real modesty, and with an accurate self-assessment of what the writer concerned can and cannot do. This would be true of a writer like Barbara Pym, whose novels I have always enjoyed and reread, together with those of Raymond Chandler, C. S. Forester, Anthony Powell, and one or two others. I can read them over and over, as if indulging in a private and comforting vice.

I recommended Pym's novels to Iris, and put them in her way, but I don't think she read them. She hardly ever read a contemporary novel, except when a friend or the friend of a friend had written one and asked if she could bear to give an opinion, whereupon she would read every word of it conscientiously. Having done so, she was very often enthusiastic; sometimes, it seemed to me, if I also read the work submitted, disproportionately so. I think this came not only from the warmth and loyalty of friendship but from a kind of innocence: She had no experience of what novels today were like, and was impressed by what I could have told her was just the current way of doing it, a mere imitation of contemporary modes and fashions. I had the feeling that in the past, and before I met her, she had not so much read as absorbed the great classic novels, and in our early days she used to read and reread Dostoevsky or Dickens, sometimes Proust. We got in the habit of reading at lunchtime, each with a book, and she read them with something of my own absorbed addict's pleasure, though she never minded my interrupting her with something I was reading myself, and which had entertained me.

She always shared in these moments of entertainment, and during my most addicted Pym period, she liked me to read out comic scenes to her, at which she laughed with real amusement, though I think partly because I was laughing so much myself as I read, and she liked that. Having comic passages read to one—those by P. G. Wodehouse, say—can be exhausting: there is the need to simulate a hilarity which on the spur of the moment it may not be easy to feel. But Pym, like Austen, does lend herself particularly well to the sharing of short passages. We met her only once, with a young friend of hers who had been a pupil of mine. We liked her and her sister very much, within the limitations of a short meeting and the usual English awkwardness. She was a very tall woman, and when her diaries were posthumously published, I was amused to find from a letter of hers to Philip Larkin that she felt she had "seemed to tower above Iris (though only in height, of course)."

Barbara Pym was as modest as she was satirical about herself, and in both those modes of being, as one sees in her diaries, wholly different from Iris. Iris had no need for consciousness of herself as an author; but there is an endearing moment in the Pym diaries when she imagines herself—as it is clear she frequently did, as most of us do—being looked at by persons who might have heard of her, and one of them saying, "There is Barbara Pym, the writer."

* * *

There is the kind of literary personality, of the sort the Germans refer to reverently as a *Dichter*, who is organised on so impressive and heroic a scale that questions of modesty, image, and attitudinising can hardly be said to arise. One such was a writer I have already referred to, whom I thought of in early days, when I first knew Iris, as the "Hampstead monster" (one of his female disciples wrote a novel on the subject of such monsters). This impressive figure had finally won, in old age, a Nobel Prize. He had come to be revered, particularly in Germany (he wrote in Ladin and in German), although he had lived when young near Manchester and spent much of his life in London.

I encountered the *Dichter* on few occasions, and only once, at a literary party, had any conversation with him. He asked me what I thought about *King Lear*. This is never an easy question to answer. My experience of attempting to "teach" the play to Oxford students was no help at all at that moment. I made some sort of reply nonetheless, to which he listened with flattering attention. "What do *you* think?" I asked, after submitting in silence for some moments to his penetrating stare.

He continued to be silent for what seemed a long time. Finally, he spoke. "Friends tell me that my book is unbearable," he said. Fortunately, I knew this to be a reference to his long novel *Die Blendung*, and I nodded my head gravely. There was a further silence. "*King Lear* is also unbearable," he pronounced at last.

I bowed my head. Shakespeare and his masterpiece

would never be paid a greater compliment than this. The mage was certainly mesmeric. The solemn atmosphere of our conclave was itself becoming unbearable, and it was a relief when we were interrupted by a bumptious but rather engaging young man who was on the crest of a wave of self-esteem. His survey of contemporary angst had itself been hailed as a masterpiece and had become an unexpected best-seller.

"What did you think of my book, sir?" he now asked in breezy tones, clearly confident that the great man could not have missed this experience.

The *Dichter's* appearance was always impressive. Squat, almost dwarfish, with a massive head and thick black hair, he looked like a giant cut short at the waist, what the Germans call a *Sitzriese*. Gazing up with an air of mild benevolence at the young man, he seemed nonetheless not fully to understand his question, not to have grasped the point at all, even though English was in fact his first language and he used it as masterfully as he did German. There was a long pause. The young man appeared to wait with growing expectation but also a growing embarrassment.

The *Dichter* spoke at last, in a wondering way and without any inflection of emphasis or irony. "You are asking me—*me*—whether I have read your book?" His sole reason for repeating the pronoun seemed to be to clear up a possible misunderstanding. Perhaps the young man thought he was addressing some ordinary mortal? There was another long pause while he continued to smile at the young man in friendly fashion. At last, murmuring something apologetic, the young man slipped away.

I felt torn between involuntary admiration and strong dislike. Dislike won, as it did on other occasions when I encountered the monster, or mage. And yet he could exhibit not only an apparent warmth of manner but a shy, almost diffident charm, which he seemed to keep, as it were, solely for you. No wonder he was worshipped. Certainly I was fascinated myself on that occasion, and I longed to see how he would continue to behave. He did so by ignoring the existence of all the writers, intellectuals, and important people present, seeming to compel them to ignore him also. After that first encounter, he moved about by himself with perfect ease, avoided by all, with no one venturing to address him. They might have decided deliberately to snub him, and if so, he found that amusing and highly satisfactory. I watched him talk to another young man, who stood on the edges of the party, clearly knowing no one there. Soon they were laughing together and deep in conversation. I could not resist approaching them, and as I did so, I recognized this man, who at close quarters had a comically villainous appearance, as an actor I had often seen in B gangster movies, to which I was at that time addicted. As this was a talking point, I told him I had often enjoyed his screen performances. He seemed pleased, but he said he had never yet had the role of chief gangster, only a subordinate one. Hailed now by a fellow actor who had just arrived, he moved off, and the *Dichter*, who seemed greatly taken with him, enquired from me what he did. "The only one here worth talking to," he added, smiling.

Feeling myself included in this judgement, I sought to escape. At that moment, our hostess fortunately claimed the *Dichter*, and the young actor returned to where I was standing. He asked me who the funny-looking cove was. "What a really *marvellous* fellow!" he said. "Really interesting. He liked me," he added, dramatising in a stage manner his own enthusiasm. "We talked about fishing. I'm mad about it—my real hobby. I don't know how he knew that, but he seemed to...."

A potent Oxford figure, Isaiah Berlin, was different from the magelike *Dichter* in almost every way—for one thing, he was truly and unself-consciously benevolent—but he shared the ability to charm anyone by the interest he took in them. He once told me he liked bores and was never bored by them. That was probably true, and certainly he made himself familiar, in a warmhearted, spontaneous Russian way, to everyone he met—shy academic wives, worldly hostesses, scientists and intellectuals, philosophers and music lovers. He had the common touch, and some people spoke patronisingly of him for that reason, implying that his fame and reputation were almost entirely due to his extraordinary powers of getting on socially, rather than to any real originality or achievement of his own.

Isaiah Berlin's favourite authors were Herzen, the Russian memoirist whose works were his bible, and the novelist Turgenev. In style, gusto, and personality, both resembled himself, though he would never have said so. The *Dichter*'s bookishness was far more mysterious, no doubt deliberately. He would indicate to his followers that a certain text was the thing, the *real* right thing, without inviting discussion of the matter, or giving any reason why it should be so. In this sibylline manner, he once urged on his disciples perusal of the *P'ing Ching Mei*, a long and complex Chinese novel of the seventeenth century. Everyone, including Iris, hastened to read it, but none of them seemed able to fathom what was so remarkable about it. Was it some sort of key to understanding, like Henry James's "Figure in the Carpet"—perhaps, indeed, the key to an understanding of the *Dichter*'s true greatness? Herzen and Turgenev are as open, as brilliant, as palpably fascinating as Isaiah Berlin himself; but what was the secret of the *P'ing Ching Mei*, or any other work to which the *Dichter* gave the seal of his approval or, come to that, himself composed? There seemed no answer to that one. Mystery always remains the hallmark of the mage.

Iris's works, at least to me, are genuinely mysterious, like Shakespeare's. About her greatness as a novelist, I have no doubts at all, although she has never by nature needed, possessed, or tried to cultivate the charisma which is the most vital element to the success of a sage, or mage. Her books create a new world, which is also in an inspired sense an ordinary one. They have no ax to grind; they are devoid of intellectual pretension, or the need to be different. They are not part of a personality which fascinates and mesmerises its admirers. Although any of her readers might say or feel that a person or an event in her fiction could occur only in a Murdoch novel, this does not mean that the personality of the writer herself is in any obvious sense remarkable.

Her humility in this respect seems itself so unpretentious, unlike most humility. She had no wish to dwell apart, but took people and what they told her on trust, at face value. I was often surprised by how easily she could be, as I saw it, taken in. She never needed to be "knowing," to see through people, to discover their weak spot. Reflecting on Napoléon's comment that no man is a hero to his valet, Hegel remarked this was true—not, however, because the hero was no hero, but because the valet was a valet. For Iris, everyone she met was, so to speak, a hero, until they gave very definite signs or proof to the contrary. I have never met anyone less naturally critical or censorious. Her private judgements—if they were ever made—remained her own and were never voiced publicly.

This is so rare in academic and intellectual circles that I suspect many more naturally animated and gossipy persons may actually have found conversation with her rather dull, even while continuing very much to respect her. Religious people, like her pupils, took to her immediately and instinctively. But she never seemed to discuss religion or belief with them, nor they with her. In some way, the "spiritual," as I suppose it has to be called, seemed to hover in the air, its presence taken for granted. When W. H. Auden, whom she had once met when he was giving a talk at her school, came to live for part of the year in Oxford, they met on various casual occasions. "He likes to talk about prayer," she reported with a smile. I asked if they had exchanged views on how it should be done. "Oh, no, neither of us do it," said Iris. "But he jokes about how he would do it if he did."

Although Iris was a scholar of Platonic philosophy, and it is so much a part of the atmosphere in many of her novels, it had no importance in her life that I could see, any more than did any kind of organised religion. This was true even of Buddhism, which she had come to know a good deal about, chiefly through her great friends Peter Conradi and James O'Neill, both of whom are practising Buddhists. I gather that the word *practising* is in fact irrelevant, just as it would be to speak of a "devout" or "serious" Buddhist. (I have sometimes been struck by the analogy with Iris as a writer: There would be no point in describing her as a practising novelist, or even a "serious" one. The Shakespearean comparison again comes to mind: In what sense was he a "serious" dramatist?) I do not think Iris would ever have taken up meditation, as done in their own way by Peter and Jim. Her sense of things worked differently and in its own way; but she at once fell in love—and that was some years ago now—with their Welsh sheepdog, Cloudy, a beautiful animal with a grey-and-white coat and blue eyes. It appears in her penultimate novel, *The Green Knight*, as the dog Anax.

Iris is and was *anima naturaliter Christiana*—religious without religion. She has never made a religion of art, and yet pictures have certainly meant more to her than any other product of the spirit, not excluding literature and philosophy. I mentioned Piero, and our experience of his *Resurrection* at Borgo San Sepolcro; and by coincidence, we were to meet in Canada, five or six years after that honeymoon time, the painter Alex Colville, who had himself been deeply influenced by Piero's art. It was the first time we had been to the New World together; although a year or so after we were married, Iris visited Yale on a month's fellowship, travelling alone and reluctantly, but enjoying it when she got there. Until very recently, going to the United States was always a problem, thanks to an act vigorously restricting the issue of a visa to any former member of the Communist Party. Iris had been briefly a Young Communist while still an undergraduate at Oxford, leaving the Communist Party before the outbreak of war, but her scrupulousness barred her from conveniently forgetting this fact, as many of her Oxford political friends had done, when filling out the visa form. She was duly restricted to single visits, for strictly academic purposes.

This proved to be inconvenient when we were in Canada, where no sort of restriction applied. Our hosts at McMaster University had planned to take us to the

Albright-Knox Art Gallery in Buffalo and to see Niagara Falls from the U.S. side. These pleasures she had to forgo, since we planned to visit Chicago on the way home, where Iris was to give a philosophy paper. She also longed to visit the Art Institute of Chicago—she had managed to visit the National Gallery in Washington, D.C., while on her visit to Yale. Such an expedition could be made only if we did not use up her precious single visa on a Buffalo visit. She insisted the rest of the party should go as arranged, and she stayed on the Canadian side by herself until we returned. There was a compensation next day when we were to go to Stratford for the Shakespeare Festival; it had been arranged I should give a talk there on the plays to be performed. We made a detour to Lake Huron, where we plunged into waves which were uncannily like those of the ocean but had no salt savour about them.

Stratford was memorable less for Shakespeare than for a performance of *The Mikado*, the best that could be imagined. But the real revelation of our Canadian visit were the pictures of Alex Colville. This quiet, reclusive artist, who lived at St. John's in New Brunswick, was then painting one or at most two canvases a year. His art is meticulous in detail, as he takes infinite pains over extreme niceties of composition, and this precision contrasts with the statuesque solidity of his human figures, as massive and mysterious as Piero's and yet wholly absorbed in the commonplace activities of contemporary life. Iris was spellbound by them. She and Colville took to each other at once, and he showed her all the portfolios he had brought with him: He had been coaxed over to take part in one of those symposia on "Whither the Arts?" which are cosy routine for so many writers and academics. It was pleasant enough in the insipid way such events are; but Colville's presence and the ease we both found in talking with him gave the days a sudden individuality. It was almost as if we had been unexpectedly received into one of his own pictures, where a husband stands naked and pondering, studying a refrigerator's contents by the dim light from within; or a woman, as massively inscrutable as any in Piero's paintings, holds the car door open for her children to enter.

We should much like to have seen more of Alex Colville, and talked to him, but he comes to Europe only rarely. On one such occasion, we managed a meeting in London, when he was en route for The Hague to repaint a tiny damaged area in the corner of one of his pictures, entitled *Stop for Cows*. The paint in this corner had been minutely scratched in the course of handling by the museum, and the authorities there had been prepared to pay for Alex to come all the way over and put it right. They must have thought highly of the picture, as well they might. A big girl with plump cheeks and buttocks is raising one majestic arm as she turns to confront an invisible motorist. In front of her are the massive backsides and tails of black-and-white Alderneys, and a wide sky suggests the sea not far away. In one way, the picture is reassuringly Dutch, robustly, even humorously physical. But it also contrives to be full of a magic strangeness in complete contrast with appearances. How Colville does this, and plans or imagines compositions that reveal it, remains a mystery, and one that I know Iris at once found familiar and sympathetic. She used to sit and study her volume of Colville reproductions by the hour. She has lost her interest in painting now that her powers of concentration have gone, but if I root out the album of Colvilles and put them in front of her, she still shows for a brief time something of her old fascination.

Part of Colville's appeal for her undoubtedly lay in his complete lack of modishness. No other modern painter is so unconscious of prevailing fashion and so indifferent to what's new in the art world. Like the woodland watercolours of our old friend Reynolds Stone, Colville's paintings have no urge whatever to get on in society, the smart society of the in-group. Nor had Iris. She never had any instinct for what constituted the "where it's at" of social or artistic success. If a criticism can be made of the social scene in her books, it might be that her sense of it is not so much innocent as nonexistent. Her world lacks any true sense of worldliness. In her grasp of how actual people behave, her novels can be both shrewd and sharply observant, but there is no indication in them of knowingness, of having, as it were, got even her own world on a lead.

Her feeling for things is far from being streetwise in the manner of Kingsley Amis, whom she knew and liked, and his brilliant son, Martin.

This unworldliness is not common among writers and novelists. Tolstoy retained to the end his involuntary fascination with high society. His zest for finding out what dances were being danced and what the girls were wearing persisted long after he had supposedly renounced all temptations of the flesh. Among writers, it is the lofty moralists, the politically and socially correct, that usually turn out in their private lives to be as pushy as Proust's Madame Verdurin. Social snobbery in the crude old sense is probably on the way out today, but the need to be in the swim is as strong as ever, itself a product of democratic hypocrisy; the need to oppose foxhunting now as much the form as foxhunting itself once was. Many of Iris's friends and fellow writers were censorious when she was made a Dame of the British Empire. They maintained such an honour to be unacceptable on democratic or political grounds, but I suspect they really saw it as out of fashion—things like that were simply not done nowadays. Iris didn't care whether it was the done thing or not. It pleased her mother and her real friends, and that was what mattered to her.

Colville must have been happy in Canada, for nobody bothered about him there, or took him up, and yet he sold his paintings internationally for what seemed to us large sums. "I like being a provincial," he remarked once to Iris in his dry way, "and you don't mind my saying, do you, that I loved your books and now you for the same reason? No striving towards Mayfair, if you see what I mean." He looked so droll saying this that I could not help smiling, and I teased him by saying that of course only provincials exhibited at the Fisher Art Gallery and stayed at Brown's Hotel, as he had already told us he was in the habit of doing when he came to London.

Iris and he were, in fact, the least upwardly mobile people one could imagine. Neither of them were in the least socially conscious, nor did they have any aptitude for making a good thing out of it. Colville's remark about provincialism was an unusual spurt of self-satire, prompted by the behaviour at the conference of a smart New Yorker and his even smarter wife, both art critics, who had been laying down the law at the discussion that morning. After it, Colville remarked to us in a conspiratorial whisper that he was becoming "a mite stir-crazy," so we got a lift into Hamilton that evening and had some drinks in a bar.

And yet I never knew Iris to disapprove of anyone on account of their pretensions, or the way they behaved. J. B. Priestley would show off to her outrageously, which she enjoyed in her benign way, without trying to enter into the spirit of things when he made efforts both crafty and elephantine to draw her out on the subject of Plato or religion, politics, or feminism. He called her "ducky," which she also enjoyed, and he affected robust irritation at the sensible and rational answers she gave him. Had he lived a generation earlier, he used to boast to her, before successful writers had their entire income removed by the government's tax policies, he would have funded an expedition to Antarctica, or set up a research institute in Oxford or Cambridge. "Cambridge wouldn't have thanked you for it," his wife, Jacquetta Hawkes, would say dryly, "I can tell you that, Jack."

They made a most engagingly incongruous pair, and their happy relationship always used to remind me of Queen Titania and Bottom in *A Midsummer Night's Dream*. Iris was deeply fond of them both. I got along well with Jack and was somewhat in awe of Jacquetta, who always made me think of an old don's remark that they'll smile in your face in Oxford and stab you in the back, whereas in Cambridge they might do you a good turn, but with a disapproving face. Jacquetta did not exactly disapprove, but her smile, though friendly, was always a little frosty, too. Her father had been an eminent Cambridge biologist, and she had a way of making unexpected confidences with a sort of scientific calm. She once told me she had jumped out of a window in Cambridge to impress a bumptious boyfriend and had seriously damaged her uterus. "You have charm," she said another time, making it seem like something one's best friends didn't tell one about. That disconcerted me a lot, but she made up for it by remarking on another occasion in an equally detached way that Iris was the only woman of whom she was never jealous where Jack was concerned. That made Titania sound quite vulnerable and human.

Jack's robust tones concealed the same vulnerability. He once asked me with a wistful look if I knew anyone in the British Academy: How could he become a member? I had no idea, but he must have thought that as an academic I should have known the answer. He also said he would once have given anything to have lived in the smart world, like Evelyn Waugh. In a weird way, he made being in "the smart world" sound the same thing as having the right views on England or politics or feminism. He could manage those all right, and they had put him on the map, but to be really on the map, one should have been in the smart world, as well. Such remarks fascinated me but also made me feel uncomfortable, and, I think, Iris, too, although she never showed it. Her way of dealing with Jack was to ask him about his life and views. He was always happy to hold forth about these. Iris was good at getting information from others while withholding it about herself. An interviewer from the newspapers once complained that she had found out all about him and he had learned nothing about her.

Iris's fondness for Jack Priestley was almost like that of a daughter, and she missed him greatly when he died.

Her fondness for Jack grew with time, but she was equally good at making instant friends. And in a sense, she still is. The other day, a caller rang up from an Irish monastery. He had long admired her work and had written to her, a correspondence I had had to take over. He asked if he could look in briefly on his way from Limerick to pick up a fellow monk from a sister foundation. He was immensely tall, dark-suited, urbane, with that indefinable air many monks have of moving in a distinctly smart world. (I thought of Tolstoy, Jack Priestley, Evelyn Waugh!) He told us the Duchess of Abercorn had sent her love; it seemed she had once met me in connection with a Pushkin Festival.

All this was momentarily disconcerting, but when the tall monk and Iris sat down together, things changed at once. They became extraordinarily animated—she starting sentences, or ending them; he appearing to know at once what she wanted to ask, and filling the gaps when words failed with a professional abundance of loving-kindness. And yet his face looked really transfigured; so, a few moments later, did hers. They were soon on about his childhood, why he joined the order, and, most of all, about his plans to make discussion of her works a regular thing at Glenstal Abbey. He assured us that two of her novels, *The Book and the Brotherhood* and *The Good Apprentice*, could be said to have inspired the recent setting up of the monastery and the way they wanted it to go. For the first time, Iris looked blank. Perhaps she had detected a note of Irish hyperbole; perhaps she was simply puzzled about the names of her novels. What were they? From whom? But she didn't enquire, only asking for the third or fourth time where he was living, where he had been born, and whether he knew Dublin.

Transfiguration doesn't last. His enthusiasms soon began to seem no more out of the ordinary than those of most religious people. Iris's own animation faded into her lost look; she seemed bewildered now by the presence of the tall, handsome monk in his incongruous city clothing. Practised in such matters, fully aware that the good minute was going, he rose swiftly, blest her, and was out of the door. The little van in which he had driven all the way from Limerick to Holyhead, and across Wales to Oxford, was waiting at the kerb. I remarked that we had ourselves once driven round Ireland in such a van, but he was not interested. I felt he had taken my measure, not because he was a clever man but because experience had taught him much about the stupidity of intellectuals, their obtuseness about the things that really mattered. He was off now to pick up his Benedictine colleague, and as a parting shot, I remarked that I had heard that the Benedictines were the most learned order. "Don't you believe it," he replied with a great laugh and a look of contempt which I felt I had fully deserved.

Inside the house, Iris had regained her animation and was full of pleasure in the visit. She grasped that the caller had been Irish, but that was about all. I tried to remind her of the time, some years before, when she had gone to lecture at Maynooth, the big Roman Catholic seminary outside Dublin. It had been at the height of the Troubles in Northern Ireland, and her host had made some reference to the IRA detainees there, "the men behind the wire," as they were known in the Irish Republic. "Aren't we all with the men behind the wire?" he had observed rhetorically, and his fellow priests had nodded their heads in approval. Iris had been incandescent with fury. She told me later that she had been hardly able to contain herself and maintain her usual civil and smiling demeanour. I am sure the priests would have had no idea of the passion they had unwittingly unleashed, assuming in their bland way that Iris, like all London intellectuals, would have the fashionably correct attitude towards Irish unity. She did not. It was the one political topic on which the presbyterian atavism of her Northern Irish ancestors completely took over.

I sometimes used to tease her by reminding her of the misprint a typist had made in one of her essays. Uncertain of Iris's penmanship, she had substituted the name Pearson whenever the word *reason* appeared in the text, thinking that this was some philosopher Iris frequently referred to. This produced a number of sentences beginning "Pearson requires" or "as Pearson indicates," and Pearson became ever after a familiar figure in our private language. But Pearson certainly had no place where Iris was concerned if any discussion arose among her friends about the future of Northern Ireland. She used to keep silent if she could, but she often burst out in the end. She once silenced me when I attempted some facetious reference to Pearson in this context by reminding me sharply of Hume's pronouncement that "Reason is, and ought only to be, the servant of the passions." It was not a view she held in any other context.

Iris's longhand was usually clear, was indeed an excellent and wholly distinctive handwriting with no resemblance to anyone else's. Taking her a cup of coffee in the morning at Steeple Aston, I sometimes used to stop and watch as her pen travelled across page after page of loose-leaf paper. Occasionally, it raced, and then her writing did become hard for the typist to decipher. The business of typing her manuscript was always arranged by Norah Smallwood at Chatto, an admirable managing director who had the reputation of being closefisted but who always treated Iris with maternal firmness and kindness. Norah, who had no children of her own, behaved like a tyrant to her young female employees, except when they were in trouble, or if she found them in tears as a consequence of her severity.

Iris was always happy to stop for a chat, never minded being interrupted, whereas if I was trying to type something in bed, I used to find interruptions fatally dismantled whatever insecure pile of syntax my mind was endeavouring to set up. If it collapsed like a house of cards, I had trouble starting over again, or remembering what I had been trying to say. But Iris, good-natured as ever, never minded my snarling at her briefly if she put her head round the door to ask some question about the day's activities. She would murmur something pacific and withdraw with a smile. Nowadays, I remember those occasions when she anxiously trails after me in the house, or if I look up from a book and see her peering at me in the doorway.

Once when I was standing by her side while she

wrote, I saw a fox strolling about on the lawn and pointed it out to Iris, who was always glad to see the creature, even though our foxes were a well-known family, as much in residence in a corner of the wild garden as the rats had once been in the house. Our neighbour's cats were also frequent visitors. A cat was crossing the lawn when we heard, a few moments later, a tremendous sound of screeching and spitting. The fox was dancing round the cat, which revolved to face the fox, making these noises. Impossible at first to say whether the fox had intended to attack and perhaps even to eat the cat or if it was all in play, an idea suggested by the way the fox would lie down between its leaps and manoeuvres and put its muzzle between its front paws. Finally, it seemed to weary of the game, if such it was, and strolled off, leaving the cat to its own devices. While the confrontation was going on, I had the greatest trouble to dissuade Iris from tearing downstairs and rushing between them, like the Sabine women between their embattled Roman husbands and their Sabine relatives. Fascinated, I had longed to see how the situation would end, even though Iris kept distractedly saying, "Oh, we must separate them—we must."

Her instincts were always pacific, and she hated the idea of animals harming one another as much as she did human beings doing so. When the local hunt killed a fox in the neighbouring field, she was up in arms at once, remonstrating with a civil and perplexed huntsman who sat his horse with an apologetic air and said, "Oh, I'm so

sorry, Miss Murdoch, I understood you were a supporter."
This was perfectly true, but there was a difference between being mildly in favour of country sports and hearing
one of her own foxes, as she supposed it must be, des-
patched close by, especially as she might well have known
the creature when it was a cub. If we walked very quietly
to that secluded corner of our garden by the drystone wall,
where bramble bushes and elder flourished and mounds
of earth had been mysteriously raised, we would often see
a small face with myopic pale blue eyes peering out at us.
The vixen usually raised five or six young there each year.

Iris felt the foxes were part of her household. To me,
they were signs, as the rats had been, that the place didn't
belong to us, that we were there on sufferance. This didn't
trouble Iris at all. She was often away, seeing her mother
and her friends in London. Possessions sat lightly upon
her; she once said to me that she was no more concerned
with their existence than she was with her own. I saw
what she meant, and yet it was not really true. She was
jealous of her things, like her stones, roses, and pictures,
and yet it never occurred to her to nourish or to visit
them, to clean them as real householders clean silver or
china, and to give them loving attention. They must never
be got rid of or moved, and that was all. So the house
always had a look of dereliction, as did the very small pad
or perch we acquired later in South Kensington, at the
time we found someone to live with Iris's mother in her
London flat and look after her.

I myself felt no more at home in this London pad of ours than I did in the house at Steeple Aston, although, oddly enough I settled down at Steeple Aston much more readily on the days when Iris was away. When in 1980 or so she had her visit to China (going with quite a high-powered delegation and meeting Teng Hsiao-p'ing, the Communist leader), I found myself making serious efforts to clean the house up. It was during a vacation, no teaching in Oxford, and I used to work on Shakespeare in the morning and clean and tidy in the afternoons. I got into quite a bachelor routine, all the more readily from knowing it wouldn't last.

Iris was greatly impressed when she got home, and touched, too. I think she felt, with a momentary pang, that this was the way I had always wanted things. Not true: I had no idea what I wanted in this or any other respect, provided she was there; and her own lack of identity with self or place precluded me from feeling at home there except when she wasn't. Her novels, and her ceaseless invention, from day to day and month to month, were where she lived. And so, after my tidy interlude as a bachelor householder, married demoralisation swiftly and comfortably returned.

Nonetheless, she loved the place in her own way, far more than I did. Apart from her refusal to go back there—a visit in which I would have felt retrospective fascination and morbid enjoyment—Cedar Lodge was her Camelot, where she had the original comforting future in her head:

her vision of the badgers breaking in, and herself rushing out to tell me about it when I got home. Perhaps that was her sole wifely vision; and after the vision dissolved and departed with the sale of the house, she never wanted to see either again. I once teased her by saying it was the foxes that in fact had broken in, not the badgers, but, as she pointed out, that wasn't the same thing at all. Oddly enough, I did once see a real badger there, though in a wholly inconclusive manner. It was a shabby elderly creature, but unmistakably a badger, which once shuffled past when I was sitting in the long grass down the slope, looking as if he had lost his way and didn't want attention drawn to himself while he tried to find it. In general, they are exclusively nocturnal creatures.

I told Iris about him, but she was not really interested. I suppose it was the Platonic idea that counted with her, not the real example. When UFOs became the fashion, she claimed to believe in their existence at once. And she was convinced of the reality of the Loch Ness Monster, a fabulous creature adored and probably invented by the British press. This monster was reputed to live in the unfathomable depths, surfacing at intervals to be sighted by local gillies and lucky tourists. When we visited John and Patsy Grigg, friends in the Highlands, Iris could not be dissuaded from sitting for hours in the heather above the loch, staring down hopefully. I don't think she was ever disappointed when nothing happened.

Since a child, I had myself taken pleasure in submarines

and airplanes, without becoming seriously interested in them, and Iris ordered a magazine series for me about the two world wars, in which the various types were lavishly featured. She never wanted to study them herself, but she liked to see me looking at my "aeroplane books," as we called them, and she liked me to tell her about them. She herself was devoted at that time to the adventures of Tintin, the perky young Belgian "boy reporter" invented by Hergé, whose comic strip stories are illustrated with an inspired contemporary detail, reminiscent of some of the old Flemish masters. Iris was introduced to these by the same Greek friend who had once told her how to cook the legendary *stifaclo*. Both of us became hooked at once; I think partly because of the French dialogue, which is extraordinarily witty and apt, but which does not come off at all in English. I have learnt a lot of French from the Tintin books, mostly idioms now outdated, which we used to repeat to each other on suitable occasions. There is a moment when the villains have hired a diver to go down and attach a limpet mine to the good characters' ship. Just as he is affixing it, the anchor happens to be released from up above, banging him on the head and knocking him and his mine down into the depths. "*Fichu métier!*" he remarks philosophically into his diving helmet. A comment whose pithiness is as untranslatable as poetry.

Iris wrote Hergé a fan letter, and, thanking her in reply, he mentioned that he would be signing copies in Hamley's toy shop, which used to be halfway up Regent Street, although there no longer. We were in the shop on the day, and Iris had a long chat with the great man, telling him about her time in Brussels with the relief organisation UNRRA, just after the war ended. She never spoke of this to anyone else. He was a big gangly sandy-haired man, like a scoutmaster, as we agreed afterwards, and he spoke excellent English. Iris's fondness for the boy reporter, and his moderately alcoholic older friend, Captain Haddock, had made her suppose that their creator was very likely homosexual. I think she hoped he was, for she had an odd streak of romanticism about gay men and was apt sometimes to be naïve in her assessment of who was what. I doubted she was right about the author of the Tintin books, and by chance I happened to see lately in the paper what was, I think, an obituary article, mentioning a long and happy marriage and hinting that he had also been something of a womaniser.

I recall the day we met him because it was the day we bought a gramophone. We had no TV of course, and it was some years before we even acquired a radio. Our first LP record was Mussorgsky's *Pictures from an Exhibition*, which was quite new to us; and I can never listen to it now on the radio—the gramophone and LP record have long since vanished—without remembering hearing it raptly with Iris that first evening, and how "The Great Gate of Kiev" seemed to resound in harmony with the spaghetti we were eating, and the red wine. Food and music are very contextual in that way. Later, we became fond of song albums, chiefly Scottish and Irish airs, the early Beatles, too, and we used to chant together an imaginary pop song whose words had somehow come into existence between us. In its early version, it ran something like this:

> Waterbird, waterbird, I love you
> Waterbird, waterbird, hoo hoo hoo.

I think it may have been suggested by the low clucking call of the moorhens down on our pond. Iris later tidied it up (the song, not the pond) and put it into one of her novels.

When we had a radio we used to listen to *The Archers*, a long-running soap which came on at twenty to two, during our lunchtime. We put down our books to listen to it. We then discussed the characters and their adventures, or lack of them. I was all for romance, Iris preferred the villains, who always had BBC accents, while the honest folk conversed in various sorts of rustic dialect. *The Archers* is still going, but I have lost interest in it now that Iris can no longer listen with me and make out who the people are and what they are up to. The high spot of her radio life was long ago, in the days when the Home Service, as it was then called, used to run a lengthy serial tale between five and six in the evening. Her favourite, featuring the slim dark-haired young heroine, Mary McCaskabell, was called "Dark House of Fear." The heroine's name perhaps reminded her of Northern Ireland, and she became totally gripped every evening by the lurid development of the tale. I loved watching her as she listened.

I was always intrigued by the ways in which Iris's creative mind seemed to work, never bothering itself much with "highbrow" literature, however much she might herself enjoy reading Dickens, Dostoevsky, Kafka, and so forth, but latching onto unexpectedly simple and straightforward stories with a popular appeal. These her unconscious mind could always make something of, although she never read them in book form, just heard them on the radio. I was reminded of Dostoevsky's own interest in lurid newspaper stories, which often found their way into his novels.

Seven

In some way, or so I felt, the house itself let us know when it was time to depart. That was nearly fifteen years ago. Our most ambitious project had been to remove an inner wall and turn round the lower steps of the dark, narrow staircase, making a wide and rather too obviously spacious descent into what now became a hall. Young Mr. Palmer and his helper had stood precariously on ladders, manoeuvring a gigantic steel girder into position on top of the new brick piers. Owing to some elementary miscalculation, this rolled steel joist, however massive in appearance, was barely long enough to span the gap, and one of its ends only just rested on the brickwork. After it had been shrouded over with paint and plaster, I sometimes used to give it a glance of apprehension as I descended the stairs, wondering if it would come crashing down on top of us, as on the day when Samson pulled down the temple on the Philistines.

The girder is still there and the house still stands, so I suppose that young Mr. Palmer's reassurances to me at the time were justified. But I felt that the venerable spirit of Cedar Lodge resisted this radical alteration. For one thing, the house did not, as we hoped and expected, feel at once roomier and more compact. It merely felt colder, the wide-open spaces of the new hall more difficult to heat. Our successors have made more drastic alterations, transforming the old house at some expense into a mansion that has even figured in the magazine *House & Garden*. But houses, like people, can lose their old character without gaining a new one. Iris's instinct never to return is probably justified.

Wanting very much to give her a small pool in which she could swim at all seasons, or at least splash about in, I plotted with young Mr. Palmer to make one in the derelict greenhouse. It was only a few feet square but nearly five feet deep, so that a few strokes were possible in any direction. The place was roofed in a simple fashion with polystyrene, and once filled, the pool was kept topped up with rainwater from the roof. The water became brown and clear, with the authentic river smell, the concrete sides deliciously silky and slimy to the touch. The rainwater had a softness not to be found in ordinary swimming pools and remained surprisingly pure; I never needed to put in chemicals. I put in a few small fish, green tench and carp, which seemed happy enough in the dark depths. Surrounded by the delicate greenery which sprouts in abandoned greenhouses, it was most agreeable in high summer, a paradisal plunge pool known to some of our friends as "Iris's Wallow."

My ambition was to make it possible to swim there all the year round, and I devised a method which would have been an electrician's nightmare had I allowed any electrician to become involved. The place was wired for some old electric heating pipes; and as the outlet seemed in reasonably good condition, I installed a couple of immersion-heater elements, intended for use in a domestic boiler. They lay on the bottom, and when switched on, they sent a cloud of bubbles up through the brown water. I was careful to put a notice beside the pool, advising, with the aid of a skull and crossbones, that the power must be switched off before entry into the pool. Even this elementary precaution seemed barely necessary; one does not, after all, electrocute oneself by dipping a finger in the electric kettle, and these heating elements were designed to operate when immersed. The cables could have caused trouble, however, and I did not like the idea of finding Iris floating and insensible, although she herself remained blissfully unaware of any hazard involved, and I was always careful to be present when the pool was being used in its heated state.

Like so many brilliant and inventive ideas, this one was not destined to be a long-running success. It worked beautifully, but Iris's arthritis was getting worse (today, it is inexplicably much better) and a walk in the cold, even to the now-heated pool, became uninviting. It was, in any case, destined to be my final attempt to impose innovation and improvement on Cedar Lodge. After it, I relapsed into quietism, and the house seemed to approve of that. Iris had always been pleased for me whenever I had planned anything, but not greatly concerned about it herself. The house and its garden never featured in any of her books. Perhaps in her own way, she was too intimate with it, and too close for it to become involved in her own imaginative life.

194

The grass of the former lawns grew longer and longer and more tussocky; I never attempted to mow them now. The box hedges, neat and trim when we moved in, had climbed to giant size and height, almost obscuring the front of the house, which faced north and was on the sombre side; the southern aspect, from which one went down into the garden, was much more sunny and attractive. Letting things go, a principle which we had once followed almost unconsciously, was now asserting itself as a positive force. The house seemed waiting, with benevolence and without haste or regrets, for its next occupant. It had always made clear in some way that we were not the kind of people who should be living in it. We had not been county people, or even country people, nor did we properly belong to the new race of enterprising commuters who left the village to go to their jobs in London or Birmingham, returning to improve their properties at the weekend.

There were still many good moments. A family of king-fishers was reared somewhere by the pond, and I went down one day, to find small apparitions in vivid turquoise and red exploding among the willow trees and uttering thin, piercing cries. They must have just crawled out of the fish bone–lined tunnel where they had been born, and they could barely fly. Another time, on a day in February which was as warm and humid as summer, we watched black-and-white woodpeckers drilling holes for their nest. The tree on which they operated was only a few yards from the drawing-room window.

And yet, for all these felicitous distractions, the moment seemed to have come. I remembered Mary, Queen of Scots, just before her execution, telling her ladies-in-waiting that it was time to go. Anachronistic fancy might imagine her raising a black-sleeved arm and looking at a watch. Mustn't keep Queen Elizabeth and her executioner waiting. For us, too, it was time to go, but we didn't know where. Should we try to find another place in the country? That seemed pointless—nothing could be so good as what we had. To Oxford, then? Yes, that seemed the obvious choice. I still had my job; Iris was deep into what proved in the end to be the most lengthy, arduous project she had yet undertaken—the Gifford Lectures, to be delivered in the Faculty of Theology and Philosophy at the University of Edinburgh. Later, she was to incorporate them in her book *Metaphysics as a Guide to Morals*.

In retrospect, we seem to have become absentees about this time, like the rentiers in *The Cherry Orchard*, who spend their time in German resorts while feeling a real and profound nostalgia for their estates back in Russia. Cedar Lodge was still very much home, but we seemed less and less to be there. Almost unconsciously, we came to spend more and more time with hospitable friends, who themselves appeared to take for granted that we had become permanent waifs and strays, needing a home now rather than a home from home. We spent weeks in this way at Cranborne with my old tutor and colleague, David Cecil, whose wife, Rachel, to whom I had dedicated my first novel, had recently died. He was often visited for tea in the afternoon by Janet Stone, herself now a widow, living in a small house in an old street on the riverbank, just outside the close in Salisbury. From her tiny garden, we could bathe there in the river in the shadow of the ancient stone bridge over which the high road had continued to Salisbury Plain, past the cathedral, and down to the coast. I was never much impressed by the cathedral, but it always made me think of Thomas Hardy and that haunting tale of Salisbury, "On the Western Circuit," the story of which I was to be reminded in sadder circumstances after Iris had developed Alzheimer's.

From Janet Stone's drawing-room window, opening on

the river, we fed the Avon's busy population of coots, mallards, and swans. Janet would stand there to watch us bathing, her gravely beautiful face always sad in repose. She had never got over the sudden death of her husband, Reynolds, nor, I think, the move from Litton Cheney and the magic vicarage under the Dorset hill where they had lived for years. A wonderful hostess, and also an outstandingly good photographer, she seemed made to live among a lot of people, caring for them, amusing them. Widowhood did not suit her at all. She loved visitors; she taught Iris grospoint embroidery, a simple skill but one to which Alzheimer's, alas, swiftly put a stop. When she died at last, quietly in her big four-poster bed, she looked like the effigy of a mediaeval saint stretched on a tomb.

We had also taken to going abroad again, not on our own, as we used to do when younger, but shepherded and looked after by a pair of great friends, Borys and Audi Villers, the dedicatees of one of Iris's novels. Audi, a Norwegian—Borys was Russian-Jewish-Polish—had formerly been a travel courier. She suffered from severe asthma, which was why they had built themselves a charming little house in the interior of the Canary Island of Lanzarote, where the volcanic air—at least that is what it feels like—is particularly pure and dry. Their house, high up, is surrounded by black hills and fields of lava, growing the tenderest and mildest garlic and onions in the world. This seems inexplicable, as it never rains, and the only other vegetation is an occasional withered-looking fig or palm tree. Lanzarote is a nice place if you avoid the beaches, which are black not only with lava but also with German and British tourists. Audi used to take us to swim in the small harbour, where the steamer left for the next island. The fish population there was considerable; an extremely handsome purple fish which sometimes appeared in the dark blue depths was my undoing. In my excitement at the sight of him through the glass mask, I took in water, then inadvertently spat out with it my lower denture. For the remainder of that stay, I had to give up eating delicious crisp tapas and crustacea. Even a mild Canary onion was too much for me. It was like trying to cut with one half of a pair of scissors. Ironically, my dentist was himself on a Canary holiday when we got home, but on his return, he regaled me with warning stories. Watch out for your dog if you are a denture wearer, he told me: the Airedale belonging to one of his patients had once found and eaten his master's set. He also tried to cheer me up by pointing out the timelessness of tooth acrylic: It is the last thing to go in the crematorium. My teeth, uncorrupted, would lie five fathom in the harbour ooze forevermore.

But some lessons are, as it were, too improbable to be learnt. I forgot this one when swimming in Lake Como a couple of years later. We were guests at some academic conference; I managed to repeat the accident. This time, it was a school of perch, cruising sprucely striped among the lake weeds, that were my undoing. Italian doctors of philosophy were charmed by what they regarded as a peculiarly English misfortune. Hearing of my accident, the waitress in the villa dining room trilled with mirth like a stage soprano. "*Niente al dente per il professore inglese!*" she would cry merrily. Only Iris remained firmly sympathetic, and she did her best, wearing my mask and upended like a duck, to probe the shallows where the teeth had vanished. No luck, of course.

Borys and Audi loved to visit Italy and often took us with them. Since they were also picture lovers, we saw again the Piero *Resurrection*, and we became knowledgeable about frescoes, and the isolated churches that cherish a single masterpiece. Audi had once taken her flock on guided tours of Capri and the Amalfi peninsula, and one year she decided to revisit. My instinct was to shun such picturesque places, but Audi said, "Just you wait," flashing a smile like the goddess Freya's, and she was right, as usual. Iris fell specially for Sorrento; I think the old-fashioned seafront reminded her of Dublin, the Kingstown harbour of her childhood, and the saltwater baths where her father taught her to swim.

The bathers down below our hotel room windows at Sorrento were all deeply bronzed, but on our first morning, there suddenly appeared a tall woman—she must have been well over six feet—with black hair and very white skin. Wearing a deep purple bikini, she looked immensely dignified but also rather sinister, like the goddess of death herself, come to claim a victim. I was fascinated, and I pointed her out to Iris, whose less romantic view was that she must be a female drug dealer. I knew better than to try to nudge Iris's inspiration, which rarely or never began with an incident from real life, but I hoped nonetheless that the scene below might alchemise at some time into one of her plots. To my surprise, however, she nodded down at the woman and said, "Why don't *you* write a story about her?"

From their balcony, Borys and Audi had also glimpsed the apparition, which made a little fantasy for us to laugh about at breakfast. It was 1992. Encouraged by them all, I dreamed up a possible scenario, which ended as a novel, *Alice*, the first I had tried to write for nearly forty years. *Alice* produced a sequel, *The Queer Captain*, and eventually the third of a trilogy, *George's Lair*.

Although it was not until two or three years later that Iris's Alzheimer's symptoms became fully apparent, I have sometimes wondered if she knew that her own career as a novelist was nearly over. Was she encouraging me to start again? Sorrento was somehow a sad place, in spite of its charms. It was also, alas, Borys's last holiday. He died a few months later, and Audi missed him terribly. She went on living in Lanzarote, and we went on seeing a great deal of her. For me, too, one of her holiday schemes was again a source of inspiration. She took us to The Hague for the Vermeer exhibition. The crowds made it difficult to see the actual pictures, but *The Girl with the Red Hat* was reproduced on posters and tickets. A story suggested itself.

I told it to Audi and Iris as we sat in a peculiar little restaurant which itself began to take part in the plot.

My story, *The Red Hat*, ended in a locale we knew well. Stephen and Natasha Spender had acquired the ruin of an old stone farmhouse in Provence, and Natasha had skilfully rebuilt it over the years. It was very isolated, up in the limestone Alpilles district near St. Rémy, and at first there was no water. Iris and I enjoyed fetching cans from the well in the nearest village. In the great heat of July, we used to plunge into the ice-cold "agricultural," an old irrigation canal that wound through the steep contours of the hills, running swiftly among the dense thickets of green canes and rosemary and cypress that bordered abandoned apricot and olive groves. They seemed to have reverted to a wild state. Nightingales sang there in June, even in July. A gripping sequence in Iris's novel *Nuns and Soldiers* was inspired by our discovery of a tunnel in the maquis-covered hillside. We could see light at the end of it and ventured to wade through. The hero of the novel had a more exciting adventure in a subterranean stream. But the magic place, the overpowering heat of midday, and the grey alpine water rushing on its mysterious course through the abandoned country—these were just as Iris described them.

Once, a dowser came to try for water on the Spenders' small property. He was a polite man, forthcoming about his craft, and it was uncanny to hold his willow switch in both hands and feel it stir and tremble. Iris stood mo-

201

tionless and enthralled for minutes, until the dowser eventually had to remove it from her hands with a courteous *"S'il vous plaît, madame."* He found water all right, but it was far down; the well that was at last built was over a hundred feet deep. It solved the problem of a domestic water supply, but Iris and I always rather regretted we no longer needed to visit the well in the village square—it had been a chore we could perform together, like Jack and Jill—and going to wash at noon in the ice-cold agricultural.

In the evening at Mas St. Jerome, we used to play Scrabble, Stephen and Natasha being great experts. Outside in the warm night, tree frogs made a soft soporific din. Stephen had an innocently cunning smile which was delightful to watch as he coaxed improbable words onto the Scrabble board. Picking up my seven letters once, I found they made the word *bunfish*, which I attempted to pass off as an authentic marine species. The others weren't having any of it, but the word found its way into our language, and that of the Spenders, too. "Doing a bunfish" became quite an expressive term for trying to get away with something.

Back in Oxford after a holiday with the Spenders, we drove about a bit, looking at FOR SALE signs. I loved now the idea of a small house. Iris was sorry to see that there didn't seem to be any big ones, not for sale at least. With a rush of warmth and relief, we mutually decided to abandon the whole idea, only to go home to Cedar Lodge and find the house expectant in some way, but not of our return. It was waiting for us to go away, and for all the accumulated dirt and *débris* of our long sojourn to go with us. It gave me a slight feeling of horror; and Iris and I looked at each other. We were becoming too anthropomorphic by far. The house was just a house, after all, and couldn't order us about.

And yet it did. Or it seemed to. Iris went to London. I went to Oxford, and after my day of a lecture and classes visited a house agent and was equipped with the prospectus for a number of desirable residences. I drove to the first, up a long, straight street in Summertown, a leafy suburb of north Oxford. There it was on the corner, a pleasant little brick house. My heart warmed to it at once. I felt we would really own that house. No more living on sufferance in a place that had always been the haunt and the property of other beings.

Without bothering to look at other houses whose particulars he had supplied, I rushed back to the estate agent. I was in a fever to buy that little house before it could be snapped up by someone else. I knew that all the residences in this part of Oxford were extremely sought after. I all but besought the agent to let me pay for the house straight away. He pointed out that he would first have to consult the owner, but he was kind enough to accept a deposit. I don't suppose so naïve a purchaser had ever come into his hands, and he played my enthusiasm craftily, regretting that so many other candidates were in the market, some of whom were only awaiting a mortgage approval before they established their right to number 54 Hartley Road. The thought of these effective and determined purchasers made me more agitated than ever.

Early next morning, with Iris still in London, I went to view the house. The owners had gone to work. Their young daughter, eating her breakfast before setting off for school, appeared baffled by the purpose of my visit, but raised no objection to my wandering about. She seemed herself a delightful emblem of urban pastoral. The clean, sunlit little rooms had a fresh and fragrant smell. A canary sang in its cage; a cat lay asleep on the dresser. A whole new mode of existence, original, unsampled, never even encountered in married life before, seemed to offer itself, seductively yet modestly. I felt sure that the poet John Betjeman, who sang of the joys of suburban life, would have approved that house and its occupants. I saw myself sitting reading by the gas fire while Iris worked upstairs. Presently, we would stroll down to the shops to make some simple purchase for our supper. There were no shops to speak of in Steeple Aston, and nowhere much to stroll to, either, outside our own wild garden.

Iris took it wonderfully well. I think she saw at once that it was no use arguing with me in my besotted state. The power of a new daydream had overwhelmed me. Nor was it, as fantasies go, at all an ambitious one. It was commensurate, as no previous lifestyle of ours had been, with my own instincts for living; and those instincts had apparently been lying in wait for years. I think Iris saw that, and even felt a kind of guilt about it. Although a stricken look rapidly crossed her face when she saw my dream house, she threw herself into the dream like a Roman matron putting her hand into the fire. She acted as if her enthusiasm matched my own.

I saw that it didn't of course. But I was obdurate—why shouldn't I be obdurate for once? And yet the dream faded even before the new house was bought and the old one sold. I realised—we realised—what a mistake we were making, but it seemed as if such a mistake was inevitable, was all we could do in return for all those years—more than thirty of them—spent together in the country in the happy shadow of Iris's own original daydream. Those badgers of hers had come home at last, so to speak. The old house was in a terrible state and we left it like that, still full of every kind of rubbish. But much of the rubbish, including all the dusty old stones, had to be taken to the new establishment. Poor Iris had been so good that I could not even try to prevent that happening.

Number 52 Hartley Road was a predictable disaster, but I continued to feel a dogged loyalty to it, even when the children round about screamed all day and the neighbourhood burglars payed us routine visits at night. We stuck it for three years, longing to go, and finally found a quieter and more suitable small house which a colleague of mine was preparing to sell in 1989. Oddly enough, Iris had done some of her best work at Hartley Road, including the Gifford Lectures. She had driven her pen there day after day, and all the more determinedly because the place was, as I well knew, so uncongenial to her. Needless to say, we never seemed to stroll together down to the shops; nor, so far as I recall, did I ever sit cosily with a book in front of the gas fire, "like a picture of somebody reading," as Keats chortles in one of his letters.

The colleague who was selling us her house (she taught economic history) enquired if we would be wanting Mrs. Shostakovich two days a week. As a cleaning lady, she could be highly recommended, and she was familiar with the house. Mrs. Shostakovich, married to a Polish ex-serviceman of that name, turned out to be a genial, rather bossy Irishwoman who saw through us in the first seconds of our meeting. We were not serious householders. She could start on Monday, she told us, implying not unkindly that by the time she had finished that day, we would know what was what so far as our own domestic duties were concerned. We behaved in a craven fashion. We thanked Mrs. Shostakovich effusively and then told my colleague that we would be making our own arrangements. We had not come through thirty-three years of home life together to be bullied by a cleaning lady who would regard our house as her own property.

Our own arrangements were easily made, and we heaved a sigh of deep relief at having escaped the Irish dominatrix. Spick-and-span at the time of our arrival in August 1989, number 7 Norbury Road soon found itself joining the seedy but, as I privately hoped, not undistinguished club of our former residences. All the miscellaneous rubbish arrived, and the books, and the armchairs grey in our service, impregnated with the dust of four decades. Perhaps the house welcomed them with a secret relief. There were little flecks and blobs of fixative on the walls, relic of posters and drawings stuck on by my colleague's little boy, and Mrs. Shostakovich had spared these. I started to get some of them off as I hung our own pictures, but Iris soon stopped me. They belonged to the house, as our own things would soon do.

Number 7 has not much in the front garden beyond two tall trees, which almost wholly conceal the front of the house. Iris fell in love with these when she saw them. In 1925, when the house was built, they must have been intended as rather unusual miniature ornamentals. Nobody seems to have known then that this new import, *Metasequoia glyptostroboides*, the Chinese dawn redwood, was a serious semi-conifer that would grow to a hundred feet, even though not aspiring to quite the height and girth of its majestic cousin, the true sequoia. Now when the wind blows, lithe reddish twigs and bigger branches rain down incessantly, creating a sort of shadowy Tannenburg. A Russian caller, come to ask Iris questions for a thesis on Iris's novels, eyed this area with some respect. "*Diky sad*," she murmured, meaning "A wild garden." I think she began to look instinctively, as a good Russian would, for forest mushrooms poking their heads through the mat of brown needles.

The back garden is also full of trees, including three gnarled and ancient Japanese prunus, which in summer form a deep bower of foliage, amethystine in spring, with white blossoms like English windflowers, turning in summer and autumn to a dusky red. Beneath them in May shoots up a wilderness of bluebells and Queen Anne's lace, so that the small garden seems to recede into the endless enchanted wood of *A Midsummer Night's Dream.* When we arrived, I put a heavy teak garden chair out for Iris to sit in, and for the first time she started on fine days to write outdoors. I feel now it was a sign that things were beginning to slow down; and when I looked at her through the window and saw her sitting tranquilly, with the pen idle in her hand, I felt a slight qualm. It was scarcely to be called a premonition, but Iris was enjoying the garden, as she still does, in a way that she never seemed to do at Steeple Aston, where it would not be glanced at while work was in progress. On the wall at the back is a fine fig tree, with leaves large enough to make biblical loincloths. The college gardener told me that one must never feed a fig tree; otherwise, it will produce a mass of foliage but no fruit. I had given it bonemeal conscientiously, until it was too dark in summer to see out of the windows: Our drawing-room concealed its dust and dirt and became a shadowy bower of deepest green. After the gardener's wise words, I hastily stopped the bonemeal treatment, and the next year figs abounded. Blackbirds as tame as cats reposed in a gorged state among them, taking an occasional languid peck. They left plenty for us. The leaves remained huge, too, the drawing-room as umbrageous as ever.

At the foot of the fig tree, I put the bronze bust of Iris, done in 1963 by Tolkien's daughter-in-law. The birds did not respect it, but Iris's serene features remained unperturbed. Faith Tolkien also did an excellent head of her father-in-law, looking like the Lord of the Rings himself, which broods benevolently on a plinth in the Oxford English Faculty Library.

Eight

*I*n 1994, we were invited by the University of the Negev in Israel to take part in an international gathering whose purpose was to celebrate, I think, the university's coming of age. I was to read a paper on "Aspects of the Novel," or "The Novel Today," one of those comfortably vague prospectuses which make few demands on either speaker or audience. Iris asked not to give a paper, saying she would rather take part in a discussion in which she would answer questions on her novels or philosophical writings. She had often done this before, and it was always a success, because while never holding the floor, she had the knack of taking seriously anything that was put forward by a questioner, then investigating its potential in a friendly and sympathetic way, which was both flattering and rewarding for the audience.

This time, it all went wrong. The chairman was sympathetic, but he soon became baffled and uncomfortable by Iris's inability to summon the words she seemed to want. Her delivery had always been slow and thoughtful and a little hesitant, and at first I was not perturbed, sure that she would recover in a few minutes, when she got the feel of the gathering. It was hard to say how conscious she was of her own difficulty, but the effect soon became paralysing, for the listener as well as for her. The audience was polite, but the liveliness and curiosity in their faces was gone: They began to look concerned and embarrassed. Israelis are straightforward in their reactions. Several people simply got up and left the conference room.

I thought she would tell me afterwards how awful it had been, and that for some reason she simply hadn't felt up to it, but that did not happen. She seemed unaware and to shrug the incident off, together with my cautious solicitude: I tried to avoid giving any impression that a fiasco had taken place. The chairman and one or two others came up to her afterwards and she talked to them and laughed in her natural way. One asked about her last novel, *The Green Knight*, and produced a copy for her to sign. It was at that moment I remembered being surprised at her telling me, several months before, that she was in trouble over her current novel, the one that appeared the following year as *Jackson's Dilemma*. Often before, if I asked her, or sometimes if I didn't, she would complain she was stuck, that she couldn't get on with the current novel, and, in any case, that it was no good at all. I used to make reassuring noises, knowing this would pass and that in a few days she would suddenly seize pencil and paper while we sat eating or drinking at the kitchen table and write something down. I would say, "Better?" and she would reply, "I think so."

But this last time, it had been quite different. "It's this man Jackson," she said to me one day with a sort of worried detachment. "I can't make out who he is, or what he's doing." I was interested, because she hardly ever spoke of the characters in a novel she was writing. "Perhaps he'll turn out to be a woman," I said. Iris was always indulgent about my jokes, even a feeble one, but now she looked serious, even solemn, and puzzled. "I don't think he's been born yet," she said.

Inside marriage, one ceases to be observant because observation has become so automatic, its object at once absorbing and taken for granted. The mysteriousness of Iris's remark seemed to me at the time quite normal. "Don't worry—I expect he'll be born any day now," I said absently, but she continued to look worried and upset. "I shan't do it, and shall never do another," she said, still in that quiet, detached tone. She had often said such things before, though not quite like that. I had known before that the mood would pass; and this one, though much odder, would, too—I could not imagine anything else. But suddenly, standing blinking in the dry, dusty sunlight of the Negev, I realised for the first time that something might be seriously wrong.

I "realised" it, but without any feeling of alarm, because I was somehow sure that everything would carry on just as usual. In a sense, I was right. When the Alzheimer's patient loses touch with time, time seems to lose both its prospective and its retrospective significance. For the partner, that is. Knowing that Iris would always be the same, I felt that the tiny disturbing eccentricity I had noticed then, when we talked about Jackson, must always have been present and would go on undisturbed into the future. Nothing that Iris could do and nothing that could happen to her could possibly make her any different. As we stood in the Negev sunshine, the matter simply drifted out of my mind. The eeriness of Alzheimer's beginnings is also its reassurance. Part of me knew that I ought to be seriously worried about the future; part knew that neither future nor past was of any consequence. The shortest possible view, even shorter than the kind the Reverend Sydney Smith recommended...

Nonetheless, the disquiet returned in full force when the extremely nice Israeli novelist Amos Oz came up to speak to me the next day. He said nothing about Iris, but from the way he looked at me, I was suddenly aware that he knew all, so to speak. Perhaps as a fellow novelist, perhaps just because he was an extremely shrewd, observant, and knowledgeable man. He said casually that he lived in the Negev Desert not far away and would love us to come and stay with him. Any time, for as long as you want, it would be no bother. I could not make out whether this was pure kindness on his part, whether he meant it, whether he was lonely, whether he had taken a fancy to Iris, or whether he wanted to study a fellow novelist who had gone off the beam, or was going off it. Oz's handsome and youthful face, which reminded me a little of Lawrence of Arabia, seemed far too natural and too independent to be concerned with any of these motives. I think it was natural for him to say, and to want, what he suggested. I have sometimes wished that we could have gone, but it is much too late now to take someone up, even this seraphic man, on such an offer. I have always enjoyed his novels. He might—looking back—have been a kind of angel of the desert, like the one who appeared to Jacob.

215

That was in the spring of 1994. Jerusalem, "city of light, of copper, and of gold," was looking marvelously beautiful. In the autumn, by coincidence, we received another exotic invitation, as if such things had begun to arrive—for one reason or another, it was years since we had been abroad for academic reasons—at a time when Iris's ability to respond to them, and to do a good job, had begun to falter. This invitation was to take part in the ceremony of awards at the South-East Asian Writers' Conference in Bangkok. All went well. Possibly the writers from Thailand, Singapore, Malaya, and the Philippines were not sufficiently in fine tune with their European colleagues to detect when a novelist like Iris, who happened to be the only writer from the West present, was in trouble with what had begun to amount to speaker's as well as writer's block.

Writers are not usually behindhand in talking about themselves, their projects and methods of work, and Iris's backwardness in this respect may have seemed at this voluble Asian gathering a becoming sort of modesty. Or perhaps they were too polite to notice. Even when the crown prince awarded the prizes and we each had to make a little speech, Iris acquitted herself well. I had rehearsed her and had written out in block capitals a suggested version of what she should say. Each writer who attended the ceremony was required, on reaching the podium, to present a sample of his or her work to the crown prince. Iris duly presented a Penguin edition of *Under the Net*. This the prince accepted and passed behind him without looking round. A courtier received it at the crouch, at once passing it to another official behind him, as in a game of rugby redundant. The book eventually reached the end of the scrum and disappeared through a doorway. I wondered what happened to the books at the end of the day: whether they were preserved in the royal library or quietly incinerated in some remote compound.

I was the more reassured during this visit because an extremely nice Englishman who worked on the *South China Times* sought us out whenever his duties permitted, and himself seemed to find Iris's company and conversation reassuring. He told us he often felt extremely lonely and depressed out there. That didn't seem surprising. We ourselves felt weighed down by a sort of Far Eastern melancholy, not wholly attributable to the monsoon weather, for the monotonous rain and soft overpowering warmth was something to be enjoyed, at least for a time. The broad river spilled over the hotel frontage like tea brimming over a saucer, and we used to stand watching it, fascinated by the huge branches wreathed in green creepers that floated past at high speed, level with our eyes. They did nothing to intimidate the drivers of the slender craft that buzzed about the river, propelled by a sort of egg whisk at the end of a powerful engine that roared and echoed down the *klongs* like an express train. It was a special relief to stand outside in the warm rain because the hotel rooms, heavily air-conditioned, felt icy. Our suite, furnished in ornate colonial style, advertised itself as the favourite stopping place of Somerset Maugham on his Far Eastern trips. His chilly presence certainly seemed to pervade it.

The *Jackson* novel had been finished at last. Iris was gloomy about it, but so she was about any novel she had done with, and I did not feel unduly perturbed. For the first time, I took to enquiring about her ideas for a next novel. She had ideas, she said, but they wouldn't come together. She was trying to catch something by its tail, and it always eluded her. She sounded resigned. Hoping against hope now, I worried and importuned her every day. "Any luck? Is anything happening? You must go on trying." If I went on too long, she would start crying, and then I stopped quickly and tried to console her. After the Far Eastern trip, the sardonic face of Somerset Maugham, smiling from signed photos all round the hotel room, still haunted me at moments when I was telling Iris that all writers at some time suffer from writer's block. I never had writer's block, he seemed to be saying, with an air of contempt.

Nor did Iris have it. That soon became clear. Alzheimer's is, in fact, like an insidious fog, barely noticeable until everything around has disappeared. After that, it is no longer possible to believe that a world outside fog exists. First, we saw our own friendly, harassed GP, who asked Iris who the prime minister was. She had no idea but said to him with a smile that it surely didn't matter. He arranged an appointment at a large hospital with a specialist in geriatrics. Brain scans followed; and after an article appeared about this famous novelist's current difficulties, the Cambridge Research Unit of the Medical Council took a special interest, giving her a number of exhaustive tests in memory and language, which she underwent politely, seeming both to humour the researchers and to enjoy working with them. *Jackson's Dilemma* came out and got exceptionally good reviews. I read these reviews to Iris, a thing I had never done before because she had never before wanted to listen. Now she listened politely but without understanding.

The irony did not bother her or even occur to her. Nor did I tell her that there had also been a number of letters about the reviews, pointing out small errors and inconsistencies in the narrative of *Jackson's Dilemma*. It was clear that these points were mostly made by fans, fondly indicating that the writer they admired so much could sometimes get things wrong. Meanwhile, I was anxiously canvassing medical opinion about the possibility of ameliorative drugs. An old friend and fan, a Swedish expert on autism, sent some pills to try, a mild stimulant of the intellectual processes. The new experimental drugs were not recommended, and no doubt wisely, for they have since been shown to be all too temporary in their effect, and apt, during a brief period of possible effectiveness, to confuse and even horrify the recipient. The friendly fog suddenly disperses, revealing a precipice before the feet.

When writing about the onset of Alzheimer's, it is difficult to remember a sequence of events—what happened when, in what order. The condition seems to get into the narrative, producing repetition and preoccupied query, miming its own state. I remarked on this to Peter Conradi, Iris's future biographer, who had already become a pillar of close friendship, support, and encouragement. He and his friend and partner, Jim O'Neill, are long-standing friends of Iris, who had in former times often visited them in Clapham. Peter is a passionate admirer of her books and knows them inside out. Even more important, he loves her and the atmosphere in which she lives and moves. He knows her thoughts, and he responds to her own knowledge with deep feeling. The same goes for Jim, whose sense of Iris's being gives her a unique kind of comfort. He, too, is widely read in her novels and a shrewd, practical critic.

Iris loved seeing their blue-eyed sheepdog, Cloudy, and she loved talking to this extraordinarily dedicated and relaxing couple about books and philosophy and Buddhism. Both, as I said, are practising Buddhists, somehow fitting a routine of meditation, retreats, and hospitality to visiting dignitaries from Tibet or Bhutan into their own working lives. Jim's a psychotherapist, and Peter a professor of literature. In now-distant days, Iris used to return to Steeple Aston or Hartley Road full of her visit to them, and of what they had told her about their Welsh cottage, a converted schoolhouse. They told her of the pool they had built in the field beneath it, the kingfishers and otters that came to visit there.

They were always pressing us to come and stay. By the time we managed it at last, Iris already needed all the support this great pair could give her. *Jackson* was published in 1995: Iris's condition deteriorated steadily over the next eighteen months. Like someone who knows he cannot for much longer avoid going out into the cold, I still shrink from the need for professional care—helpers, the friendly callers of Age Concern, even the efforts of kind friends. All that is to come, but let us postpone it while we can. Iris becomes troubled as well as embarrassed if she feels a visit is to keep her company or to look after her if

I have to be absent. In fact, I am hardly ever absent, and helpers are not now needed. We are lucky to be able to go on living in the state to which we have always been accustomed.

Peter and Jim make this still easier. They do not bother about the dirt in the carpet or the stains on the glasses, although their own home is kept like a new pin and so is the Welsh cottage. They pick us up as often as it can be done and carry us off there.

> When life fails
> What's the good of going to Wales?

221

We proclaim Auden's lines joyously together sometimes, sitting in the back of the car. It's a joke, for we know better. So, it seems, does Cloudy, who opens her muzzle to smile, while her blue eyes shine with anticipation.

Now

Nine

January 1, 1997

*D*idn't *Margaret Thatcher*, at mention of whose
name Cloudy always starts barking, used to
say there was no such thing as "society"? She
didn't put it in quotes, of course: She knew what she
meant. But her point wouldn't have been so obviously
untrue if she had said there is no such thing as the
"people," a word that today only achieves some sort of
meaning if placed, whether accidentally or deliberately, in
a given context. But "the people" are a fictitious body,
invoked by politicians in the interest of democratic emo-
tionalism, whereas "society" is still a neutrally descriptive
word, making sense in any context. The only way "the
people" can be contextualised is as "ordinary people," another purely emotive phrase which has just been used by
the Archbishop of Canterbury in his New Year's speech

on TV. Every "ordinary" person is, in fact, extraordinary, often grotesquely so, and in every sort of way.

I pondered such matters while making Iris her drink, after the Archbishop's speech. Important to make a routine of this. Around twelve o'clock or a little before. The drink itself slightly dishonest: a little drop of white wine, a dash of Angostura bitters, orangeade, a good deal of water. Iris likes it, and it has a soothing effect, making her sit watching TV for longer periods. Otherwise, she is apt to get up and stand with her back to the TV, fiddling incessantly with her small *objets trouvés*—twigs and pebbles, bits of dirt, scraps of silver foil, even dead worms rescued from the pavement on our short walks. She also puts water—sometimes her drink—on the potted plants by the window, which are now wilting under the treatment. But she never does this with a real drink, an alcoholic one. Sensible girl— her old fondness for bars still stands her in good stead.

February 20, 1997

Teletubbies. They are part of the morning ritual, as I try to make it. I have to insist a bit, as Alzheimer's now seems to have grown inimical to routines. Perhaps we all know by instinct that an adopted routine preserves sanity.

Just after ten, as part of the BBC 2 children's programme, the Teletubbies come on. One of the few things we can really watch together, in the same spirit. "There are the rabbits!" I say quite excitedly. One of the charms of this extraordinary programme is the virtual-reality land-scape supplied: an area of sunlit grass—natural—dotted with artificial flowers, beside which the real rabbits hop about. The sky looks authentic as well, just the right sort of blue, with small white clouds. The Teletubbies have their underground house, neatly roofed with grass. A per-iscope sticks out of it. A real baby's face appears in the sky, at which I make a face myself, but Iris always returns its beaming smile.

The creatures emerge, four of them, in different-coloured playsuits. How are they animated? What is inside their plump cloth bodies? The way they trot about and smile is almost obscenely natural, as are their grown-up male voices. Twiggy or something, Winky, Poo...They trot about, not doing anything much, but while they are there, Iris looks happy, even concentrated.

This form of childishness is itself like virtual reality. We used to have a more genuine, spontaneous kind. It began, just before we were married, with a postcard of a very clueless-looking kitten putting its nose wonderingly round a door. Appropriately labelled "Ginger." Iris sent it to me, making a balloon on the front and writing in it, "Just coming." She became Ginger, and then Gunga.

"Haunted by Gunga," I teased her the other day, will be the title of the first section of my autobiography. She laughs and is pleased to be talked to that way, but I don't think she recognises the word anymore.

Something about the Teletubbies reminds me of going

to see the bluebells in Wytham Wood. Since living in Oxford and finding out about this amenity, we have been to see them every year. Coming on them if the sun is shining has something of the beautiful dubiousness of Teletubby land. Can they be real? Do they really exist? They are in a thick and distant part of the wood, under dark conifers that stretch away downhill, and as they recede into darkness, they light up into their most intense colour. They vanish as if into a strange land where an endless dark blue lake begins. Close at hand, they look much more ordinary—greyish, purplish.

We stand and look at them. Last May, for the first time, Iris seemed not to take them in at all.

On the way there are real trees. Two gigantic sycamores, overpowering as a cathedral. But Iris has now a great fear of trees and I hurry her past them. I thought, This had better be the last time we come here.

As we got in the car, I said to her reassuringly, "Soon be back in Teletubby land." But I don't think she remembered what Teletubbies were. I would quite like to be able to forget them myself.

The sense of someone's mind. Only now an awareness of it; other minds are usually taken for granted. I wonder sometimes if Iris is secretly thinking: How can I escape? What am I to do? Has nothing replaced the play of her mind when she was writing, cogitating, living in her mind? I find myself devoutly hoping not.

When Iris's mother was taken to the mental hospital, we did not tell her where she was going. I had doped her, but the drive seemed interminable. As the nurse took her away, she looked back at us with a lost, unreproachful look.

The same look's on Iris's face when I manage to leave her for an hour with a friend.

Like school. Being left there. Probably such moments would not be so painful now if they hadn't started all those years ago at school, inside one's own ego.

I knew where I was going when I was taken to school. But being left there felt the same as the look on Iris's face, and her mother's. In fact, we retrieved her mother after she had been in the asylum a few weeks. Back again later. So it *was* like school.

Associations of that look. Seeing it, I remember the first little boy I met at school, after being left there. He was wizened, like a little old man, with a pale, leprous skin. I shrank from him, all the more because he was extremely friendly, confidential. He said, "Shall I tell you what my father told me? My father said it was the most important thing there was. He said, 'There is no difference at all between men and women. *Absolutely none at all.*'"

I regarded the little boy with horror and fear. It all seemed part of this nightmarish new world of school. At the time, it seemed the worst thing I had ever heard, or was ever likely to hear.

Long piece in *London Review* on Iris's essay collection *Existentialists and Mystics*. The critic made a great thing of the contrast between Iris's views on the novel—the importance in it of free and independent individuals, character creations, *et cetera*—and her own practices in writing fiction, which instead of giving her characters "a free and realised life make them as unfree as pampered convicts." This has always interested me, too. In one way, it is an obviously true point; in a more important sense, it is irrelevant. For Iris makes a free world in her novels, which carries total conviction because it is like no other, and like no one else's. That is what matters, and that is why this world has such mesmeric appeal for all sorts of different people.

It is bound to be a tautology to talk about "freedom" in a novel, in which only the author is free to do as he likes. Pushkin, and Tolstoy following him, liked to emphasise that their characters "took charge," and that they were surprised by what they did, and by what happened to them. Once again, there is a kind of truth in that, but it won't really do. It is a cliché which novelists invent or repeat. What matters is whether the world created is both convincing and wholly *sui generis*, and here, of course,

Pushkin and Tolstoy pass with top marks. So does Iris, in her own way.

I remember that time, years ago, when I was working on a study of Tolstoy, and Iris and I endlessly used to discuss the sort of perplexing questions that arise in the case of great novelists. I used to make the point that Tolstoy's greatest and least visible strength, or "freedom," was the cunning way he blended many different novel tactics when creating a character. At one moment, they behave, as if deliberately, like "people in a novel"; the next, they are suddenly like people we know, as inconsequential as people in life. They seem entirely themselves, as created characters, but the next moment they are behaving just as we might do, so that one can ask in a rather eerie and disquieting way, How does this writer know what I am like?

Tolstoy's people are both completely particular and completely general. At this point in my argument (such as it was), Iris used to look thoughtful. As a philosopher, she wanted to get things more clear than that; and I used to think that perhaps there was a real incompatibility between the philosophic mind and the simple undifferentiated muddle in which free characters and creation must move. Tolstoy, I felt, was not clearheaded at all; he merely picked up one thing and dropped another. Plato wouldn't have cared for that, or for Tolstoy—or for the novel generally.

Your characters, I used to tell her, have contingent aspects because you know that there are so many contingent things in life, and therefore the novel must have them, too. But contingency in some novels is not like that; it is glorious in itself and has no other purpose than to be itself. It's always funny, like the dog in *Two Gentlemen of Verona*.

"Is there a dog in *Two Gentlemen of Verona*?" she asked.

"I think so. I hope so, but I may have got the play wrong. Anyway, you see what I mean?"

Iris always, and as if indulgently, did see what I meant, though it didn't necessarily mean anything to her. We loved those conversations, usually over food or wine. Only for a few moments or minutes did they last, with the gramophone playing in the background. It all seemed funny, too. But I was surprised how much of what we touched on, all clarified and sharpened, is there in the essays collected in *Existentialists and Mystics*, superbly edited by Peter Conradi. Peter pointed out to me a lot of things about this collection, things which he said were like things in *The Characters of Love* and *Tolstoy and the Novel*. It hadn't struck me before, because those words between Iris and me, now vanished, just seem part of us both, although how that can be when our minds were so different—hers clear, mine muddled—remains a mystery.

We can still talk as we did then, but it doesn't make sense anymore, on either side. I can't reply in the way I used to do then, but only in the way she speaks to me now. I reply with the jokes or nonsense that still makes her laugh. So we are still part of each other.

March 30, 1997

The horrid wish, almost a compulsion at some moments, to show the other how bad things are. Force her to share the knowledge, relieve what seems my isolation.

I make a savage comment today about the grimness of our outlook. Iris looks relieved and intelligent. She says, "But I love you."

233

Iris surprised me when the radio was on and we were having lunch—toast, cheese, beetroot, and lettuce salad—by asking, "Why does he keep saying 'education'?" She sounded anxious. Anxiety and agitation are so much a part of her speech now, like the unending query "When are we going?" But lunch and supper are usually quite peaceful times. Trying to make everything as much a reassuring routine as possible. But now something on the radio has very much unreassured her. Government ministers say "education" so often. It ought to be a soothing word, even if a comparatively meaningless one.

It occurs to me that Iris is worried that it might mean something different now, which she has failed to grasp. In a sense, of course, that is true. It refers to skills with computers and such, which we know nothing about. But I think it is the frequency of the word in political speech that bothers her. It becomes almost like her own queries.

I try to say something about the importance of education, and everyone getting enough of it. Iris still looks anxious. "Do they read books?" I wonder whether education now chiefly means reading books, as it did when she was at school and college. Her coherence perturbs me. Normally now, sentences trail off, become deadlocked—start again in another place. Only anxiety queries complete themselves, and this seems to be one. I remember the kindly specialist at the hospital advising that another word suggested from outside can clear the circuit, as it were, temporarily allay the language anxiety. "It's a question of learning, I suppose. As we used to," I say. Her face does clear a little. *Learning* is not a word one hears much now, and certainly not *book learning. Education* has taken over. But *learning* is, or used to be, the more specific term.

> *When land is sold and money spent,*
> *Then learning is most excellent.*

The old rhyming proverb returns to my head—is it borne on the same mysterious circuitry that has failed in Iris's case?

* * *

"When are we going?"

"I'll tell you when we go."

Iris always responds to a jokey tone. But it is sometimes hard to maintain. Violent irritation possesses me and I shout out before I can stop myself, "Don't keep asking me when we are going!" Only a short time ago, it seems, this would have registered as a "tantrum," and the circuit would have visibly adjusted itself and responded with that mixture of amusement and forbearance, complete understanding, which survived as an automatic but infinitely welcome response. One notices that a lot of women respond to snappish husbands in public, and no doubt in private, too, with what Milton, describing Eve, tellingly refers to as "sweet austere composure." The opposite of understanding. Eve was the first to rail herself off in sex disapproval.

Iris never did that. She never got cross herself, and she never does now; but when I did so in the past, she would soothe me by a particular sort of reassurance, implying that I was most lovable and close to her when I was being angry, silly, or tiresome.

Now her face just crumples into tears. I hasten to comfort her, and she always responds to comfort. We kiss and embrace now much more than we used to.

Often something that Iris says now, or a word she repeats, starts me off, too, on some more or less dotty train of association. I remember her mother with the early stages of Alzheimer's—not diagnosed or labelled then. She used to repeat a word in a touching way, as if it were a talisman or portent. If somebody said "journey" or "Baron's Court," where she lived, she would go on repeating it at intervals, and the same if someone happened to say "shandy" or "ham and cheese." Once the mind attends to this involuntary habit, it becomes a conscious one. I become aware that the word *learning* has been popping up at intervals in my mind, and so I play with it idly.

Significant, perhaps, that it is in some way a competitive word. A learned man stands out from his fellows, an educated man does not especially do so. Hence, *education* is a more okay word, something we can all have if the government goes about it the right way. It used to be normal to try to shine, to have read some book or books that others had not, to be able to quote. Lord Birkenhead, or someone like that, proclaimed in the thirties—was it in Oxford?—that there were still "plenty of glittering prizes for the sharp sword." The comment was adapted, ironically, by Auden in his poem "Oxford," so attitudes to that sort of thing must already have been changing. If prizes are given now, they must be given to all—in theory at least.

It's a relief in a way that things have changed. The atmosphere of "learning" is always tiresome, can be oppressive. Even my dear Barbara Pym, whose novels I am so fond of, must have been awful when she was young, and all her set, too, because they were always trying to dazzle with clever remarks, or by neatly capping quotations. Innocent enough, and rather charming in her early novels, but it must have been fatiguing in life. Socially speaking, people thought they had to *try* in those days.

Iris is a great contrast with all that. When young, she was already formidably learned, but I'm sure it never showed. Perhaps considered unsuitable for serious women to show it? Male dons certainly vied with each other, and I remember disliking it while trying to keep up with it. Nowadays, Common Room conversation is blessedly untaxing. But does "learning" require some sort of overt display, like a bird's feathers, to show how important it still is, or should be? It would have been thought odd if Prime Minister Blair had proclaimed his new government's policy to have been "learning, learning, learning," instead of "education, education, education." In spite of its competitive nature, learning is ideally an end in itself, and no government particularly wants to encourage that, or to pay for it, either.

April 15, 1997

Moving from stage to stage. How many are there? How many will there be? I used to dread Iris's moment of waking, because the situation seemed to strike her then in full force, at least for a minute or two. Reassuring noises, so far as possible, and then she would go back to sleep, and I would sit beside her, reading or typing. The sound of it seemed to help as reassurance. Iris's greed for sleep had something desperate about it, and yet she slept, and still sleeps, so easily and so long in the morning that it was a great mutual comfort. Lying beside me, she is like an athlete who had passed on the torch to a back-up member of the relay. I couldn't do what she had done, but I was doing something.

Not a good metaphor, though. It would be truer to say that I myself was reassured by her unawareness of anything that I might be doing on my own. It would have been unbearable if she had shown her old friendly interest. Where work was concerned, we had always left each other alone, so that being cut off now about such things was positively welcome. The simpler and more primitive our needs and emotions now, like those of babies for their mothers, the more absolute they feel. The exasperation of being followed about the house now by Iris is as strong and genuine as is my absolute need for it. Were she to avoid me, or "tactfully" leave me alone, I would pursue her as anxiously, if not quite so obsessively, as she now pursues me. I don't feel any particular pleasure or emotion when her whole face lights up at the sight of me when I return to the car after ten minutes of shopping. But I remember it if I wake up in the night, and then I reach out to her. The "lion face" of Alzheimer's used to be transformed in that way when her mother saw daughter Iris. Not that Iris's face has grown as expressionless as her mother's used to be. Sitting waiting for me in the car, she looks quite alert and amiable, and passing strangers smile at her.

But thank goodness that the stage of that old despair on waking seems to be over. Now she makes a soft chuckling sound and looks at me like the Teletubby baby in the blue sky on TV. No anxious queries. We exchange a few of the old nonsense words before she goes to sleep again. As the condition gets worse, it also gets better. It seems to compensate each new impoverishment. Should be more thankful for that.

The agony of travel nowadays. Iris has always loved travelling, and she craves it now more compulsively than ever. I have always detested the business of leaving home, and I was so thankful in the old days to drive her to the station and wave her good-bye. Now I have a fever of travel angst—taxis, tickets, train times. Iris never worried about all that. She used to arrive at the station like a Russian peasant and wait for the first train to arrive.

The worst of both worlds. Although Iris is compulsively eager to be "going"—somewhere, anywhere—she is in as much of a flap in her own way as I am. At the station, she keeps repeating, "Why didn't you tell me we were going?" I had told her many, many times. Now I tell her again sharply, and with her own degree of querulous repetition. People look round at us. I am fumbling in my wallet, checking the tickets. They are hard to separate, and after shuffling them wildly again and again, I can still find only one return ticket. The whole system is absurd; why must they give us four separate tickets when two would do? It's definitely not there. I rush to the ticket office, where a queue is made to unwind in serpentine fashion between rope barriers. The ticket man has drawn his little curtain and gone off. The customer at the other guichet seems to want a round-the-world ticket, and to be in no hurry about getting it. He and the ticket clerk canvass the possibilities in leisurely fashion. Iris clutches me anxiously, urging us to run to a train which has just come in, the wrong train, I hope. At last, the ticket man is free. I produce the receipt and the delinquent tickets. No, he can do nothing—it wasn't his sale. I turn away in despair. Why can't we just go home?

Iris has not understood the problem and keeps urging me towards the wrong train. At that moment, a man comes up to us and holds out a ticket. It is the original ticket man himself, strangely naked and unrecognisable now he's not behind the counter. He doesn't explain what happened, but just gives me a small collusive smile and walks rapidly back to his place of work.

On the train, I keep counting the tickets. The elderly couple opposite look sympathetically at Iris. I am clearly the one who's become a problem.

Utterly exhausted and drenched in sweat. Vague heart sensations, too. And the whole thing so trivial. Alzheimer's obviously has me in its grip, and the ticket man, too. As well as Iris, and probably everyone else.

Does the care-giver involuntarily mimic the Alzheimer's condition? I'm sure I do.

Sitting exhaustedly in the train, I suddenly recall a droll moment at the time when Iris seemed more or less to have decided to marry me. She was going down to her old school—to give the prizes or something—and suggested I should accompany her. After her business there was over, she wanted to call on the retired headmistress, a famous old white-haired lady who lived in a flat on the school premises. In her bleak way, the headmistress had been very kind, regarding schoolgirl Iris as the jewel in her crown. I was introduced, and after a few minutes I managed to slip away, leaving the pair of them together. When Iris came out, she was looking much amused. "Do you want to know what BMB thought about you?" she asked. I expressed a natural curiosity. "Well," said Iris, "she just said, 'He doesn't look very strong.'"

I didn't bother about being strong in those days. Now I have to try, but I'm sure the attempt wouldn't deceive BMB.

Kind friends up our street are giving a Sunday-morning drinks party. I used to enjoy the quiet of Sunday mornings, the Sunday paper, leisurely breakfast, with Iris working upstairs, absence of morning anxiety about what I had to do that day. In those days, I should have made some excuse, Iris acquiescing. She wouldn't have minded going but knew I wouldn't want to. Now it offers a welcome distraction. I say nothing about it until eleven. If I did, she would panic, demand why I hadn't told her sooner. She does not distinguish now between what she wants to do and what is happening.

"Are we going to London?"

"No, just up the street. You'll know them when we get there. They're very nice. You'll like it."

I know this is true, but it produces a "trouser grimace," as I now call it in my mind. Every evening, we have the battle of the trousers. She wants to go to bed in them, and in everything else she is wearing, too. My resistance to this is halfhearted, compared with the determination she shows on the issue. Sometimes I win, more or less dragging them off. Iris gives up the struggle, but she produces a frightful grimace, an expression wholly new and different from anything her face ever did in the past. It always unnerves me, and it is becoming more frequent in other situations.

Not that I care about her trousers. Our habits have never been exactly hygienic; and yet distinguishing day from night now seems vital to our saving routines. Twice in the day, at ten in the morning and five in the evening, panic and emptiness descend, not because there is something we have to do, but because there isn't. Routine has no suggestions to make. All I can do then is to promise the next thing soon: a drink, lunch, or supper.

Iris's fear of other people if I'm not there is so piteous

that I cannot bring myself to arrange for care-givers to "keep her company," or to take her to the age therapy unit. All that will have to come. Meanwhile, I am ruthless about getting her ready for the party, confident that she will enjoy it when she gets there, as they used to tell us in childhood.

She does. It is a nice party. I marvel, as I have often done before, at the way in which guests enjoy being guests. Standing opposite someone and keeping going, holding eye contact in the same practised, precarious way that one holds glass and canapé. Like a naval battle in Nelson's times: ship to ship, yardarm to yardarm. Sometimes another ship looms up through the noise of battle. Should I switch targets, or redouble broadsides against the present opponent? There is something remorseless about the concentration required. No one wants to be drifting aimlessly through the battle, guns silent, disengaged....

The extraordinary thing is that Iris can serve her guns and return fire, as it were, just like everybody else. I wouldn't have brought her if I hadn't known it would be so. Her face becomes animated—no trace of trouser grimace; she is playing her part just like the rest of us. Mustn't this be good therapy? I should like to think so, but exercise in that sense would imply improvement, recovery. This happy distraction can be only for the moment. I close cautiously on the stern (still automatically Nelsonian) of the guest who is talking to Iris. He is giving a tremendous impression of being good at his work, and happy at it. Half-listening, while at the same time engaging my own opponent closely, I overhear a lively account of the way things are done in an insurance adjustment office. Smiling, Iris listens closely—her attention must be flattering. Then I hear her say, "What do you do?" From the face opposite her, it is evident that the question has been repeated several times in the last few minutes. Undiscouraged, he begins all over again.

Some people might actually find it more restful at a party to talk to someone more or less with Iris's condition. I think I should myself. Apart from making you feel you are performing a service to the community, it is also in the short run less demanding and taxing than the conventional art of party intercourse.

Coming up to me, the hostess says, "Isn't Iris wonderful?" She sounds surprised, perhaps thankful that there is no squeaking or gibbering going on. I am conscious of a base sense of annoyance, even exasperation. People who see Iris on such occasions assume there must be nothing much to worry about. Suppose I were to say to our hostess, "You should see how things are at home." Thank goodness one cannot or does not say things like that at parties.

When we get home, I try to keep Iris interested in the party, saying how much people had liked seeing her. In retrospect, the party does seem to have been a happy time; I am already looking back on it with nostalgia. But it is not remembered. Iris begins to say anxiously, "When do we go?" I wonder how many times she asked the insurance man what it was that he did.

I *am continually* surprised by the way in which the most unexpected people look a little embarrassed if I make some flippant remark about the caring services, the welfare ethic, even "lone" mothers (previously single mothers). Can it be that nice people don't mock such things, even as a joke? No one needs to be nice about sex anymore, or religion. But the modern feeling about social or state "compassion" is uncannily like the old silence about sex, or the reverence about religious beliefs. It's puritanical, too, blasphemy not now recognised as a part of faith, as it was in the older religions.

"Niceness" is always with us, and a good thing, too, but it shifts its ground, even though still clinging precariously to its ambiguities of meaning. Iris's novel *The Nice and the Good* implied these in a masterly way, with as much humour as precision. Does that novel—her others, too—nonetheless demonstrate in some way the inescapability of innocence, perhaps arising from a secure and happy childhood? Iris was both a nice child and a good one, and her parents were the same. None of the three had religion; all were, in the theological sense, naturally Christian souls. Like many philosophers, Iris is impatient with wickedness,

245

its commonplaceness, its knowing conceit. The bad despise the good, confident, and with some justification, that the hapless good may think they "understand" the bad, but in fact can have no true awareness of them. In the characters of her novels, Iris substitutes the desire for power, which fascinates her, for commonplace, disgusting wickedness, which she is neither fascinated by nor understands. To understand wickedness, you must resemble it, at least possess some of its knowing conceit and its inherent dullness. You must be, as Isaiah Berlin said of Dostoevsky, "not a very nice man."

An argument with Iris once about that—or rather, about the good man, Alyosha Karamazov. A projection of the author's will, I said, whereas Dostoevsky's Underground Man slides effortlessly and absolutely into existence. Why? Because Dostoevsky was as boringly familiar with his Underground Man as he was with himself, while Alyosha is basically an idea, a good idea, of course. Iris objected that great novelists were explorers as well as natural knowers. Wasn't Dostoevsky going to send Alyosha into the pit of hell in a later volume, make him commit all the sins of man? Not real sins, I objected, because they wouldn't have been dull enough, nor conceited enough. Not *natural*. They would have been sins in the author's will, not in the book's reality.

I said this, as it made a reasonably smart point, but I knew my position was undermined by Iris's quiet good sense, by her niceness, in fact. I was point-scoring, something she never did in her novels, nor in her daily life. At the same time, I think one reason we fell in love, and got on so well, is that both of us have always been naïve and innocent, at some deep healing level. Finding it in each other, but not saying so, or even knowing so. Iris is good. I'm not good inside, but I can get by on being nice. A wit remarked of Cyril Connolly, from whose features amiability did not exactly shine, that he was "not so nice as he looked." Iris is just as nice as she looks; indeed, in her case, the feeble though necessary little word acquires an almost transcendental meaning, a different and higher meaning than any of its common and more or less ambiguous ones.

Knowingness. Have got it in my head today, instead of "learning." Peter Conradi told me that the French word for it is *déniaiserie.* Fear of being naïve?

And that awkward word, which I can hardly believe really exists, reminds me in some Proustian way of a disgustingly knowing boy at school. Haven't thought about him for years, if at all. One Sunday, his eye lit up with malicious glee when the lesson was read in school chapel. I couldn't help being curious, and he was delighted to tell me why. It was the story of the woman who anointed Jesus' feet with a precious ointment. "Jesus was awfully pleased with himself. When they said the ointment should have been sold and the money given to the poor, he said, 'Bugger that for a lark—I'm the one who matters, not the poor.' I'm going to take the piss out of God Clark about that."

"God" Clark was the chaplain. When I enquired how, as I was meant to, he said he'd do it in the Divinity Essay we had to write at half term. He did, too. But he failed to get a rise out of the chaplain. All too knowing about the ways of boys, the chaplain returned the essay without comment, merely congratulating the crestfallen youth on the fact that it was "well written."

"God" Clark, a saintly-looking old fellow with white hair, had a dark-haired young assistant chaplain with saturnine good looks, who was known as "Jesus" Steed.

Now why should I have remembered that? Having done so, I would once have rushed to tell Iris, sure that the story would amuse her. Now it wouldn't, alas. I can see her face if I were to tell her, with its bothered and confused look. We can still have jokes, but only very simple ones. Not anecdotes. Least of all anecdotes about "knowingness."

Iris once told me she had no "stream of consciousness." She did not talk to herself. She did not say to herself (I had said that I did), I am doing this—and then I must do that. Sainsbury's—the clouds—the trees are looking nice.

No trivial play with inner words? Did all once go into the world of creation, which lived inside her?

They say people with a strong sense of identity become the worst Alzheimer's patients. They cannot share with others what they still formulate inside themselves. Does Iris speak, inside herself, of what is happening? How can

I know? What is left is the terrible expectancy. "When?" and "I want."

Is she still saying inside herself, like the blind man in Faulkner's *Soldiers' Pay*: "When are they going to let me out?"

Escape. The word hovers, though she never utters it.

Home is the worst place. As if something should happen here for her, which never does. Anxiety pushing behind at every second. Picking up things, as if to ward it off. Holding them in her hands like words. Wild wish to shout in her ear, "It's worse for me. *It's much worse!*"

This after the TV breaks down. It is I who miss it more obviously than Iris does, but in its absence she becomes increasingly restless. The recommended sedative seems not to help.

When are they going to let *me* out?

June 4, 1997

Nightmare recollection of a day in the hot summer last year, just before or after our only swim in the Thames. What provoked the trouble, apart from the heat and a drink or two I had at lunch (when I normally try not to drink, Iris has her few drops of white wine with orangeade)? I must have been feeling unusually low. Rows like that are unpredictable, blowing up like squalls out of nowhere and subsiding as quickly. Then the sun is out, the water calm. One can even forget it is going to happen again. Quite soon.

The cause, though? The reason? There must be one. I remember being struck once, when reading Tolstoy, by his description of anger and emotion, a description which resembles the one theorised about by William James, the novelist's philosopher brother. According to James, at least as I recall, the anger or fear or pity is itself its own cause. I doubt this means much, but in Tolstoy, the notion becomes extraordinarily graphic: as when the movement of the tiny wrinkled fingers of Anna's baby are imitated involuntarily by Karenin's own fingers and face. His pity, even love, for this child of another man by his unfaithful wife existed purely in physical terms.

Was it for me some memory of the smell of Iris's mother when she was daft and elderly, arising now from Iris herself in the muggy heat, which expressed itself not in love and pity but in repulsion and disgust? Smell, as Proust knew, can certainly coincide with pleasure and relaxation, and become identified with those things. Or with their opposites? Iris is not responsive to subtle smells, but I have a very acute sense of them. Perhaps that divides us. I like almost all smells that one becomes conscious of without having to sniff at them, or recoil from them. All our houses have had their different smells, neither good nor bad in the obvious sense, but characteristic—that of Hartley Road, ironically enough, was especially memorable and attractive.

To me, the smell of Iris's mother's flat, though quite faint, was appalling. I had to nerve myself to enter; but Jack, who for quite a while looked after the old lady, never seemed to notice it; nor did Iris herself. The ghost of that smell certainly comes now from Iris from time to time: a family odour and a haunting of mortality. But it wasn't that which caused the row I made, although if William James was anything near right, physical causes are too wrapped up in their emotional results to be disentangled.

The trouble was, or seemed to be, my rage over the indoor plants. There are several of these along the drawing-room windowsill—cyclamen, spider plant, tiger plant, as we called a spotty one—to which I had become rather attached. I cared for them and watered them at the right intervals. Unfortunately, they had also entered the orbit of Iris's obsession with her small objects, things she has picked up in the street and brought into the house. She began to water them compulsively. I was continually finding her with a jug in her hand, and the windowsill and the floor below it slopping over with stagnant water. I urged her repeatedly not to do it, pointing out—which was certainly true—that the plants, the cyclamen in particular, were beginning to wilt and die under this treatment. She seemed to grasp the point, but I soon found her again with a jug or glass in her hand, pouring her water. Like Danaïds, those sad daughters in Greek mythology, condemned forever to fill their sieves with water, punishment for having killed their bridegrooms on their wedding night.

I was not put out at the time: I was fascinated. I took to coming very quietly through the door to try to surprise Iris in the act, and I frequently did. Once when her great friend and fellow philosopher Philippa Foot (her mother, born in the White House, daughter of President Grover Cleveland) had come to see her, I found them both leaning thoughtfully over the plants, Iris performing her hopeless destructive ritual, Philippa looking on with her quizzically precise, polite attention, as if assessing what moral or ethical problem might be supposed by this task. I was reminded of their colleague Elizabeth Anscombe, absently bringing up her immense brood of children, and once amusing her audience at some philosophical gathering with a sentence to illustrate some subtle linguistic distinction. "If you break that plate, I shall give you a tin one."

Whether or not the fate of the plants, or the ghost of an odour, had anything to do with it, that day I went suddenly berserk. Astonishing how rage produces another person, who repels one, from whom one turns away in incredulous disgust at the very moment one has become him and is speaking with his voice. The rage was instant and total, seeming to come out of nowhere. "I told you not to! *I told you not to!*" In those moments of savagery, neither of us has the slightest idea to what I am referring. But the person who is speaking soon becomes more coherent.

Cold, too, and deadly. "You're mad. You're dotty. You don't know anything, remember anything, care about anything." This is accompanied by furious aggressive gestures. Iris trembles violently. "Well," she says—that banal prelude to an apparently reasoned comment, often heard in that tone on BBC discussions, usually followed by some disingenuous patter that does not answer the question. Iris's "Well" relapses into something about "when he comes," or "must for other person do it now," or "dropping good to borrow when." I find myself looking in a mirror at the man who has been speaking. A horrid face, plum colour.

While I go on doing horrible things, as if kicking a child or a lamb, I suddenly think of the bursar of St. Catherine's College, a charming scholarly man, a financial wizard, a Parsee, who was telling me about his little son Minoo, a year or two old. "He's very tiresome. He's always breaking things. But it's not possible to be angry with him."

The bursar looked surprised and interested by his own reaction. I wonder briefly, if we'd had a child, would I have learnt not to be angry with it? In which case, would I not be angry with Iris now?

November 20, 1997

Anger sometimes seems now to be a way of still refusing to admit that there is anything wrong. Like a sincere compliment. You are just the same as ever, bless you (or curse you), and so shall I be. I wouldn't insult you by pretending otherwise.

A happy stay, with our friend Audi in her little house in the middle of Lanzarote. Getting there is an ordeal, the charter flight always packed to the doors with holiday-makers. I am reminded of the old joke about Géricault's painting *The Raft of the Medusa*, with stricken castaways clinging on at all angles in the last stages of exposure and thirst. Reproduced with a holiday brochure caption: "Getting there is half the fun." But Peter and Jim come with us and look after us, so the whole ordeal is almost pleasurable.

Return a fortnight later. I have a heavy cold and feel unnaturally tired, although the journey up to this point could not have been easier. Peter puts us on the bus for Oxford. I sink back thankfully. Nearly home. The bus cruises steadily on through the dark, seeming to shrug off the rush-hour traffic on either side of it. The few passengers are asleep. But we have no sooner started than Iris is jumping up and down in agitation. "Where are we going? Where is the bus taking us?" She won't sit still, but rushes to the front and looks out anxiously ahead. I manage to get her sitting down. I say, "We're going back to Oxford. Back home." She replies, "No! No home. Why travelling like this? He doesn't know."

Before I can stop her, she is speaking agitatedly to the bus driver. She has caught hold of one of the bags, whose contents begin to spill on the gangway. I pick the things up, then push Iris into a seat opposite a sleeping woman. I apologise to the driver, who remains ominously silent. When I get back, the woman, a nice-looking person, is awake, and distraught, desperately trying to regain the handbag and other possessions which had been on the seat beside her. I take them from Iris and put them back, apologising again in a whisper. Iris says, "So sorry," and gives the woman her beautiful smile. I get Iris into another seat and give her a surreptitious violent punch on the arm by which I am holding her.

Gatwick to Oxford in the late Friday rush hour is a long way, every second of it occupied by tormented squirrel-like movements and mutterings. Iris grips the seat in front and stares ahead. A feeling of general distraction and unease eddies through the calm of the darkened bus. I can make out faces now alert and fixed resentfully. As the bus at last nears Oxford, I try to point out things she might recognise, but the agitation gets worse.

Clumsy escape from the stares of the passengers. Only one ancient taxi left, driven by a villainous-looking Indian with a gentle cultured voice. He starts to go the wrong way half-way up Banbury Road, and I distractedly put him right. He says, "Oh, no, I should know better, really. Very sorry about that." I give him a ten-pound note through the wire grille and get very little change, but I can't be bothered about that. I give some of it back as a tip and he says nothing. Open the door. Get inside the gate. The house feels deathly cold. I find Iris looking at me in a wonderful way, just as she used to do when we returned home together from some trying outing. I ignore her look, rush to the central-heating switch. Then I come back and say in a cold, furious voice, "You behaved disgracefully on the bus. I felt ashamed of you."

She looks surprised but then reassured, as if recalling an old cue. She would just be defending her corner by the kind old method—that is to say, not defending it. Leaving me to work out my nastiness, as if I were a child. "Well," she says. Her equivalent now of what might once have been a soothing "So sorry." I have lost my voice, can't hear, and am drowning in a cold that seems more ominous than an ordinary cold, as the bus driver's silence seemed more ominous than words. My chest hurts when I cough. After a few more ugly words, I say that I've probably got pneumonia. Hasn't she noticed I'm ill? She looks uncomprehending again. The moment of realisation and reassurance has gone with my own fit of cold fury, which brought them on. My appeal for sympathy leaves her lost and bewildered.

What'll she do if I die? If I'm ill and have to go to hospital. If I have to stay in bed—what'll she do then? Still exasperated by the bus business, I make these demands with increasing hostility and violence. I am furious to see my words are getting nowhere, and yet relieved, too, by this, so that I can continue to indulge my fury. She knows none of these things can or will happen. While I am still screaming at her, she says, "Let's go. There now. Bed." She says this quite coherently. We squeeze together up the stairs, huddle under the cold duvet, and clutch each other into warmth. In the morning, I feel a lot better.

Iris, I think, has never felt bad. She never caught my cold, as if the Alzheimer's is a charm against mere mundane and quotidian ailments. Jim washed and cut her hair in Lanzarote; Audi gave her a shower and a bath. She said to Audi as they stood together in the shower, "I see an angel. I think it's you." Having caught my cold, poor angel was in fact suffering from asthma and a serious chest in-fection, for which she had to start taking tetracycline, for-tunately available over the counter on the island. How sensible, because Audi has never found a proper doctor there, though she has lived on the island on and off for years. Her temperature went up to nearly 103 degrees, but then came down quickly, much to our relief. I think we were all grateful in some way that Iris knew nothing about it. She reassured us by not knowing of troubles, and the tears of things.

Or rather, troubles touch her heart in invisible and mysterious ways. To Audi's cats, which she was once very fond of, she now seems almost indifferent. She strokes them absently. Peter and Jim's dog, Cloudy, whom she once loved to make much of, now seems to have, for her, the distance and impersonality of an angel. When she sheds tears, softly and for short periods, she hides them with an embarrassment which she no longer feels about any other physical side of herself.

In the old days, she used to weep quite openly, as if it were a form of demonstrable and demonstrated warmth and kindness. Now I find her doing it as if ashamedly, stopping as soon as she sees I have noticed. This is so unlike the past; it is disturbing, too, in another way. It makes me feel she is secretly but fully conscious of what has happened to her and wants to conceal it from me. Can she want to protect me from it? I remember as a child finding my mother crying, and she stopped hastily, and looked annoyed. In Proust, the grandmother has a slight stroke while taking little Marcel for a walk in the park, and she turns her face away so that he should not see it all puckered and distorted.

There are so many doubts and illusions and concealments in any close relationship. Even in our present situation, they can come as an unexpected shock. Iris's tears sometimes seem to signify a whole inner world which she is determined to keep from me and shield me from. There is something ghastly in the feeling of relief that this can't be so; and yet the illusion of such an inner world still there—if it is an illusion—can't help haunting me from time to time. There are moments when I almost welcome it. Iris has always had—must have had—so vast and rich and complex an inner world, which it used to give me immense pleasure *not* to know anything about. Like looking at a map of South America as a child and wondering about the sources of the Amazon, and what unknown cities might be hidden there in the jungle. Have any of those hidden places survived in her?

Showing me a tracing from the most elaborate of the brain scans Iris underwent a year or so ago, the doctor indicated the area of atrophy at the top. The doctors were pleased by the clearness of the indication. I thought then— the old foolish romantic idea of the Amazon—that her brain world had lost its unknown mysteries, all the hidden life that had gone on in it. It had been there, physically and geographically *there*. And now it was proved to be empty. The grey substance that sustained its mysteries had ceased to function, whatever a "function," in there, can possibly mean.

Twice, Iris has said to Peter Conradi that she now feels that she is "sailing into the darkness." It was when he asked her, gently, about her writing. Such a phrase might be said to indicate the sort of inner knowledge that I had in mind. It seems to convey a terrible lucidity about what is going on. But can one be lucid in such a way without possessing the consciousness that can produce such language? And if consciousness can go on producing such words, why not many more, equally lucid?

Were I an expert on the brain, I should find it hard to believe in such flashes of lucidity revealing, as it were, a whole silent but conscious and watching world. It would be as if—to use a clumsy analogy from my hidden city in the jungle—a flash of lightning were to reveal its existence, and then the explorers found that it didn't exist after all. The words which Iris used with such naturalness and brilliance cannot be stacked there silently, sending out an occasional signal. Or can they? I notice that the eerie felicities which Iris has sometimes produced, such as "sailing into the darkness" or "I see an angel," seem to come with a little help from her friends. They are like the things a young child suddenly comes out with, to the delight and amusement of parents and friends. But it was the friends or parents who unconsciously did the suggesting. Must have been.

Iris has heard nothing from a great friend, a novelist whom she had once befriended and inspired, counselled and consoled. Had this now famous friend left her, abandoned in her silence? Was it in resignation or in bitterness of spirit that she spoke those words? Sailing alone into the dark...

In my own daily intercourse with Iris, words don't seem to be necessary, hardly appear to be uttered. Because we don't talk coherently, and because we talk without seeming to ourselves to be talking, nothing meaningful gets said. The clear things Iris does sometimes come out with are intended for public consumption. They are social statements. They have the air of last remarks before all the lights go out.

I always liked Sunday mornings, but Iris never noticed them. She still doesn't, but now I find TV a great help. Looking in on her as I potter about, I am relieved to see her sitting intently, like a good child, watching the Sunday-morning service. Later, she is still there; the service has changed to an animated cartoon featuring Bible history, Roman soldiers, and so on, in which she is equally engrossed. Thank goodness for Sunday-morning TV.

There are occasions when I have such a strong wish to remind Iris of something we did or saw that I find myself describing it hopefully, in great detail. I don't say, "You probably don't remember, but..." Instead, I now have the feeling that she is trying to follow something I am creating for her. Spring is more vivid when you talk about it in winter, and I find myself telling her about one of our visits with Peter and Jim to Cascob, in Wales, at the end of last May. The small schoolhouse, where twenty or thirty children were once taught, lies on a rising knoll at the end of a steep and narrow valley. It is an old place, a single large high-roofed room. Adjacent to it is the schoolmistress's house, one room up and one down. Although they were once separate buildings, Peter and Jim have joined the two and made some alterations, but the basic structure remains intact. The crown of the hillock on which their home stands slopes sharply down to their pond, with a little island in the middle, thick with alder and willow and with flowers in summer. Just beside the school is an extremely old church, half-buried in green turf nearly up to the window openings on one side, so that the sheep can look in. An immense yew tree, much older even than the church, makes a kind of jungle beside it, dark red with shadows.

On that visit to this enchanting place, we soon found a special routine. A pair of redstarts were nesting just above the back doorway. If we sat motionless in the little courtyard, or looked out of the schoolhouse window, we could see them come and go: small flamelike birds, looking much too exotic to be seen in the British Isles. The breast and tail (*steort* means "tail" in Old English) were bright cinnamon red, the head jet black, with a white ring on the neck. When they hovered near the nest, wary of a possible watcher, they were as jewel-like as hummingbirds.

After watching the redstarts, our ritual was to go round to the churchyard, where we could have quite a different experience. Jim had fixed a nesting box on a great ash tree where the graveyard bordered their copse. He told us a pair of pied flycatchers were nesting there. A flycatcher is a little bird, even more rare than the redstart, a migrant who now only comes back to the borders of south and central Wales. We stood by a gravestone, watching. Nothing happened for a long time. Suddenly and soundlessly, a neat little apparition in black and pure white appeared by the hole in the nesting box. It was motionless for a moment and then vanished inside. We looked at one another, hardly believing we had really seen it. It seemed like a pure speck of antiquity, robed in the hues of the old religion, almost as if a ghostly emanation from the church itself.

After this, we could not keep away from the grave mound by the edge of the copse, a vantage point only a few feet away from the nest on the ash tree. The little birds seemed unaware of us, just as ghosts would have been. Their busy movements had a soft spirit-like silentness. Peter and Jim told us they did have a small song, but we never heard them make a sound. Although we saw both birds, and identified the male and the female, we could not really believe in their physical existence at all. Like the ghosts in *Macbeth*, they came like shadows, so departed.

In the winter, I find myself telling Iris all this, and she listens with a kind of bemused pleasure and toleration, as if I were making up a fairy story. She doesn't believe it, but she likes to hear it. I myself find that these bird memories, and the whole memory pattern of summer sunshine and green leaves, become subtly different from what it was like at the time. It really is as if I were making the whole thing up.

I remembered that Kilvert, the Victorian parson who once lived not far off in the same part of Wales and had so much loved writing his diary about his days, his walks, and his priestly duties, had once confided to it that what he wrote down was more real to him than what he had actually seen that day or the one before and was now writing about. Only memory holds reality. At least this seems to have been his experience, and that of a lot of other writers, too—romantic souls who, like Wordsworth (worshipped by Kilvert), made the discovery that for them to remember and to write was to create their lives, and their sense of living things. The actual experience was nothing beside it, a mere blur always on the move, always disappearing. Proust or D. H. Lawrence must have felt the same, however much Lawrence himself might protest about "Life—Life" being the great thing. Wordsworth only *really* saw his daffodils when he lay on his couch and viewed them with his inward eye.

Iris's genius as a writer is rather different, I think, more comprehensive. Nor does one think of Shakespeare as creating this wonderful vision after the event. It seems to be a Romantic discovery, this sense that all depends on memory. But like all such generalisations, this is not altogether true: Some writers or artists—Vermeer for instance—create such vanished moments but without bothering to make a song and dance about it.

As I create, or re-create, those birds for Iris, I wonder what is going on in her head. Is she cognisant of an invention, a fairy tale instead of a memory? For a writer of her scale and depth, the power of creation seems so much more important than memory, almost as if it could now continue independent of it. And yet the one seems to depend on the other. So what are we remembering when we invent?

The main thing is, she likes to hear me talk about the birds. They must be just a part, a coming-and-going part, of the me she is always with. Once I was outside her, a reality quite separate from herself, her mind, her powers of being and creating. Not now.

Now I feel us fused together. It appalls me sometimes, but it also seems comforting and reassuring and normal.

Reminded of *The Girl with the Red Hat*, the Vermeer portrait that for me haunted our short but happy stay in The Hague. When we were there, I at once began to have that fantasy about it, which I told to Audi and Iris, separately I think. For Audi, I wanted it to be comic, a comical adventure fantasy, with sinister overtones, which we could laugh at together. Could it be that for Iris I instinctively tried to make it sound a bit like something in her own novels? As if I were trying to remind or inspire, or even carry on the torch by a kind of imitation? However that was, the story I wrote about it does not sound in the least like Iris, except perhaps to me. It came out much more like the fantasy I told Audi, who kindly said she enjoyed it when the book appeared a year later.

Life is no longer bringing the pair of us "closer and closer apart," in the poet's tenderly ambiguous words. Every day we move closer and closer together. We could not do otherwise. There is a certain comic irony—happily, not darkly comic—that after more than forty years of taking marriage for granted, marriage has decided it is tired of this, and is taking a hand in the game. Purposefully, persistently, involuntarily, our marriage is now getting somewhere. It is giving us no choice—and I am glad of that.

Every day, we are physically closer; and Iris's little "mouse cry," as I think of it, signifying loneliness in the next room, the wish to be back beside me, seems less and less forlorn, more simple, more natural. She is not sailing into the dark: The voyage is over, and under the dark escort of Alzheimer's, she has arrived somewhere. So have I.

This new marriage has designed itself, as Darwin once speculated that fish perhaps designed their own eyes, to bring to an end her fearful anxieties of apartness—that happy apartness which marriage had once taken wholly for granted. This new marriage needs us absolutely, just as we need it. To that extent, it is still a question of "taking for granted."

The phrase "taking for granted" was in my head because I had just received a letter from the Japanese psychologist Takeo Doi. Admiring Iris's novels, he had once corresponded with her, and his ideas had interested her. As pen pals, they had got on, and the three of us had once met in Tokyo. He had read a piece of mine on marriage which had been commissioned by The Times. The paper had naturally wanted it to be about Iris's Alzheimer's, but I had also made our old point about taking marriage for granted, quoting Iris's character in *A Severed Head* who had lamented that her marriage "wasn't getting anywhere." This had struck the distinguished psychologist, the explorer of *amae*, the taken-for-granted bond which supplies the social cohesion of the Japanese people, and he had titled the essay which he now sent me "Taking for Granted." Japanese husbands and wives, he said, do not make a fuss about marriage, as in the Western style, but take it for granted. I wrote thanking him for the piece, and remarked that marriage was now taking us for granted, rather than we it.

As in the old days, nothing needs to be done. Helplessness is all. Yet it's amusing to contemplate "new marriage." Like New Labour, the New Deal, and so on? Not quite like that. Hard, though, to contemplate one's arrangements without their becoming, at least to oneself, a private form of public relations. I need our closeness now as much as Iris does, but I don't feel I need to cherish it. It has simply arrived, like the Alzheimer's. The best as well as the fullest consciousness of it comes in the early morning, when I am beside Iris in bed, tapping on my typewriter, and feel her hearing it in her doze, and being reassured by it.

In the past, she would have been up and in her study, in her own world. I am in mine, but it seems to be hers, too, because of proximity. She murmurs, more or less asleep, and her hand comes out from under the quilt. I put mine on it and stroke her fingernails for a moment, noticing how long they are, and how dirty. I must cut them and clean them again this morning. They seem to grow faster by the month, and I suppose mine do the same.

As I am sitting in the kitchen, trying to read something, Iris makes her mouse noise at the door. She is carrying a Coca-Cola tin picked up in the street, a rusty spanner—where on earth did she get that?—and a single shoe.

Single shoes lie about the house as if deposited by a flash flood. Never a matching pair. Things in odd corners—old newspapers, bottles covered in dust. A mound of clothing on the floor of the room upstairs where she used to write. Dried-out capless plastic pens crunch underfoot. A piece of paper in her handwriting of several years ago with "Dear Penny" on it.

Rubbish becomes relaxing if there is no will to disturb it. It will see out our time. I think of the autumn in Keats's poem "Hyperion": "But where the dead leaf fell, there did it rest."

An odd parallel between the rubbish on the floor and the words that fly about the house all day. Words the equivalent of that single shoe.

Tone is what matters. All is okay with a child or cat or gunga exclamation. "The bad cat: What *are* we going to do with her?" I stroke her back or pull her backwards and forwards till she starts laughing. I imitate the fond way her father used to say in his mock-exasperated Belfast accent (she told me this long ago), "Have you got no sense at *all*?" Iris's face always softens if I mention her father in this way. Instead of crying, she starts to smile.

I rely on the bad-child ploy, which can easily sustain some degree of frenzy. "You bad animal! Can't you leave me alone *just for one minute!*" Or sometimes I sound to myself like Hedda Gabler needling her lover. But if I give it the tone of our child talk, Iris always beams back at me.

She never showed any interest in children before. Now she loves them, on television or in real life. It seems almost too appropriate. I tell her she is nearly four years old now— isn't that wonderful?

The Christmas business, it's all come round again. Iris has always enjoyed Christmas, and the socialising that goes with it. The festive season always makes me feel glum, though I go through the motions. Why not get away from it all? In the old days, Iris wouldn't have liked that. Now I am not so sure. Change in one sense means little to her, yet a different scene of any sort can cause her to look around in astonished wonder, like Sleeping Beauty who when she stirred among the cobwebs saw—must have seen, surely—spiders and rats and mice running away in alarm. (I am assuming that the prince who woke her would have stepped tactfully back into the shadows.)

Wonder on the edge of fear. That shows in Iris's face

if we go anywhere unfamiliar to her. A momentary relief from the daily pucker of blank anxiety. A change only relieves that anxiety for a few minutes, often only seconds. Then anxiety returns with new vigour. The calmness of routine has more to recommend it. But no choice really—Hobson's choice. Routine needs a change, and change finds some relief again in routine, like the people in Dante's hell who kept being hustled from fire into the ice bucket, then back again.

Well, not as bad as that. The point about Christmas could be that it combines a change with a routine, a routine of custom and ceremony that has at least the merit of a special occasion, of coming but once a year. Years ago, our friend Brigid Brophy and her husband decided to go to Istanbul for Christmas. "To eat our turkey in Turkey," as they explained. Iris then laughed politely, but she was not amused. Indeed, I am not sure she was not really rather shocked. Christmas to her was not exactly holy, but it meant something more important than the opportunity for a witticism about turkey in Turkey.

I think she welcomed at that time the idea of inevitability—something that has to happen. Mary and Joseph in the stable could do nothing about it—why should *we* need to?

Now I must encourage that instinct towards passivity, taking refuge in blest, or at least time-honoured, routines. No point in getting away from it all, nowhere to get away to. Alzheimer's will meet you there, like death at Samarra.

So we'll go to London as usual, visit my brother Michael, have Christmas dinner with him. We'll do all the usual things.

It's Christmas morning. And we are doing all the usual things. Routine is a substitute for memory. Iris is not asking the usual anxious questions: "Where are we? What are we doing? Who is coming?"

Someone, or something, is coming. The silence it brings makes no demands. London is uncannily silent on Christmas morning. Nobody seems to be about. If there are churchgoers and church bells, we see none, hear none. The silence and the emptiness seem all the better.

We walk to Kensington Gardens up the deserted street, between the tall stucco façades falling into Edwardian decay, but still handsome. Henry James lived on the left here; Browning farther up on the right. We pass their blue plaques set in the white wall. A few yards back, we passed the great gloomy redbrick mansions where T. S. Eliot had a flat for many years. His widow must be in church now.

Our route on Christmas morning is always the same. We have been doing this for years. As we pass their spectral houses, I now utter a little bit of patter like a guide. Henry James, Robert Browning, T. S. Eliot. On former mornings like these, we used to gaze up at their windows, talk a bit about them. Now I just mention the names. Does Iris remember them? She smiles a little. They are still familiar, those names, as familiar as this unique morning silence. Just for this morning, those writers have laid their pens down, as Iris herself has done, and are taking a well-earned rest, looking forward to their dinners. Thackeray, the gourmet, whose house is just round the corner, would have looked forward to his with special keenness.

Now we can see the park, and beyond it the handsome Williamite façade of Kensington Palace. When Princess Diana died, the whole green here was a mass of cellophane, wrapping withered flowers. And the crowds were silent, too. As quiet, the media said in an awed way, as it is in this morning's calm. The grievers were like good children at bedtime, folding their hands in ritual prayer. It was a tranquil ceremony, like our Christmas, as we wander now vaguely over the deserted road, usually a mass of traffic, and up the expanse of the Broad Walk.

A few dogs here, unimpressed by Christmas, but seeming merrier than usual in contrast with the silence. There is one bell now, tolling somewhere on a sweet high note. Up in the sky, the jet trails move serenely on, seeming more noiseless than usual, their murmur fainter when it comes. Christmas morning in London is always calm and mild and bright. I can only remember one time when it rained, even snowed a bit. I ask Iris if she can remember that Christmas. She smiles. No need to remember, as this ritual that has replaced memory goes on.

The Round Pond. Canada geese standing meditatively, for once making no demands. The same path as usual, downwards, to the Serpentine. Nobody round the Peter Pan statue. Not even a Japanese couple with a camera. One Christmas, we met two middle-aged ladies from New Zealand here, who told us this statue was the one thing they really wanted to see in London.

Young Pan himself, bronze fingers delicately crooked, his double pipe to his lips, has the sublimely sinister indifference of childhood. Captain Hook, his great enemy, was always made nervous by that pose. He considered Peter to have Good Form without knowing it, which is, of course, the best Form of all. Poor Hook was in despair about this. It made Iris laugh when I told her, years ago, before we were married. I read a bit of the book to her (the book is much better, and funnier, than the pantomime play). Iris, I recall, was so amused that she later put the "good form" business into one of her own novels.

Iris's amusement may even have been shared, in a quiet way, by the sculptor himself, who covered the base of the group with elves and rabbits and snails in the Victorian fairy-tale tradition. But at the top, he put the elegant figure of a much more worldly young woman, scrambling determinedly over the plinth to proposition Peter, giving the bystander an agreeable view of her polished bronze derrière. It is clad in a modishly draped and close-fitting Edwardian skirt, and she looks much too old for Peter anyway. Could it be that Sir George Frampton, as well as being an excellent artist and sculptor, had a sense of humour about these matters? It certainly looks like it, on such a quiet, sunny Christmas morning, with real squirrels hopping about all round the statue, vainly soliciting the nuts which the fat little beasts have no trouble in getting from tourists on ordinary, busier days.

As we walk round and admire, I tell Iris that my mother assured me that if I looked hard enough over the railings, into the private dells where the bluebells and daffodils come up in spring, I might see fairies, perhaps even Peter Pan himself. I believed her. I could almost believe her now, with the tranquil sunshine in the park making a midwinter spring, full of the illusion of flowers and fairies as well as real birdsong.

Iris is listening, which she rarely does, and smiling, too. There have been no anxious pleas this morning, no tears, none of those broken sentences whose only meaning is the dread in her voice and the demand for reassurance. Something or someone this morning has reassured her, given for an hour or two what the prayer book calls "that peace which the world cannot give."

Perhaps it is the Christmas ritual. It is going somewhere, but it is also a routine, even though a rare one. It is both. And now it will go on. We shall return to my brother, who has attended matins this morning at Chelsea Old Church, where Sir Thomas More once used to worship. We shall eat sardines and sausages and scrambled eggs together, with a bottle or two of a Bulgarian red wine which goes with everything. The sort of Christmas dinner we all three enjoy, and the only time of the year Michael permits a little cookery to be done in his immaculate and sterile little kitchen. The sardines are routine for him, but the eggs and sausages represent a real concession. I shall do them, with Iris standing beside me, and we shall bring the wine.

A snooze then. Iris will sleep deeply. Later, we listen to carols and Christmas music. And I have the illusion, which fortunate Alzheimer's partners must feel at such times, that life is just the same, has never changed. I cannot imagine Iris any different. Her loss of memory becomes, in a sense, my own. In a muzzy way—the Bulgarian wine, no doubt—I find myself thinking of the Christmas birth, and also of Wittgenstein's comment that death is not a human experience. We are born to live only from day to day. "Take short views of human life—never further than dinner or tea." The Reverend Sydney Smith's advice is most easily taken during these ritualised days. The ancient saving routine of Christmas, which for us today has been twice blessed.

About the Author

Born in India in 1925, John Bayley was educated at Eton and Oxford, and he served during World War II in the Grenadier Guards. He became a fellow of New College in 1955, where he taught English. In 1956, he married the novelist Iris Murdoch, who was then teaching philosophy at St. Anne's College. In 1973, he was appointed Warton Professor at St. Catherine's College.

Bayley has written numerous works of criticism, notably *The Characters of Love, Tolstoy and the Novel, Pushkin: A Comparative Commentary*, and *Shakespeare and Tragedy*. He has also published several studies about Thomas Hardy, Jane Austen, and Henry James, as well as a history of the short story. His most recent novel, *The Red Hat*, was published by St. Martin's Press in May 1998. He is a regular reviewer for *The New York Review of Books*. Bayley lives in Oxford.

THE CASE OF THE

DIAMOND DOG COLLAR

THE CASE OF THE

DIAMOND

DOG

COLLAR

MARTHA FREEMAN

Holiday House / New York

Art on page 50 by Clement Goodman

Library of Congress Cataloging-in-Publication Data

Freeman, Martha, 1956-
The case of the diamond dog collar / Martha Freeman. — 1st ed.
p. cm. — (A first kids mystery ; 2)
Summary: Seven-year-old Tessa and ten-year-old Cammie, the first female president's
daughters, investigate when a diamond goes missing from the collar of their very
rambunctious dog.
ISBN 978-0-8234-2337-8 (hardcover)
1. White House (Washington, D.C.)—Juvenile fiction. [1. White House
(Washington, D.C.)—Fiction.   2. Presidents—Family—Fiction.   3. Sisters—
Fiction.   4. Dogs—Fiction.   5. Lost and found possessions—Fiction.
6. Washington (D.C.)—Fiction.   7. Mystery and detective stories.]   I. Title.
PZ7.F87496Cas 2010
[Fic]—dc22
2011005019

For my mother,
Barbara Parks Freeman

THE CASE OF THE

DIAMOND
DOG
COLLAR

CHAPTER ONE

MY sister, Tessa, ran into our bedroom yelling: "One of the big, fat diamonds is missing!"

I didn't look up.

Tessa waved her arms to get my attention. "I'm serious, Cammie!"

There are not that many big, fat diamonds in my life, so most likely Tessa was talking about one from our dog's new collar. It had come the day before yesterday, a present from Empress Pu-Chi. She's not a real empress, she's a dog, and she belongs to the president of a nearby nation.

I sighed and closed my book. "They're big, fat, *fake* diamonds, Tessa."

"I know, I know, I know," Tessa said. "But anyway, one of 'em's missing, and you gotta come see."

Have I mentioned my sister is a drama queen?

Still, when she grabbed my arm, I went with her. I didn't have anything better to do. It was Friday afternoon, the start of our March break. Right about now my family was supposed to be on Air Force One flying to California. Only at the last minute, my mom was too busy working on the energy bill to leave Washington.

We didn't want to go to California without Mom.

Since January, when she got to be president of the United States, Tessa and I don't get to see her that much.

Tessa pulled me out the bedroom door and headed for the West Sitting Hall, which is kind of like our living room. Our dog, Hooligan, was there, dozing in his old bed. I was surprised to see him. Usually about now Mr. Bryant would be taking him for his afternoon walk on the South Lawn.

Tessa let go of me and ran over to Hooligan. "Look!" She pointed at the collar, which was bright red, with twelve big, fat, fake diamonds all around it.

Make that eleven.

Hooligan must've heard us because he stretched his paws and opened one eye.

"We should find that missing diamond, Cammie," Tessa said. "It looked real to me. I bet the letter's wrong."

Tessa meant the letter that came with the present. Here is what it said:

Greetings to Hooligan, Esteemed Dog of the First Children of the United States of America,

On behalf of my master, President Manfred Alfredo-Chin, democratically elected leader of a certain nation nearby to your own, I am pleased to offer you the gift of this canine accessory. Please accept it as a token of our admiration and respect, as well as evidence that President Alfredo-Chin bears you no hard feelings for the unfortunate incident earlier this year.

While President Alfredo-Chin's own dog (me!) is practically perfect in every way, he wisely recognizes that in most cases, dogs will be dogs.

> *Supreme Regards,*
> *Empress Pu-Chi*
> *Pekingese*

P.S.—In keeping with the laws on gifts to the pets of presidents, the stones adorning the accessory are not genuine diamonds but attractive facsimiles.

Tessa and I didn't know the word *facsimile*, but our Cousin Nathan did. He is ten like me and lives with us here in the White House along with his mom, my aunt Jen. According to Nathan, *facsimile* is pronounced *fak-**si**-mi-lee*, and it means "copy"—in other words, fake.

Also, I should explain that when President Manfred Alfredo-Chin visited earlier this year, Hooligan did something that almost caused an international incident. I was glad to know there were no hard feelings.

"What do you mean you think the letter's wrong?" I asked Tessa. "You think someone's lying about the diamonds?"

Tessa shrugged. "All I'm sayin' is they look pretty sparkly."

Hooligan opened his other eye and wiggled his ears. At the same time, I heard canary hysteria from the second-floor kitchen.

"What is wrong with Granny's new—?" Tessa started to ask, but before she could finish, Hooligan jumped like a string had yanked him.

"Hooligan?" I made my voice all calm and soothing. "Be good now."

Hooligan cocked his head as if I had made an excellent suggestion, one worth thinking about...but not right now. Right now he was too busy...

...going *crazy!*

He does this sometimes: lunges forward, thumps his paws, springs high in the air and spins so fast he turns blurry.

"*Catch him!*" I yelled.

Tessa dived, but too soon, and Hooligan, long tail flying, made a neat leap over her and ran like he'd seen rabbits in the distance.

Twee-twee-twee! came from the kitchen, and then the clatter of canary wings against the cage.

Distracted, I turned and didn't see Tessa's body, which I kicked—"*Ow, Cammie!*"—before falling over onto the floor. Lying there, I heard a squeal from down the hall. Then there was an *oof*, a *thump*, a pause and a *thwack*.

Oof and *thump* mean Hooligan's crashed into someone and knocked 'em over. This happens a lot.

But *thwack*? What did that mean?

Twee-twee-twee!

And then: *Aah-rooo!*

Hooligan had started to howl.

Tessa and I untangled, scrambled and ran.

In the center hall, we found a body.

"Are you okay, Mrs. Hedges?" Tessa asked.

She was lying on her back with her eyes closed. Her hands clasped a feather duster to her chest.

"Go away." Mrs. Hedges is one of the maids. She is usually grumpy.

"Hooligan's not really bad," I explained. "He just has—"

"—too much energy. I know." Mrs. Hedges did not open her eyes. "Don't worry about me. I'll just lie here till my strength returns."

"What if it doesn't?" Tessa asked.

"Then someone will cart me away."

Aah-rooo!

"We'll be back!" I told Mrs. Hedges.

We found Hooligan outside the Lincoln Bedroom, singing to the ceiling. High up on the closed door were the unmistakable marks of doggy toenails. Hooligan must've leaped at the door—*thwack*.

"*Hooligan! Be QUIET!!*" Tessa yelled.

This had no effect.

Then the door opened.

A beautiful blonde woman stood there. She was dressed all in white except for a gold necklace and gold earrings. She was smiling...luckily. "Why, Hooligan, shouldn't you be out walking? Hello, Cameron. Hello, Tessa. *Oh!*"

The "*oh!*" was Hooligan pushing past her into the bedroom.

"Hello, Ms. Kootoor," Tessa said. "Sorry about—"

"Never mind, Tessa," said Ms. Kootoor. "You know how I love dogs. Be with you in a moment." The door closed.

Ms. Madeline Kootoor is a friend of my mom's from high school. She used to be a supermodel, then she married somebody rich, then he died. She's been staying with us for a week. According to Dad, we can't throw her out because she raised so much money for my mom's campaign. Plus she and Tessa get along great. They talk about clothes and purses and junk.

The door opened again. Ms. Kootoor came out, holding Hooligan by the collar. At the same time, Mr. Bryant walked up behind us.

Hooligan was thrilled to see Mr. Bryant. He wagged his tail, smiled a big doggy smile and lunged—pulling Ms. Kootoor right over on her face.

"Hooligan!" Mr. Bryant is usually patient, but now he was angry. "Can't a man grab a cup of coffee without all be-whatz-it breaking loose?"

Hooligan finally figured out he was in trouble and dropped to the floor with his paws over his ears. For a moment, he and Ms. Kootoor were lying side by side. Then Ms. Kootoor pushed herself up on her elbows, squinched her eyes, and shook her head.

"Are you okay?" Tessa asked.

Ms. Kootoor tried to smile, but her lipstick was smeared, so the smile came out crooked. "Nothing a mirror won't fix," she said bravely, "and maybe some aspirin."

From down the hall we could still hear Granny's canary: *Twee-twee-twee!*

CHAPTER TWO

WITH things under control outside the Lincoln Bed-room, Tessa and I went back to check on Mrs. Hedges. She was gone.

Did her strength return? Or was she carted away?

To find out, we decided to go with Mr. Bryant and Hooligan on their walk. On the way to the South Lawn, we could stop and ask Mr. Ross if Mrs. Hedges was all right. Mr. Ross is the chief usher, in charge of taking care of the White House.

We found him in his office on the state floor, also known as the first floor. We live mostly on the second floor.

"She's a little shaken up but otherwise fine." Mr. Ross looked at Mr. Bryant. "I thought Hooligan was supposed to be supervised?"

After Hooligan caused the almost international inci-dent, some changes were made in the White House. Like Hooligan has his very own bedroom where he goes to bed in his crate at nine every night. Also,

Mr. Bryant, who used to run the presidential elevator, got the job of taking care of Hooligan from morning till dinnertime every weekday. On weekends, there's a new guy, Mr. Ng, which is pronounced *ing*. He is from Vietnam. At night, the family—meaning me, Tessa, Granny, Nate and Dad when he's in town—take care of Hooligan till bedtime.

"I left Hooligan napping in his old bed in the West Sitting Hall so I could get a cup of coffee," Mr. Bryant said. "Until yesterday, he'd been behaving so much better. I didn't expect any—"

"Hmm," said Mr. Ross. And he wasn't smiling.

The White House South Lawn is like the biggest backyard ever. During a war a long time ago, a president kept sheep here so he could save money on mowing. Now, there's a swing set and a fountain and a putting green. There are mini forests of trees, a vegetable garden and a basketball court. There is a hidden garden that has paving stones with the hand prints of presidents' kids and grandkids from long ago.

There is also a swimming pool, but we can't use it till the weather gets warm enough.

It was a cool, clear March day. I was wearing a sweatshirt, but Tessa had refused to put one on. She said she didn't have one the right color to go with her outfit. To keep warm, she started to bounce up and down, which made Hooligan hyper all over again. As soon as Mr. Bryant unbuckled the leash, he took off, sprinting in circles.

Mr. Bryant looked down at us. "He had been doing better, hadn't he?"

"Up till yesterday," I agreed.

By now I guess you're wondering about yesterday. Short version: Hooligan broke his leash, and because of that, my sister, a bunch of marines, half the Secret Service and the vice president of the United States almost got blown to Kansas in a helicopter hurricane!

Long version: After school, Nate, Mr. Bryant and Hooligan, Tessa and I had been standing under the awning outside the Diplomatic Reception Room waiting for my dad's helicopter to land.

When anyone in our family travels in a helicopter, a couple of extra ones go along, too, to fool bad guys. So three helicopters were descending toward the landing pad when some birds burst out yakking, and Hooligan went so crazy he busted his leash and raced right toward the spinning blades!

Tessa ran after him. I closed my eyes. The Secret Service agents yelled into their headsets: "South Lawn emergency. Fireball in danger! Repeat, Fireball in danger!"

Fireball is the Secret Service code name for Tessa. Mine is...well, never mind what mine is. For our family, they all have to start with *F*.

Anyway, to avoid squashing anybody, the pilots kept their helicopters hovering in the air, and the blades acted like giant fans. When I opened my eyes, it looked like a massive game of wind-whipped tag, one that turned into hide-and-seek when Hooligan got himself lost in the trees by the tennis court.

Meanwhile, the vice president had been working with his staff in the West Wing. When he saw all the excitement, he came out through the Rose Garden to help.

The scene was frantic and confused with people running every which way, and for a few minutes I couldn't see Hooligan at all. Finally, he reappeared sprinting toward us on the driveway, and that's when Mr. Bryant cut him off.

"How come his paws were so muddy?" I asked Mr. Bryant now. "It's not like it rained this week."

"With the dry spell we're having, the gardeners had been watering," said Mr. Bryant. "I had mud on my shoes, too."

One thing about living in the White House, there are always news guys around, which is why every dinky thing ends up on TV. I mean, sure, my dog and my sister and the vice president and the marines and the Secret Service almost got mixed-up in a helicopter crash in the White House backyard...but is that supposed to be news?

Anyway, the helicopters finally landed, and my mom came over from the Oval Office to meet my dad—same as she does every week.

By then, Ms. Kootoor had joined us under the awning. The news guys love Ms. Kootoor. Dad calls her "cameraman catnip." When she air kissed my dad, their cameras clicked and whirred.

"Whatever was all the fuss, girls?" she asked Tessa and me.

When Tessa explained, Ms. Kootoor laughed her tinkly laugh. Then she knelt and spoke to Hooligan. "Silly puppy. Didn't anyone ever teach you not to chase helicopters?"

Hooligan smiled a big doggy smile and licked her face. He had forgotten all about being in trouble.

CHAPTER THREE

MR. BRYANT, Tessa, Hooligan and I were on our way back upstairs when we ran into Aunt Jen. Her job is being White House hostess, which is like First Lady now when there's a woman president.

Aunt Jen was walking with a skinny, black-haired man. He looked kind of familiar, but what I noticed most were his clothes—jeans, red plaid shirt, cowboy boots. Usually, everyone in the White House except my family is wearing a marine uniform or business clothes. This man looked out of place.

"Just the people, and the dog, I wanted to see," said Aunt Jen. "I'd like to introduce—"

Tessa interrupted. "*Oh my gosh!*" Her eyes were huge. "You're Julius Mormora! Star of Canine Class on TV!"

"Indeed I am, Miss Tessa Parks," said the man. "And this would be your sister, Cameron?"

I was so surprised I answered automatically. "How do you do?"

"I am *fabulous*, as always," said Julius Mormora, and then he spoke to Hooligan. "How are you, my new friend? Ready for Canine Class, I hope?"

Like us, Hooligan was awestruck. He sat right down and put out his paw.

"*Whoa*," I said. "He never did that before."

"Usually with new people," Tessa explained, "he knocks them over and slobbers."

"Mr. Mormora has come for a week to teach Canine Class," Aunt Jen said. "We all recognize, I'm sure, that Hooligan's behavior still needs a little, er...tweaking."

Mr. Bryant said, "Hmmph."

Aunt Jen said, "Mr. Mormora, meet Mr. Bryant. He takes care of Hooligan."

Mr. Mormora offered his hand.

Mr. Bryant hesitated before he shook. "If you don't count yesterday," he said, "Hooligan's behavior has improved."

Aunt Jen didn't look convinced. "We're lucky Mr. Mormora's schedule would accommodate us. In fact, he has already been here to tour the house and grounds."

"It was yesterday afternoon that I happened to visit," said Mr. Mormora. "I would have met you then, but there was that incident—"

"—It really wasn't Hooligan's fault," Tessa said.

"Oh?" said Mr. Mormora.

Tessa shook her head. "He never did anything like it before."

"Never ran away before?" asked Mr. Mormora. "Or never broke his leash?"

"Actually, he does that stuff all the time," Tessa said.

"Never, was, uh...chased by so many people before?" asked Mr. Mormora.

"Not in at least a week," I said.

"So what is it exactly that he has never done?" asked Mr. Mormora.

"Never tried to catch helicopters," Tessa said.

"I see," said Mr. Mormora. "Well, we will work on resolving all undesirable behaviors—starting tomorrow when I meet my students."

"We've invited several members of the staff to bring their puppies and participate," said Aunt Jen. "In fact, Mr. Bryant, I believe you have a couple of puppies yourself. Would you like to bring one for Canine Class?"

"We begin promptly at eight a.m.," said Mr. Mormora. "And after that, eight a.m. each day through Wednesday—five days in all."

"But Hooligan likes to sleep in!" Tessa protested.

Mr. Mormora shook his head. "No, no, no! Regular hours and regular habits. This is the way of the Canine Class."

This is also the way of Aunt Jen. No wonder she had invited Mr. Mormora. "Because of the early start," she said, "Mr. Mormora is staying with us in the White House. He'll be joining us for dinner this evening, too."

"Downstairs?" asked Tessa. *Sweet!*

Most nights we eat with the family in the second-floor dining room next to our own kitchen. Getting to eat downstairs is a treat.

Mr. Mormora put his hand over his heart. "I came to

this country as a young child. For my first job, I cleaned dog kennels. It is beyond my dreams to be a guest in the White House."

I looked around. We were standing in the center hall on the ground floor. It has cream-colored, arched ceilings, statues of the heads of important dead people, and paintings of kind, smiling first ladies. Now that my family has lived here a few months, I am getting used to the whole White House deal. But Mr. Mormora reminded me it's special.

Mr. Bryant looked at his watch. "Would you mind taking Hooligan back upstairs, girls? I have an engagement this evening."

I took Hooligan's leash and said, "see you at dinner," to Aunt Jen and Mr. Mormora. Then Tessa and I started back upstairs. On the way, Tessa asked, "What's engagement?"

"Date," I said.

Tessa looked confused. "Isn't Mr. Bryant too old for that stuff?"

Sometimes it's my job to educate my sister. "There's lotsa kinds of dates, Tessa. I bet it's only with his daughter—the grown-up one who's always broke."

Back upstairs, we saw there was still time before dinner, so we decided to study Hooligan's collar for clues. The diamonds that were left were each attached with eight silver prongs. Looking closely, we saw four of the prongs for the missing diamond were bent back, and the other four had broken.

"I don't think there's any mystery, Tessa," I said. "I think Hooligan caught his collar on a bush when he was running yesterday, and the diamond got yanked off."

Tessa looked at me and sighed. "Well, *that* would be disappointing."

CHAPTER FOUR

DINNER was pink fish with green-speckled sauce. Mom was delayed—this happens a lot—and Granny had gone out. So it was Dad, Ms. Kootoor, Mr. Mormora, Aunt Jen, Nate, Tessa and me around the table. Tessa, Aunt Jen and Ms. Kootoor talked about fashion. Ms. Kootoor owns this big plaid purse with buckles that to me looks like a big plaid purse with buckles. But according to Tessa and Aunt Jen, it's a Blueberry Bag, and that makes it just about the coolest thing ever. Tessa's Fashionista Barbie even has a teeny tiny one of her own.

"I don't get it," I said. "If it's a 'Blueberry Bag,' why is it plaid?"

"Blueberry is the designer label," said Ms. Kootoor.

"Oh," I said. "And it's special because . . . ?"

Ms. Kootoor gave me a look like I was crazy. "The *style!*"

Tessa leaned toward me and whispered, "Also, it cost a *ton*."

For dessert we had strawberries with lemon ice.

That's what we were eating when Mom finally came in. She was dressed in her Madam President clothes—blue skirt and jacket, stockings and high heels. She looked tired. After kissing Dad on the cheek, she turned to Mr. Mormora. "A pleasure to meet you." She gave him her hand. "I'm so sorry I couldn't be here earlier, but there's a senator behaving badly, and then that typhoon in Asia..."

Mr. Mormora shook his head. "Sometimes I am glad all I must worry about are dogs."

"Helping people and pets live in harmony is important," said Mom.

"We could use a little more harmony around here," said Aunt Jen.

"My methods are very effective," said Mr. Mormora. Then he told us about some dogs he had met, like a Rottweiler that dug up flowers but only red petunias, and a poodle that ate whole rolls of toilet paper.

Honestly? None of them sounded as bad...I mean as full of energy... as Hooligan.

"I, for one, like Hooligan the way he is," said Ms. Kootoor.

"Oh, please do not mistake me," said Mr. Mormora. "I like all dogs. That is...all dogs except one."

"Which one?" Tessa asked.

Mr. Mormora frowned. "A certain Pekingese dog of my unlucky acquaintance."

"I only ever heard of one Pekingese dog," said Tessa, "the one who sent Hooligan his diamond dog collar, Empress Pu-Chi."

Mr. Mormora dropped his spoon. "But this is the dog to whom I refer!"

"She's not like a close personal friend," I said quickly. "We never even met her."

"Still, the collar is cool," said Tessa. "And guess what?" She paused dramatically. "*One of the diamonds is missing!*"

Tessa was hoping for a big reaction.

But she didn't get it.

Ms. Kootoor took a dainty bite of dessert. "They're only rhinestones, I believe?"

"A rhinestone is the same as a diamond fac-si-mi-le," said Nate.

"But what if they're *not*?" said Tessa. "What if there's a diamond thief loose right here in the White House?"

For a second we all looked around, like, Which one's the thief?

Then Aunt Jen laughed. "I think someone's imagination is running away with her. But tell us, Mr. Mormora, how do you know this Empress Pu-Chi?"

"I have family in that nearby nation," he said. "And a few years ago I was hired to train the animal. The training did not, shall we say, go well."

"Are Pekingese generally difficult?" Dad asked.

Mr. Mormora shook his head. "It is not the breed but only this particular dog. She is very spoiled." Mr. Mormora turned to Mom. "What do you think, Madam President, of Manfred Alfredo-Chin's leadership?"

Mom smiled at Mr. Mormora, took a sip of coffee,

then set down the cup. "I'm so sorry. I have a briefing that begins"—she looked at her watch—"five minutes ago. So if you'll excuse me. . . ."

"*Mo-o-o-om!?*" Tessa whined. "Don't go! What about Monopoly?"

Friday night Monopoly is a tradition in our family. But sometimes Mom's too busy. "You don't need me tonight," Mom said. "You've got plenty of players! Later I'll be up to give you a kiss."

CHAPTER FIVE

MS. KOOTOOR took Mom's place at Monopoly, and you never saw anyone go bankrupt so fast! Only a half hour into the game, she landed on Boardwalk and couldn't pay the rent.

We were up in the Solarium, which is like our family room. It's on the third floor, and, at night when the monuments on the Mall are lit, the view is beautiful. Besides me and Ms. Kootoor, Tessa, Dad and Nate were playing. Mr. Mormora was preparing for his class in the morning. Aunt Jen doesn't like games.

When Nate won, he punched the air. "Loser puts the game away! Loser puts the game away!"

Ms. Kootoor raised her hand. "That would be me."

Nate looked embarrassed. "Oh...but you don't count."

"Because you're a guest," Tessa said. "Anyway, Cammie doesn't mind."

I said, "*Me?!*"

Ms. Kootoor shook her head. "No, no, Cameron. Let me. I lost fair and square."

Granny came in while Ms. Kootoor was collecting the pieces.

"Past your bedtime, isn't it, Judge?" Dad said.

Granny laughed. "I'm wide awake! Must be that splash of coffee late in the day."

"Maybe some news will lull you to sleep," Dad said. He punched the remote . . . and you'll never guess what picture came on the screen: a big, fat diamond!

Tessa squealed.

". . . missing from the National Museum of a certain nearby nation, Jan. Officials are calling the sixty-karat stone known as El Brillante an 'irreplaceable national treasure.'" It was Larry who was talking. He and pretty, blonde Jan do the local news we always watch.

Now there was a close-up of Jan, who looked concerned. "And the gem was kept in a sealed vault, Larry?"

"Locked up tight, Jan." Larry looked concerned, too. "The theft was discovered this morning, but authorities say it's possible the diamond had been missing for as long as a month."

Tessa said, "*See!* I told you a diamond was missing!"

Nate said, "Earth to Tessa. Different diamond."

Tessa shook her head. "But it's the exact same nearby nation! There's gotta be a connection."

"I don't see how," Dad said. "El Brillante is one of the largest diamonds in the world. Even if Hooligan's was real—by comparison, it's puny."

Tessa was offended. "*Puny*?"

"And besides," Dad said. "That diamond was missing from a vault a thousand miles away. The fake stone is missing from Hooligan's collar."

Behind me, Granny cleared her throat. "If anyone is interested," she said, "I think Tessa has a point."

Before she was a judge, Granny was a police officer, so she is the only one in the family with actual crime-fighting experience. Dad, Nate and Ms. Kootoor tried to argue with her, but she wouldn't budge.

"It's like I told the girls last time they were detecting," she said. "Something illogical just might be a clue. This time, the incidents may seem unrelated, but happening together like that? An unlikely coincidence."

CHAPTER SIX

WHEN Mom came in to say good night, she was wearing an old gray Stanford hoodie and pink plaid pajama bottoms.

Tessa groaned. "*Mo-o-o-om!* I don't get how you and Ms. Kootoor ever even got to be friends. She is so stylish! Like that Blueberry Bag—"

"What's a Blueberry Bag?" Mom asked.

I put my hands over my ears. "If I hear 'Blueberry Bag' one more time, I will scream."

Tessa shrugged. "We can talk about diamonds instead. Did you hear one is missing from a certain nearby nation, Mom? It's called El Brillante! And you wanna know what I think?"

Mom nodded and yawned. "Uh-huh, muffin. What do you think?"

"It's got something to do with the diamond missing from Hooligan's collar!"

"Uh-huh," said Mom. "Interesting."

"You should tell the FBI that, Mom. They will want to know," said Tessa.

"Uh...okay. But first, let's see what develops," Mom said.

Tessa crossed her arms over her chest. "Well, if *that's* your attitude, then me and Cammie will investigate ourselves."

"Cammie and *I*," said Mom.

"Great!" said Tessa. "We could definitely use your help."

"Oh, dear, muffin, I didn't mean..." Mom tried to tell Tessa she was only correcting her English.

But Tessa wasn't listening. She was too busy planning our investigation. "First, we interview witnesses," she said. "I know—how about President Manfred Alfredo-Chin? One thing I want to know is who really wrote the letter from Empress Pu-Chi. Is he sure those diamonds on the collar aren't real? After that—"

"Muffin?" Mom interrupted. "It really wouldn't do for you to phone the president of another country and ask questions. The secretary of state would have a fit. But I do have an idea. If you're interested in diamonds, one of the most famous in the world is right here at the Smithsonian Museum of Natural History. It's called the Hope Diamond. What if you and your sister and Nate go see it this week? It's not a trip to California, but at least it's a project."

"Can you come with us?" Tessa asked.

Mom hesitated. When she used to be a plain old senator from California, we could do regular things like go to the mall or the zoo. Now that she's president, there has to be loads of security anytime anyone in the family goes anyplace—even school. For Mom, if she even takes a walk, they shut down streets and surround her with officers and motorcycles.

I bet she wanted to come with us, but the hassle would never be worth it. "I'm sorry, girls," she said. "But Granny would love to go."

Tessa rubbed her eyes and sniffed like she was going to cry, but really she was just being dramatic. I know because as soon as Mom kissed us, said good night and closed the door, she was totally fine again. "Cammie?" she whispered. "You agree with me about the missing diamond, right?"

"Wrong," I said.

"Oh," said Tessa. "Well, okay. But you'll still help me investigate?"

"I guess," I said.

"Because you don't have anything better to do?"

"Right," I said. And I closed my eyes. And I know this sounds weird, but I think I heard my little sister smiling.

CHAPTER SEVEN

THE next morning arrived with Granny at seven a.m. "Rise and shine, girls! Canine Class today!"

Tessa pulled up the covers and grumbled, "I already know 'sit' and 'stay.'"

"Me, too. I can even roll over." I demonstrated.

Granny laughed but there's never any point in arguing with her. Ten minutes later we were dressed and brushed and ready to name the canary. He lives in a cage in our family's kitchen and belongs to Granny, but she won't tell us where he came from.

It's a minor mystery.

That day it was Tessa's turn, and she tried "Sunny."

"Because he's yellow," she explained.

"*Boring.*" I said.

"I have to agree," Granny said. "Nate's turn tomorrow—if he gets up in time."

So far, my cousin still hadn't come down from his bedroom on the third floor. No surprise. He may know everything, but he's so lazy he's always missing breakfast.

Tessa and I sat down at the table. I barely had my napkin in my lap when she crossed her arms over her chest. "We already found something illogical," she said. "So next we interview witnesses."

I shook my head. "Huh?"

Tessa pointed at the pink baseball cap on her head. "*Duh*, Cammie!"

It took a second, but then I got it. The pink cap is what she wears for detecting.

"You mean two missing diamonds at the same time is illogical," I said. "But we don't know for sure that Hooligan's was even stolen. So what if first we look around and see if we can find it?"

This was the most obvious idea ever, but Tessa nodded like I had said something smart. "That could work. But where do we look?"

"Good morning!" Ms. Kootoor was standing in the kitchen doorway. "Here—let me take those." She took bowls of cereal from Granny and brought them to us at the table. "Did I hear you girls say you're looking for something?"

"The diamond!" Tessa said.

"Ah." Ms. Kootoor nodded. "And where do you think it might be?"

I explained about the bent and broken prongs. "We think it came off yesterday when Hooligan was being chased."

"So here's the plan," said Tessa. "We'll start looking in the shrubs and trees on the South Lawn—right after Canine Class."

A few minutes later, we ran into Mr. Mormora and Aunt Jen's secretary, Mrs. Crowe, in the Dip Room.

"Oh my goodness!" said Mr. Mormora when we stepped out under the awning. "The backyard is enormous!"

Mrs. Crowe laughed. "You haven't been out to the South Lawn yet?"

He shook his head. "I have not had the chance. I believe everything has been made ready for us, though?"

"Follow me," said Mrs. Crowe.

The class was going to be held on the grass in the middle of the driveway—the same place the helicopters land.

To my surprise, Nate was already there waiting.

And guess who else?

Puppies!

Big ones, small ones, all different breeds plus mutts—but here's the thing: They were all around six months old...and Hooligan is two *years* old! When Mr. Ng brought him out a few minutes later, Hooligan looked big and goofy—like a fifth grader repeating kindergarten.

Hooligan wasn't embarrassed, though. Dragging Mr. Ng by the leash, he charged right in, bumping the little guys with his nose and rolling them over to get a good sniff. Soon there was a spiderweb of leashes, and Mr. Ng and the rest of the humans were going over and under to sort things out.

It took a while, but eventually Hooligan's leash was attached only to Hooligan. That's when Mr. Ng came over and handed it to me. "Good luck, Cameron," he said.

Mr. Ng is tall and skinny and kind of serious. Mr. Bryant says he's shy, but he makes me a little nervous.

Now—and it wasn't his fault—he made me a lot nervous. "What?!" I said.

Mr. Ng shrugged. "Somebody's got to be the Canine Buddy. Your dad talked to me about it, and..."

I took the leash but immediately held it out to Tessa. "Don't you wanna—?"

Tessa put her hands behind her back. "No, no, no, Cammie! You're the responsible older sister."

"Nate?" I tried. But that was hopeless. He's into piano, not pets.

Mr. Mormora was calling the class to order when the last puppy pupil arrived, a black puffball mutt, along with his owner, Mr. Bryant. Of course, Hooligan was thrilled to see Mr. Bryant! He lunged and would've pulled me over, but I leaned back with every ounce I own. *"Hooligan! Stay!"*

Too bad he actually did, which I never expected. Unbalanced, I sat down on a cockapoo. The cockapoo wasn't hurt, but he snapped at me, which made the owner squeal and Hooligan growl. This got the rest of the dogs excited, and we were on the verge of total puppy upset when Mr. Mormora dropped to dog's-eye level and spoke: "*Amigos, perros,* dogs of my heart..."

And like magic, every pup was quiet.

In Canine Class, the people are known as Canine Buddies, CBs for short, and the dogs are Canines in Training, or CITs. To start with, we all went around in a circle and introduced ourselves.

Hooligan and I were first, and then the woman next to me with the cockapoo. "I'm Ann Major. I'm an assistant press secretary to President Parks. And this is my dog, Pickles."

After that, nine more Canine Buddies introduced themselves and their CITs. There was a poodle, four golden retrievers, a labradoodle, a Chihuahua and two I'm-not-sure-whats. Last was Mr. Bryant. He is always very dignified.

"I am Mr. Willis Bryant," he said, "and this is my canine, Cottonball."

In case you have never seen Canine Class on TV, this is how it goes: Mr. Mormora takes one of the CITs as an example and gives him a command—like "sit."

The dog sits. This could be a mean dog or a dumb dog or a dog that speaks Chinese, it doesn't matter. The dog sits. No one knows how Mr. Mormora does this, but he does.

That day, all the other dogs and their trainers watched Mr. Mormora convince a CIT golden retriever to sit several different times from several different angles. Then he turned toward the rest of us. "All right, Canine Buddies, it is now your turn. Please, command your CITs to sit."

Instead of watching the golden retriever, Hooligan had been making friends with a Chihuahua. I did not have a good feeling. But I stood up straight like Mr. Mormora did, and I tried to copy the way he talks: "Hooligan—*sit*."

Hooligan didn't move. Pickles scratched herself, and the I'm-not-sure-what on our left tried to dig a hole. Only a poodle and Mr. Bryant's dog, Cottonball, actually sat.

Then...so did Hooligan.

It was a miracle! From where the spectators were standing, I heard Tessa squeal. When I looked over, I noticed a whole bunch of cameras were aimed at Hooligan. The press loves him almost as much as they love Ms. Kootoor.

After that, all the CITs tried sitting again. And again. And Hooligan sat every time! Later, when we tried "stay," he did that every time, too.

Canine Class only lasts forty-five minutes because, as Mr. Mormora explained it, "canine concentration is not powerful." Even so, there's some waiting around, so I asked Ms. Major about being an assistant press secretary. She told me she used to be a TV reporter, but then she went to work for my mom's campaign. Now her job is mostly keeping track of what's written and broadcast about our family, and Hooligan, too.

The end of Canine Class is always the same. Mr. Mormora thanks everyone for participating and gives out Canine Cookies. They are the shape of ordinary dog biscuits, but they have red and yellow stripes.

"You see how it is that Hooligan is a star pupil?" said Mr. Mormora. "It is the positive peer pressure. With the younger dogs, he wants to be a leader."

I hadn't noticed Ms. Kootoor with the other spectators, but now she was walking toward us with Dad and Tessa. "Great job, puppy!" she said, and scratched him behind the ears. He nosed her hand and whined.

Then Mr. Bryant came up, pulled along by Cottonball.

"Sit!" said Mr. Bryant. Cottonball looked at him, trying to remember what that word meant.

Tessa said, "Like this," and sat down on the grass. Cottonball didn't copy her, he tackled her! Then Hooligan piled on.

Mr. Bryant and I were trying to pull them off when Mr. Mormora spoke: "Gentlemen?"

Right away the dogs backed off and sat down.

Tessa wasn't hurt—unless dog slobber hurts. She wiped her face and asked Mr. Mormora, "How do you *do* that?"

He smiled. "It is just having the confidence. Dogs respect confidence. By the time we hold graduation on Wednesday, each of these dogs will be a fine example of Canine Class, and one will be Top Dog—the number one student. That dog will receive a blue ribbon, and its picture will appear on boxes of Canine Cookies. Hooligan, what do you think? Have you the makings of the Top Dog?"

CHAPTER EIGHT

WHEN Tessa was four, she got a pink Barbie watch for her birthday. She still wears it, even though I tell her she's too old. Now, according to Barbie, it was nine thirty—still early for a Saturday morning. But already Canine Class was over, the puppies were gone, and Tessa, Hooligan and I were riding a mini-tractor past the tennis court on the South Lawn. Behind us on the tractor was a load of very smelly compost.

It was Mr. Golly, one of the groundskeepers, who was giving us a ride. Tessa was next to him in front, and I was on the little bench seat in the back, holding tight to Hooligan. We had been trying to follow his trail from Thursday on foot, and Mr. Golly had picked us up like hitchhikers.

"Your parents won't mind, will they?" he called as the tractor bump-bumped along.

Tessa and I chorused: "No!" because—both of us were thinking—*we will never tell them*.

And if we were lucky, nobody else would tell either.

The thing is, wherever Tessa and I go, we're being watched by the Secret Service. Like right then, I could see two agents: Malik was standing by the fountain in the middle of the lawn, and Jeremy was over to our right on the basketball court. It was the weekend, and they were assigned to the White House residence, so they didn't have to wear suits. Instead they had on khakis and polo shirts, but with their straight posture, short hair and shiny shoes, they still looked like Secret Service.

Mr. Golly's compost was bound for the new kitchen garden near the far fence. The ride down there gave Tessa an excellent opportunity to do some detecting.

"Mr. Golly," she asked, "have you or any of the other groundskeepers seen a big, fat, fake diamond lying around the South Lawn since Wednesday afternoon? Or possibly a big, fat, not-fake diamond?"

Mr. Golly adjusted the brim on his hat. "Hector found an orange flip-flop last week. And we're always finding Frisbees and footballs and kites. I don't remember diamonds, though—fake or not fake. Why are you asking?"

Tessa and I took turns explaining how one was missing.

"If you're looking for clues," said Mr. Golly, "there are plenty of dried footprints in the flowerbeds."

"I don't think footprints will work," I said. "We already know a zillion people were down here—chasing Hooligan and flattening flowers."

Mr. Golly agreed it was a mess. "But a crew and I raked up the dead stuff yesterday."

Tessa and I looked at each other. Had the diamond been raked up, too?

"What happens to the dead stuff?" I asked.

"We grind it for compost," Mr. Golly explained.

"And did you do that already?" Tessa asked.

"Yesterday afternoon," Mr. Golly said.

Sometimes my sister and I don't have to say anything. We just understand: If Hooligan had dropped the diamond in a flowerbed, by now it was diamond dust.

Mr. Golly pulled the tractor up next to the kitchen garden, which was only a big, bare patch of dirt. Later in the spring, vegetables would be planted. Aunt Jen had told Tessa and me we could help.

"Does your dog have any bloodhound in him?" Mr. Golly asked.

"According to Dad, he's got everything," said Tessa.

"So maybe you can get him to track down that diamond," said Mr. Golly.

This seemed worth a try, so, while Mr. Golly scooped compost with a pitchfork, Tessa took Hooligan's leash off and explained the idea to him. Meanwhile, I looked around. The South Lawn is more like a big park than a backyard. Assuming the diamond still existed, how were we ever going to find it?

Tessa stood up. "Okay, he gets it," she said.

"Are you sure?" I asked.

"Totally," said Tessa. "Ready, Hooligan? *Go!*"

Hooligan lunged, thumped, sprang, spun—and then he was off, with Tessa and me sprinting to keep up.

Soon we were in the trees, and sure enough,

Hooligan had his nose to the ground like a vacuum cleaner. I was just thinking this plan could actually work when he stopped dead in his tracks and Tessa, ahead of me, almost tumbled over him.

"Cammie, look!" she said. "He found it!"

CHAPTER NINE

SOMETHING told me that was just too easy.

And something turned out to be right.

I didn't know what it was Hooligan had found in the trees, but it wasn't a diamond.

Dogs don't eat diamonds.

"Bad dog!" I scolded him.

But my sister scratched his ears. "Don't listen, puppy. She doesn't mean it."

"I do, too!" I said.

"Maybe I didn't explain it to him right." Tessa unbuckled his collar and held it up so he could see the space where the diamond used to be. "That's what you're looking for, puppy," she said. "Okay?" She buckled the collar back on. "Ready, set—find that diamond!"

Have I mentioned Hooligan has too much energy?

First he led us over by the west fence, then we ran up past the pool, across the driveway and around the putting green twice before we cut south again. I play midfield on the D.C. Destoyers soccer team, but even so I was out of breath. The only reason I kept up at all was that he kept pausing and gobbling junk—probably crucial pieces of evidence.

It was a warm day for March, and I was getting sweaty when Hooligan solved that problem—he ran through the fountain, so of course Tessa and I did, too. If we weren't already in trouble for riding the tractor with Mr. Golly, we for sure were in trouble now, but there was no time to worry about that. Hooligan was bee-lining for the kitchen garden—right back where we started.

"Watch out!" I yelled to Mr. Golly. He was forking up the last smelly scoop and didn't see Hooligan, who sideswiped him—*ka-bam!*

"Are you all right?" I asked when we got to him.

"Are you mad?" Tessa asked.

Before Mr. Golly could answer, Jeremy and Malik appeared. Jeremy is a really big guy with a deep voice. Malik is my second-favorite Secret Service agent after Charlotte. They had seen the whole thing.

Now Malik reached out a hand to help Mr. Golly, and Jeremy asked, "You okay there?"

Mr. Golly was wiping compost from his eyes. He said, "Reckon I'll live," and shook his head. Black bits flew out of his hair.

"I think we should escort you girls back to the house," Malik said. "You're going to want to get out of your wet shoes and socks."

"Mr. Ng will be here for Hooligan shortly," said Jeremy.

Tessa had grabbed Hooligan's leash and run over to where he lay in the shade. Now she called me over, too. "Look," she said and pointed at the fur around his snout. There was plenty of plain brown dirt. But there was something else besides—a whole lot of crumbs, bright red and bright yellow.

Only one thing leaves red and yellow crumbs.

"Canine Cookies!" I said.

"That must be what he kept stopping to eat," Tessa said. "But who dropped them?"

"Mr. Mormora most likely," I said. "But didn't he tell Mrs. Crowe he'd never been out here? There's no reason he'd lie about that . . . is there?"

CHAPTER TEN

ALL the Secret Service agents wear radio headsets so they can keep in touch. That's why, when we got to the Dip Room door, Granny was waiting with our slippers and frowning.

"Sorry, Granny," Tessa and I chorused.

"Hmmph," said Granny, then she held out our slippers. "Change out of your wet shoes and socks so you don't make a mess or catch pneumonia. After lunch, you'll each write an apology to Mr. Golly."

Oh well. It could've been worse.

On weekends, we eat lunch in the family kitchen. Usually, either Granny or Dad makes it. Granny is better because she takes special orders. Like my sandwich doesn't get mustard, Tessa's doesn't get mayonnaise and Nate doesn't eat anything green, like lettuce.

Dad makes all our sandwiches the same, and if we complain, he says, "How would you like to make *my* lunch for a change?"

Today Granny put plates down for Nate, Tessa and me, then made a surprise announcement: "We're going to go see the Hope Diamond tonight!"

It turned out Mrs. Crowe had phoned the Museum of Natural History, and Saturday at seven p.m. was the best time for our visit. The museum would be closed, so keeping us safe would be easy. Plus we wouldn't be bugging the regular visitors with all the hoo-ha that happens when we go someplace.

"One of the assistant curators, a Mr. Rubio, has agreed to meet us and talk about the diamond," Granny said. "And Ms. Kootoor is coming, too. She's always been fond of diamonds."

"That's for sure," Tessa said. "She's got loads of diamond jewelry, and even a diamond whistle!"

Granny raised her eyebrows. "Why on earth—?"

"Her dad gave it to her," Tessa explained, "when she moved to New York City to get famous. If she's ever in danger, she's supposed to blow the whistle."

"Has she ever used it?" I asked.

Tessa shook her head. "Nope. But she keeps it with her just in case."

Granny nodded. "You know? A safety whistle might be a good idea. But I don't see the point of the diamonds."

Tessa's mouth opened. Luckily, it was empty. "How can you say that, Granny? The diamonds are for style!"

When we had finished our sandwiches, Granny looked at her watch and pushed back her chair. "With this warm weather, I've made a tennis date—the first of the year. Can you entertain yourselves?"

Nate said a friend of his was coming over. They were going to shoot hoops.

Lucky, I thought. All my friends were out of town for March break.

But Tessa said we'd have no problem keeping busy.

"We won't?" I said.

"*Hello-o-o*?" She crossed her arms over her chest. "We've got a mystery to solve? Remember?"

After lunch, we sat down at our desks to write to Mr. Golly. Along with our beds and posters, the desks came with us from our old house. But the rest of the furniture in our room belongs to the White House collection. Aunt Jen helped Tessa and me pick what we wanted. When we leave someday, it will go back in storage—or maybe the new president will have kids that pick the same stuff.

I spent a long time writing. I really did feel bad that Hooligan had knocked Mr. Golly into the compost. It was going to take a lot of shampoo to get the smell out of his hair.

Tessa drew a picture of a man lying down and a brown dog with a frowny face. Over the dog it said: "Sorry!"

When we were done, we folded our notes and put them in envelopes for Granny to address.

Then it was time for detecting.

In the West Sitting Hall, where Hooligan's old wicker dog bed is, there's a comfortable stripe-y sofa that's good for thinking. By now, Mr. Ng had brought Hooligan back inside. After his busy morning, Hooligan was napping. Tessa and I sat down on the sofa, and I wrote down everything we knew about the case so far:

- Hooligan's diamond probably disappeared Thursday during helicopter incident.
- Prongs on collar broken or bent back.
- Acc. to Jan/Larry: El Brillante was missing Friday morning from museum.
- But could have been missing a month.
- Connection between El Brillante and Hooligan's missing diamond?
- Gardeners found flip-flop last week but no diamond this week.
- But did they by mistake grind up diamond?
- Or is it on South Lawn somewhere?
- Canine Cookie crumbs on Hooligan's nose.
- Used to be Canine Cookies all over South Lawn.
- Not anymore.
- Did Mr. Mormora drop them?
- But Mr. Mormora said he hadn't been on South Lawn.

By then, my hand was tired so I shook it out. Tessa had been reading over my shoulder and making suggestions.

"I don't like it if Mr. Mormora lied to us," she said.

"He's nice though," I said. "I like the way he talks to dogs."

"You should write down what he said at dinner, too," Tessa said. Then she dictated:

- Mr. Mormora has family in nearby nation.
- Mr. Mormora doesn't like Empress Pu-Chi.
- Mr. Mormora asked Mom about President Manfred Alfredo-Chin.

"I don't think Mr. Mormora likes President Alfredo-Chin either," she said.

"So what?" I said.

Tessa waved her arms dramatically the way she does. "So I don't know what! But isn't it suspicious?"

"Isn't what suspicious?" Granny had come in from tennis. She was pink and a little sweaty. Hooligan looked up when he heard her voice.

"Do you want to help us do detecting?" Tessa asked.

Granny said sure, and together we read through the notes. We had to explain about the cookies and the diamond maybe being ground up.

"If I were the detective," Granny said thoughtfully, "I'd say the next move was obvious. It's time to interview Mr. Mormora."

CHAPTER ELEVEN

MR. MORMORA was staying in a guest room on the third floor, down the hall from Aunt Jen and Nate. We were going up there when Charlotte came into the West Sitting Hall. Charlotte is my favorite Secret Service agent.

"Mr. Mormora?" Charlotte said when we told her what we were doing. "He's out sightseeing—one of those bus tours."

Tessa dropped back down on the sofa. "Well, *that's* disappointing."

Charlotte said, "Sorry," then she held an envelope out to me. "For you, Cammie."

Tessa and I get letters all the time—not as many as my mom or Hooligan, but too many for us to sort ourselves. First they go to the office that handles White House mail, and most get answered by volunteers. When there's a special letter, we see it after it's checked out by the Secret Service.

"Is it a good one?" I asked.

"You're going to like it," she said and winked.

"What the...?" But then I looked at the address, and instantly forgot about Mr. Mormora, missing diamonds, and even Hooligan. This is what it said:

Camron Parks
The White House
1600 Pensylvania Ave.
Washingtun, DC 20500

Tessa read over my shoulder. "Hey—somebody's as bad a speller as you! So that must mean it's from—"

I sighed. "Paul Song." And I guess my face went moony because Tessa rolled her eyes.

"Oh, brother," she said, "and you make fun of *me* for having crushes!"

Paul Song, in case you don't know, is part of the best band in America, The Song Boys. Not that long ago, he and his brothers played a concert at the White House, and I got to meet him. He was really nice, not stuck up at all.

And now he'd actually written me a letter!

> *Dear Cammie,*
>
> *You will probably think I'm a dork for writing you an old-fashion letter with a stamp and everything. But right now we were sitting here in the hotel, and I saw this writting paper and I thought it would be funny to write you.*

On TV yesterday I saw how that TV dog guy is staying with you and giving Hooligan dog lessons! That is so cool! I wish he could give my dog dog lessons, too. I miss my dog when we are on tour. Did I tell you about him? He was a puppy at the pound when we picked him, and he grew up to be funny-looking but not as funny-looking as Hooligan. (Don't let Hooligan read that part. JK.) My dog's name is Singalong because when he was a puppy he liked to howl with us.

My brothers don't know it, but Singalong likes me best. That's because I sneak him dog biscuits. I am going to have to stop, though. Or else he will be funny-looking AND fat. Here is a picture:

Okay, so gotta go do the show. After LA, we go to San Fransisco and then Orgon.

See you later. I hope?

Best—Paul Song

PS—If I just wrote "Paul," would you know it was me, or do you know lots of people named Paul?

"It's not a very interesting letter," said Tessa.

"Hey!" I flipped it over and elbowed her. "It's personal!"

"Like a cartoon dog is *so* personal," said Tessa. "He didn't sign it 'love.' And he can't even spell your name."

"You're just jealous," I said.

"Am not."

"Are too."

"Girls?" It was Granny. She had gone to shower and change her clothes. Now she was back. "We need to eat early if we're going to get to the museum on time. Go get yourselves cleaned up, and I believe Aunt Jen has put clothes out."

Pretty much any time we go anywhere, the news guys are there with their cameras. That's why Aunt Jen picks our clothes. If she didn't, I would wear gym shorts, and Tessa would wear pink party dresses.

Usually I don't mind changing, but now I was grumpy after arguing with Tessa. "I look fine already!" I insisted.

Tessa looked me up and down. "You'd at least better fix your hair, Cammie. What if icky old *Paul Song* sees you on TV?"

CHAPTER TWELVE

THE Smithsonian Museum of Natural History is located on the National Mall, less than a mile from our house. So you'd think we could have walked there, right?

Wrong.

To keep us safe, we had to be driven. Tessa, Nate and I went in a van with Charlotte. Granny, Dad and Ms. Kootoor followed in another van.

You're probably thinking: *Lucky-y-y! She gets to have a driver to take her places!*

But sometimes I feel more like I'm trapped. I mean, it would have been nice to walk to the museum with nobody knowing or caring who I was—to be like I used to be, a normal kid.

Of course, back then, I didn't appreciate how normal was nice.

The museum building sits at the top of some big wide steps, and it's full of cool stuff like dinosaur bones, crazy-looking bugs, pretty rocks and stuffed wild animals. Usually, it is also full of people. But when we walked through the big heavy doors, there were only a couple of guards and a man in a suit and tie. That was Mr. Rubio, the assistant curator. With so few people, the museum was kind of spooky and quiet. I felt like I was in church.

Tessa didn't. She tore through the doors, past the stuffed elephant in the lobby and around Mr. Rubio— "Hi, nice to meet you!" Charlotte ran after her, trying to keep up.

The Hope Diamond has its own room on the second floor. Over the doorway is a helpful sign that reads, THE HOPE DIAMOND. It sits on a white velvet pedestal in a glass and metal case. It's more than an inch long, which is big for a diamond, and it's gray-blue, which is the main reason it's special.

Mr. Rubio and the six of us clustered around the case. I got out my notebook, ready to write. Tessa was wearing her pink detecting hat.

"Over the centuries the Hope Diamond has been owned by millionaires, lords, ladies and kings," Mr. Rubio explained.

Nate, who knows everything, said he heard there was a curse.

Mr. Rubio nodded. "The story goes that the diamond was stolen from the eye of a statue of a goddess, and the goddess cursed all future owners."

Uh oh. Were the museum walls going to crumble?

"But there's no evidence for the story at all," Mr. Rubio continued. "What is true is that a lot of people who owned this diamond were unlucky and died broke."

"Well, that's crazy," Tessa said. "If you had this big diamond, you could sell it and not be broke anymore!"

"Sell something so *beautiful?!*" Ms. Kootoor was horrified.

"If the diamond's unlucky," Granny said, "why is it called 'Hope'?"

Mr. Rubio said it was owned by the Hope family in the 1800s, and that was the name that stuck. "The diamond was actually mined in India in the 1600s, then sold to the king of France," he said. "At that time, it was known as the French Blue. Later it disappeared and turned up in London, but by then it was smaller. It had been cut and reshaped."

"I didn't know diamonds were cut more than once," said Granny.

"Oh, yes," Mr. Rubio said. "Sometimes they're recut to eliminate a flaw. Sometimes a particular shape goes out of fashion. Other times, a diamond will be divided into smaller stones."

Dad asked, "What is it that makes a diamond special in the first place?"

"Diamonds are rare," said Mr. Rubio. "It takes billions of years for one to form deep under the surface of the earth. And the pressure makes a diamond one of the hardest materials known."

"But can't they be manufactured?" Dad asked.

"Yes, but the process is as expensive as finding one in nature," said Mr. Rubio. "Of course, there are also diamond facsimiles. They can be made out of all sorts of minerals, or even plastic."

"So how does one tell the difference between real and fake?" Granny asked.

"It's not always easy," Mr. Rubio said. "But I can demonstrate one test. Is anyone wearing a diamond?"

Granny took off her engagement ring and held it out. Mr. Rubio took it, and raised it to his mouth. *"Ewwww!"* said Tessa. "You're not gonna lick it, are you?"

Mr. Rubio opened his mouth like he just might... but he was kidding. Instead, he made his mouth into an O and blew a sharp little puff.

"See that?" he asked us.

"The diamond didn't fog up," Granny said.

Mr. Rubio nodded. "That's because it's real."

"Well, I hope so," said Granny.

"A real diamond has special physical properties that keep it slightly cool at all times," Mr. Rubio said. "That's why an old-fashioned nickname for diamonds is 'ice.' Those same properties mean that a diamond clears condensation almost instantly. A fake typically requires several seconds, or else has to be wiped clean."

Tessa crossed her arms over her chest the way she does when she's interviewing a witness. "Mr. Rubio," she said, "what would happen if a diamond got stuck in a compost grinder?"

Mr. Rubio raised his eyebrows. I don't think anyone had ever asked him that before. "Uh...how big a diamond?" he asked.

Tessa showed him with her fingers.

"I should think a diamond that big would break the

mechanism . . . and probably make a horrible noise, too," he said.

"Write that down, Cammie," Tessa said.

"But the diamond we're looking for is fake," I said.

Tessa sighed and recrossed her arms. "Mr. Rubio," she said, "what would happen if a *fake* diamond got caught in a compost grinder?"

"I'm no expert on fake diamonds," he said. "But I should think it would grind up just fine."

A diamond, even a famous blue one, is only interesting for so long. We looked around at the other things in the room—a meteorite, a crystal and a huge sheet of copper—then at some fancy jewelry in the room next door. It was almost time to go when Nate asked Mr. Rubio, "So how much money is the Hope Diamond worth?"

"*Nate!*" Tessa delivered her best Aunt Jen look. "Money's rude!"

But Mr. Rubio said he didn't mind answering. "You see, the Hope Diamond is worth two things at once: everything and nothing."

"Huh?" said Tessa.

Mr. Rubio explained. "Looked at one way, the Hope Diamond is worth so much money it can't even be calculated. There is not another like it in the universe! But looked at another, it's worth nothing. That's because it's so famous, it couldn't possibly be sold. Any buyer would recognize it and know it had been stolen."

I thought of something. "Is El Brillante the same amount famous?"

"The diamond that disappeared in a certain nearby nation?" said Mr. Rubio. "I would say so, yes."

"So same thing," I said. "No one could sell it. And if that's true—why would anybody steal it?"

Mr. Rubio shrugged and shook his head. "That's one question I can't answer."

CHAPTER THIRTEEN

THAT night it was Dad who came in to give us our kisses.

"Where's Mom?" Tessa asked.

"She's sorry, girls," Dad said. "Something came up."

"Something more important than us?" Tessa said.

"Nothing's more important than you," Dad said. "But some things are more urgent."

"Hmmph," said Tessa. "Hey—did you hear Cammie got a *letter*? From Paul *So-o-o-ong*."

"Aren't there any secrets in this house?" I said.

Dad smiled. "What did the letter say? Or don't you want to tell?"

"I'll tell!" Tessa said. "He can't even spell, and besides that—"

Dad held up his hand. "All right, Tessa. Cammie's entitled to some privacy. But, uh, sweetie...do you think you'll write him back?"

"Maybe," I said. "But not right away. Tessa and I have a mystery to solve."

*　*　*

Tessa woke me before I knew I was asleep.

She was bouncing on my bed. "*Cammie!*"

"Go away."

"No, *seriously*! I thought of something! We have to do some detecting!"

I didn't want to, but I opened my eyes. It was still dark. "What time is it?"

Tessa didn't answer, just pulled me out of bed. A weird dream had woken her. In it, Hooligan's diamond collar was on display in the Hope Diamond's case. Mr. Rubio was there, and he wrote on the foggy glass with his finger: "Are they real?"

"Do you get it, Cammie?" Tessa asked.

I shook my head to clear the sleep out. Then… "Oh—you mean the breath test? You want to do it on Hooligan's collar!"

I had to give Tessa credit. Why hadn't I thought of that?

Without another word, we tiptoed out of our room and down the hall. Hooligan's own bedroom is next to the elevator. It's a room some first ladies have used for doing hair and makeup, but a long time ago a president's dog named Millie had her puppies here. Now it's where Hooligan goes to bed in his crate.

Tessa whispered, "You block him in, and I'll get the collar."

Hooligan's crate has a black wire gate at the front. I crouched down, unlatched it and pulled it partway open. Tessa slid her hand in to unbuckle the collar. All the time my heart was pounding.

"Got it!" Tessa whispered.

Hooligan snuffled and shifted, and I thought my heart would stop. We weren't doing anything wrong, but if he woke up, he'd wake the whole house.

Back in our room, I breathed again. Then I turned on the lamp. In the light, the collar seemed extra sparkly, and I couldn't help wondering how much it would be worth if the diamonds were real. Was I holding millions of dollars?

"Your breath or mine?" Tessa asked.

"It was your idea," I said.

Tessa made her mouth into an *O*.

"Wait a sec," I said.

"What?"

"If it's real, we're gonna want to scream, right?"

Tessa nodded. "*Oh*, yeah."

"But we can't," I said. "If the president's kids start screaming in the middle of the night…"

"Good point," Tessa said. "So how 'bout if we scream silently?"

"Pinky promise," I said. We hooked our fingers.

Tessa took a breath. "Here goes." She put one of the diamonds next to her face, made her lips into an *O* again and exhaled. I leaned close, and together we looked.

No fog.

No fog?

The diamond was real!

We closed our eyes, we opened our mouths, we pumped our fists—and we screamed!

Silently.

To somebody watching, it would've looked like the sound was on mute.

After that, Tessa and I took turns testing the other diamonds. And guess what? They were real, too. Every single one.

Hooligan must have been super tired because Tessa and I sneaked the collar back onto his neck without waking him. After that, the two of us were so excited there was no way we could go back to sleep.

So instead we brushed our teeth, washed our faces, got dressed, and made our beds. Ready to face the day, I looked at the clock on my bedside table.

It was four in the morning!

"Now what are we supposed to do?" I asked.

"Let's wake up Mom and Dad. This is big news!"

I shook my head. "We can't do that. Mom's tired already, and she has a country to run."

"Then let's look at your notes again," Tessa said. "Now that we know it couldn't have been ground up, we really have to find that diamond."

Instead of telling you every word Tessa and I said for the next three hours, I am going to summarize the important parts:

- Sometimes diamonds are cut more than once.
- Diamonds break compost grinders.
- Famous diamonds are priceless and worthless.

And

- The diamonds on Hooligan's collar test real.

This brought up three fat questions:

- Did the person/dog who sent the collar to Hooligan know it had real diamonds?
- If yes, why had he/she lied?
- And why was someone sending Hooligan diamonds at all?

At seven, Granny came in to wake us. You can imagine the look on her face when she saw us up and dressed. "What in the world...?"

"Well it *took* you long enough!" Tessa jumped off the sofa. "Come on. We have something to show you."

Shaking her head like we were crazy, Granny followed us into Hooligan's room. All three of us knelt down. All three of us looked in his crate.

All three of us saw it was empty!

CHAPTER FOURTEEN

"DOES what you want to show me have to do with Hooligan?" Granny asked.

"*Duh!*" Tessa said.

"Mr. Bryant took him out for a romp with Cottonball before Canine Class," Granny said.

"But that doesn't start for another hour!" Tessa said.

Granny shrugged. "He said there was no traffic this morning so he got here early. Come on and eat your breakfast. What's all the excitement anyway?"

It seemed lame just to tell Granny the diamonds were real. We wanted to prove it. Tessa said, "If it's okay, we'd rather tell you later."

"Suit yourselves," said Granny. "But remember you've got church this morning—right after Canine Class."

On our way to the kitchen, Tessa tried to argue: "We have to interview Mr. Mormora after class! It's really important!"

Granny's look said: Mr. Mormora can wait. God can't.

"Oh, *fine*," Tessa said.

"Meanwhile," Granny said brightly, "it's time to name the canary."

It was Nate's turn. And for once he had come to breakfast on time.

"I propose 'Serinus,' " he said.

"Se-whatziss?" Tessa asked.

"The Latin name for canary is *Serinus canaria domestica*," Nate said.

Granny cut bagels in half and put them in the toaster. "Sounds too much like sinus," she said, "and that gives me a headache."

Nate didn't seem too disappointed. "Did you know most male canaries sing all the time?"

"Maybe this guy would sing more if he had a name," Tessa said. "The last time he really sang out was on Friday—right before Hooligan went crazy."

"That reminds me of something," I said. "When Hooligan went crazy on Thursday? Remember how those birds outside were yakking? You could hear them over the helicopters."

Tessa nodded. "I do remember. Only what does that have to do with anything?"

Granny set down our toasted bagels and glasses of orange juice. We thanked her. I got out my notebook and wrote down about the singing canary and the yak-king birds.

"I have no idea what it means," I told Tessa. "But it's another strange coincidence."

By the time Nate, Tessa and I got down to the South Lawn, Mr. Mormora was already there, and the puppies were starting to arrive. From beyond the fountain, Mr. Bryant, Cottonball and Hooligan were walking toward us.

Tessa and I still hadn't told anyone about the diamonds on the collar. And keeping it to herself was driving Tessa crazy. Finally, she couldn't stand it. "Nathan, can you keep a secret? Hooligan's diamonds are real!"

Nate's mouth opened, like for a second he believed her. But then he started to argue: "They can't be.... The letter said...Who would send Hooligan real diamonds?"

Mr. Bryant by now was a few yards away. "Hello, girls. Hello, Nate." And a second later, Cottonball was threading his leash around Tessa's ankles while Hooligan, tail wagging, jumped up and tried to knock me over.

"*Sit*." I said.

Cottonball ignored me but Hooligan—future Top Dog—did as he was told.

"We can prove it, Nathan!" Tessa danced her ankles out of the tangle then bent down to undo Hooligan's collar.

Only there was one small problem.

The diamond collar was gone!

In its place was Hooligan's boring old brown collar—the one we had replaced when Empress Pu-Chi's gift arrived.

Tessa fell back on her bottom. My heart went thud. But before we could ask Mr. Bryant about it, Mr. Mormora called Canine Class to order.

CHAPTER FIFTEEN

THE Canine Class topic for the day was "stay."

And that—besides how Hooligan was perfect again—is pretty much all I remember. Otherwise, I was much too sleepy and much too distracted to pay attention.

Where was the diamond collar?

And something else was bugging me, too.

The collar had either disappeared in the night when Hooligan was in his crate or in the morning when Mr. Bryant was walking him. Could Mr. Bryant have taken it? Was it possible he knew the diamonds were real, too? Was it true he got to our house early because traffic was light—like he told Granny?

That wasn't a very good reason.

Mr. Bryant is Tessa's and my friend. But his daughter did need money. . . .

I shook my head trying to get the thoughts inside to make sense. Something didn't seem right.

Anyway there was no time for questions. The moment

Canine Class was over, Dad herded Tessa and me toward the White House.

"But Dad!" Tessa protested. "Look!" She pointed at Hooligan's neck while we walked.

I thought we'd have to explain, but Dad understood right away. "That's strange. Where's the gift from the empress?"

Tessa got dramatic and waved her arms the way she does. "It's more than strange, Dad! Because it turns out the diamonds are *real!*"

Dad didn't argue like Nate did. He only raised his eyebrows. "When did you notice the collar was missing?"

Tessa took a breath. "Last night before bed I drank a glass of milk? And maybe my stomach was gurgly? Because in the night—"

Dad interrupted. "Short version."

"It was there about three thirty this morning," I said. "And gone at seven."

Dad's eyebrows stayed up. "Okay—you can explain in the car. You two go ahead and get dressed. Mom's in the Oval Office. I'm just going to touch base with her."

Mr. Ng met us outside the Dip Room.

"Good morning, Cameron. Good morning, Tessa. It's a beautiful day, don't you think?"

"Is it?" I hadn't even noticed, but he was right—blue sky and warm sun.

"Look, Mr. Ng! Hooligan's new collar is gone!" Tessa handed him Hooligan's leash. "And you know what else? The diamonds—"

"Tessa!" I said.

Tessa blinked. "What?"

But I couldn't tell her not to tell Mr. Ng right in front of Mr. Ng. It would be rude. "Nothing," I said. "Except we have to go. Come on."

"Have a good day, girls!" Mr. Ng called. And Hooligan woofed the same.

"Why did you make me be quiet?" Tessa said on the stairs. "Is Mr. Ng a suspect?"

"I don't know who's a suspect," I said. "But it can't be smart to tell everybody a bazillion dollars worth of diamonds are missing from the White House."

Tessa started to argue, but the words dissolved in a big, fat yawn. I think we were both grumpy from no sleep.

Like I said, the plan was for Mom to go to church with us, but a few minutes later when Tessa and I climbed into the car, we got another surprise. Only Dad and Malik were waiting.

Dad saw we were disappointed. "She's very sorry, girls. But something came up."

"Is it bad?" Tessa asked.

"I hope not," Dad said.

"What about Granny?" I said.

"She's going to another church today. A friend invited her."

Aunt Jen and Nate never go to church with us. They go to a different one that has mostly Korean people. That's because Nate was born in Korea, and Aunt Jen adopted him when he was a baby.

Our church is near Dupont Circle. So while we drove, Tessa told Dad the long version—how we tested the diamonds and sat up half the night. Dad didn't say much, but he listened carefully.

I complain about church sometimes, but really I like it. Instead of Sunday School, Tessa and I sit in the pew with our family. It's nice to be together. And anytime I get bored, there are the pretty windows to look at. Another part I like is hymns. Tessa sings loud, and I sing on key.

CHAPTER SIXTEEN

AT lunch, we got our first lucky break.

We didn't have to go looking everywhere for Mr. Mormora. He sat down to eat with us!

Only it seemed rude to interview a person who was eating a tuna melt. Wouldn't he get indigestion? So Tessa and I made a date to talk to him later.

Lunch was in the family dining room upstairs. The tuna melts came from the White House kitchen. They are Dad's favorite, and I like them, too, but they're messy. When I eat one the mayonnaise flies.

"So how do you think Hooligan is getting on in class?" Dad asked Mr. Mormora.

Mr. Mormora dabbed the corner of his mouth with his napkin. "Ah, you can see for yourself! He is an excellent student. He wants so much to make Cameron, his Canine Buddy, proud." He flashed me a smile, and I felt myself blush.

"There is, though, one thing that puzzles me," Mr. Mormora continued. "Hooligan is a little, uh...fleshier than I would like. And yet he is on an excellent diet with no opportunity for snacking. Can you explain that?" He looked at us each for an answer.

"Too many Canine Cookies?" said Tessa.

"No, no, no!" said Mr. Mormora. "Canine Cookies are specially formulated for good taste *and* good health."

I thought of Paul Song's dog. "Maybe someone's feeding him treats," I said.

Mr. Mormora nodded. "I have thought of this. It was the case with the dog I mentioned previously, Empress Pu-Chi. Her caregiver spoiled her with ginger snaps and liverwurst."

"*Ewww!*" said Tessa.

"What about this Mr. Ng?" said Mr. Mormora. "He is new, I believe. How well do you know him?"

Dad explained that anyone working in the White House has to be interviewed a bunch of times, then checked by the Secret Service.

"This tells us he is neither criminal nor spy," said Mr. Mormora. "But what is in his heart? Perhaps he is the kind that gives unhealthy treats to dogs to win their friendship."

And if that was true, I thought, could he also be the kind that stole diamond dog collars?

We finished our sandwiches and talked about the other dogs in Canine Class. As we were getting up, Mr. Mormora asked where we should meet.

"How about Mrs. Kennedy's Garden?" Tessa said. "There are chairs and a table out there."

"Perfect," said Mr. Mormora. "In half an hour?"

Back in our bedroom, Tessa and I changed out of

our church clothes. Then I got my notebook, and she put on her pink detecting hat. We were ready to go when Tessa asked me to bring the letter from Empress Pu-Chi. I found it in my top desk drawer and handed it over.

"But remember," I said, "Mr. Mormora is a witness, not a suspect. And we aren't gonna tell him the diamonds are real, right? It's a bad idea to blab that to everybody."

"Okay, okay. Don't give me a lecture," Tessa said. "Sheesh, you'd think I never interviewed a suspect before."

"*Witness*," I said.

"Right," Tessa said.

But I did not have a good feeling.

CHAPTER SEVENTEEN

UP till my aunt Jen, Jacqueline Kennedy was probably the prettiest First Lady ever. Her garden is outside the East Colonnade, which is the corridor that goes from the ground floor of the White House to the East Wing.

Malik came downstairs with Tessa and me, and he even offered to help us interview Mr. Mormora. "I'm a trained law enforcement professional, you know," he said.

"Thanks, Malik, but we've got this," Tessa said.

I looked at my sister. "We do?"

Tessa shrugged. "Sure. We have all the rest of March break to solve it, don't we? And not even any homework."

The Jacqueline Kennedy Garden has a lawn, hedges and flowerbeds. At one end is a pergola, sort of a stick house covered with vines. Mr. Mormora was waiting for us there. Granny said the vines would be leafy in the summer, but now they were just starting to show a little green.

Malik walked across the lawn and sat down in the shade on the other side. Tessa and I sat down on white metal chairs across from Mr. Mormora. Before I could even say hi, Tessa crossed her arms over her chest.

"Mr. Mormora," she said, "may I direct your attention to Exhibit A?"

I said, "Huh?"

Mr. Mormora said, "Huh?"

Tessa said, "*Duh!*" and waved the empress's letter in his face.

"May I see that please?" Mr. Mormora took the letter.

"Cammie and I know dogs can't write," Tessa said—like it proved we were unusually smart. "So do you know who wrote it for real?"

Mr. Mormora nodded. "I recognize the signature. It was written by the man who is responsible for the empress's personal correspondence. He is President Alfredo-Chin's chief of protocol, Mr. Eb Ghanamamma."

I was so surprised I stopped writing. "Eb Ghanamamma, the singer?"

Mr. Mormora smiled. "You have heard of him? It was very long ago that he gave up singing to become involved with politics."

"How come *I* never heard of him?" Tessa wanted to know.

"I was really little when Dad used to listen to him," I said. "He sang about people who were poor and a girl who was pretty."

Mr. Mormora nodded. "A folksinger, yes. His most famous song was a song of lost love called 'Lina.'"

"Did he ever sing about diamonds?" Tessa asked.

"Never," said Mr. Mormora.

Tessa looked disappointed. "So why would he want to send a zillion dollars worth to Hooligan then lie about it?"

If I was the kind of person who kicks her little sister, I would have kicked my little sister. "*Tessa!*" said.

"Oops," Tessa said.

But Mr. Mormora didn't look shocked...or guilty. "I do not know," he said. "And while I did not like Empress Pu-Chi, I found Mr. Ghanamamma very nice. I believe he sincerely wants to help the people. Perhaps you should ask him this question yourself? In fact..."

Mr. Mormora unhooked his phone from his belt then leaned over to show us the screen. He scrolled through pictures of dogs, tons of them, including the empress herself. She had a pouty face and a red bow tied between her ears. Then he scrolled through his contacts and found Eb Ghanamamma.

"Will this help you?" he asked.

Tessa said, "Write that down, Cammie," and jumped up from her chair. "We can phone right now! Thanks, Mr. Mormora."

"Aren't you forgetting something?" I said.

"Nope," said Tessa. "Let's go."

"The Canine Cookies?" I said. "That Hooligan found on the South Lawn?"

"Right!" Tessa recrossed her arms. "Mr. Mormora, if you were never out on the South Lawn before the first Canine Class, how come there were Canine Cookies everywhere for Hooligan to find? Did you lie to us on purpose, or what?"

Mr. Mormora looked confused.

I sighed. "You have to forgive my sister. She is very sleepy. What she's trying to say is Hooligan found a whole bunch of Canine Cookies on the South Lawn yesterday. Do you have any idea how they got there?"

"Now that I find interesting," said Mr. Mormora. "I did not drop the cookies, if that is what you mean. But we have been keeping the cookie supply in one of the outdoor sheds. Yesterday before class, a box disappeared. I thought I had miscounted, but perhaps...?" He shrugged.

I scribbled this down and stood up. "Come on, Tessa. Now we can call. Thanks, Mr. Mormora!"

He had been a big help—that is, if he was telling the truth. But if he was a diamond thief, wouldn't he have lied to throw us off the track?

CHAPTER EIGHTEEN

OTHER than Nate, Tessa and I are the only kids in America who don't have cell phones. Because of that, we would have to call Mr. Ghanamamma from a White House phone. Malik came upstairs with us, but he didn't have to stick around once we were safe on the second floor. Since we needed privacy, we decided to use the phone on the desk in the Treaty Room.

On our way, I thought of something. "What time is it in a certain nearby nation?"

Tessa consulted Barbie. "Four o'clock."

"It might be a different time zone there," I said. "We might call Mr. Ghanamamma and wake him in the middle of the night."

"Well, *that* would be embarrassing," said Tessa.

Since Nate has a computer in his bedroom, we went upstairs to ask him. "I'll go online and check," he said. And the way it turned out, Tessa was right—four o'clock in the nearby nation, too.

"But why do you need to know?" Nate asked.

Explaining took a while.

"So you're really going to call him?" Nate said. "You don't think you'll get in trouble?"

Tessa and I looked at each other. Mom had told us not to phone presidents. But she never said not to phone a chief of protocol. Right?

"We're detecting," Tessa said finally. "Someone has to do it."

"Can I come?" said Nate.

Tessa and I looked at each other. We didn't necessarily get along all the time with Nate. But Tessa shrugged okay, so I said, "I guess. It could be helpful, having someone who knows everything."

The Treaty Room is at the top of the grand stairway and next to the Lincoln Bedroom on the second floor. Sometimes Mom works there, but today she was working in the Oval Office. It's in the West Wing, which is supposedly part of the White House but really more like a separate building next door.

We took the elevator down from the third floor. When we walked out, we saw that Hooligan was in his old bed by the fireplace in the West Sitting Hall, and Mr. Ng was sitting on the comfy sofa, reading the newspaper. I had a sudden idea.

"Can we borrow Hooligan? We need a guard dog."

Mr. Ng thought for a moment. "It *should* be fine," he finally said. "I believe he is too tired to get himself in any trouble."

In the Treaty Room, I closed the door and ordered Hooligan to sit and stay.

"Your job is to guard the door," I told him. "If you hear anybody coming, bark!"

Hooligan smiled an agreeable doggy smile. Then he lay down and closed his eyes. A minute later, he was chasing rabbits in his sleep. Some guard dog.

Next, we decided Tessa would do the talking. I didn't want to say it, but I was worried about having to speak a foreign language. In school, my worst subject is spelling but my second worst is Spanish. And anyway, none of us was totally sure what language they spoke in the nearby nation.

Tessa said it didn't matter. "I'll just talk loud. Ready, Nate?"

He dialed. It was a lot of numbers. But somebody must have picked up fast because Tessa tilted her head to listen. Then she smiled and said, "WHATEVER YOU SAID, BACK AT YOU. I AM TESSA PARKS FROM THE UNITED STATES OF AMERICA. CAN I TALK TO EB GHANAMAMMA?"

There was a pause. "WARM AND SUNNY, THANK YOU. IS THE WEATHER NICE IN YOUR NATION?" Another pause. "YES. EB GHANAMAMMA. DON'T ASK ME TO SPELL IT. I CAN HARDLY SAY IT."

After a moment, she spoke to Nate and me. "I'm on hold."

"I don't get it," Nate said, "did they speak English?"

Tessa shook her head. "Of course not—*duh*. It's a foreign country."

"Then what was that stuff about the weather?"

Tessa shrugged. "Grown-ups always talk about

the weather." She tilted her head again. "MR. GHANA-MAMMA?" Pause. "WELL, *THAT'S* DISAPPOINTING. WHERE?" Pause. Then she repeated her name, gave the White House phone number, said GOOD-BYE and hung up.

"What happened?" Nate and I asked at the same time.

"HE'S IN THE JUNGLE," Tessa said.

"STOP SHOUTING!" I said.

"What jungle?" Nate said

"Whatever jungle's in a certain nearby nation. Anyway, there's no cell service there. So he can't be reached."

"Wait a sec," said Nate. "How did you know the word for jungle in a foreign language?"

Tessa thought for a second. "I don't know. I just did. Or maybe it was *beach*. Anyway, he definitely wasn't there and could not be reached."

"So when will he be back?" I asked.

"Earth to Cammie?" said Tessa. "How do I know? They weren't speaking English!"

CHAPTER NINETEEN

HOOLIGAN had slept through Tessa's shouting, but now came a noise so shrill and piercing he sprang up like a jack-in-the-box: *aw-row-row-row-row-rowff!*

"What is it, puppy?" Tessa ran and opened the door to the hall to look. Standing on the other side was Ms. Kootoor, but she hadn't made the noise. She was as startled as we were.

Hooligan is always glad to see Ms. Kootoor and shot out the door. But this time he didn't knock her over. She was ready.

Meanwhile, the nameless canary sang—*Twee-twee-twee!*—Granny and Mr. Bryant appeared in the doorway on our left, and a second later Cottonball careened between them and leaped toward Hooligan, who forgot all about Ms. Kootoor and wrestled his puppy pal to the rug.

For a few seconds the two of them played, then Hooligan broke free and sprinted toward the East Hall with Cottonball close behind. Now the second floor was a race track, with Hooligan and Cottonball neck and neck. Every once in a while a tail hit a wall, the furniture, or some fragile historic object.

Here is a piece of advice if you ever live with a dog: Don't put breakable things at tail level.

Mr. Bryant and Mr. Ng moved to the Center Hall to stop them, but it wasn't easy. There was lots of furniture in the way, and the dogs could go under and around places Mr. Bryant and Mr. Ng couldn't. Just watching made me dizzy, and then Mr. Bryant wasn't looking and collided with Mr. Ng, and they both fell back and sat down on the rug—*ouch*.

"Everyone just stay calm!" Granny said, not very calmly. "If we wait, they'll tire themselves out." But then, "*Oh!*" she had to sidestep to stay out of Cottonball's way, and "*Ooh!*" Hooligan brushed by on the other side.

It was Mr. Mormora who saved the day. The stairs outside his room come out on the second floor near the Treaty Room. When he heard the commotion, he came running down and placed himself in the dogs' path like a traffic cop. "Gentlemen?" he said. "You stop now."

And they did.

It took three maids to sweep and dust and set things right. Meanwhile, Mr. Ng took the dogs outside, Ms. Kootoor said she had a headache and went back to her room and Mr. Mormora went back upstairs. In the end, it was Granny, Mr. Bryant, Tessa, Nate and I who collapsed in the West Sitting Hall.

Maybe for the first time ever, Granny looked

embarrassed. "I guess I shouldn't have tested it with the dogs around," she said. "It seems to have upset them."

"Tested what?" Tessa asked.

From her pocket, Granny pulled two silver some-things, each one on a chain—whistles! "I thought Ms. Kootoor's father's idea was a good one," she went on. "So these are for you girls."

"Cool!" Tessa took a whistle and immediately put it to her mouth.

"*No!*" everybody shouted at once.

Tessa grinned. "Only kidding. Thanks, Granny. Even if it doesn't have diamonds, I like it better than Ms. Kootoor's. It's a lot bigger."

I took my whistle and thanked Granny, too. Then I realized this might be our best chance to interview Mr. Bryant. Tessa must've been thinking the same thing because she crossed her arms over her chest. "Mr. Bryant," she said. "Do you mind if we ask you a few questions?"

CHAPTER TWENTY

"QUESTIONS?" said Mr. Bryant. "No, I don't mind. Are you girls detecting again? I understand those diamonds on Hooligan's collar might be real after all."

"How'd you hear that?" Tessa asked.

Granny looked embarrassed again. Twice in one afternoon had to be some kind of record. "I think by now it's, uh...general knowledge here in the White House," she said.

Tessa started over. "Mr. Bryant, was Hooligan wearing his diamond collar when you got him out of his crate this morning?"

Mr. Bryant shook his head. "No. In fact, he wasn't wearing any collar at all. That's why I put the old one back on him."

"What time did that happen?" Tessa asked.

"Must've been just after six twenty," Mr. Bryant said. "I know because they clocked me in at the gatehouse at six fifteen."

"So that means the collar disappeared between—" I

started to say. But I was interrupted by the appearance of two men in almost identical gray suits standing in the doorway to the center hall. Granny seemed to know them.

"Yes?" she said.

"Sorry to bother you, ma'am," said the taller one. "Do you mind if we—?"

"No, no. Go ahead," Granny said. "Whatever you need."

"Thank you," said the other man, and they turned and disappeared back into the hall.

Some parts of the White House are public spaces, but the second and third floors are where we live. That means I usually know everyone. But I didn't know these guys.

"What's going on?" I asked.

"Are they gonna look in our room?" Tessa asked.

"They're doing their job," Granny said, which, if you think about it, did not answer the question. "Your mom will be in to talk to you later."

"Oh, *fine*," said Tessa. "As usual, the grown-ups are all in on it together."

CHAPTER TWENTY-ONE

NO way was Granny giving us more information. So Tessa and I went back to our room to look at our latest notes. Unfortunately, it seemed like they only added confusion.

Then I remembered something Granny once told Tessa and me—how a fresh pair of eyes can help you see clearly.

Could Nate's be a fresh pair of eyes?

Tessa didn't like the idea at first, but in the end I talked her into it. "Only we have to make him pinky promise not to reveal our secrets," she said.

"*Ewww!*" said Nate, when we proposed the pinky promise, but in the end, curiosity won out, and we all hooked fingers.

"Don't you ever tell any of my friends I did this *ever*," he said when we let go.

"The problem," I said after he had looked at my notebook, "is that the investigation keeps changing. At first we were only looking for a single fake diamond.

Now we're looking for a single real diamond, plus the collar."

"But that's a good thing," said Nate. "It's like a math problem. Adding a second variable limits the possible solutions."

Tessa shook her head. "Would you puh-leeze remember I am only in second grade?"

"Even you can understand this, Tessa," Nate said. "The way you've got it figured, the diamond disappeared when Hooligan was in the trees by the tennis courts, right? Then the collar disappeared between four and six twenty this morning. So if you forget all the confusing details about Mr. Ghanamamma and El Brillante, the thief has to be someone who could've gotten to Hooligan *both* times. That's fewer people than had access to him one time or the other. See?"

"But couldn't there be two different thieves?" I said. "Like, Mr. Mormora doesn't seem to trust Mr. Ng. He thinks Mr. Ng's giving Hooligan treats that make him fat."

"Yeah—and then there's these new guys," Tessa said, "the ones in the suits? Who are they anyway? There were all kinds of people on the lawn Thursday. Maybe they were there, too."

"I don't know who they are," said Nate. "But it seems illogical for there to be two thieves—too big a coincidence."

I was trying to be logical, but I didn't like where logic was going. To me, it seemed obvious that the person with the best opportunity to steal first the diamond and then the collar was—

"Mr. Bryant," Tessa said my thought out loud. "He fits Nate's math problem. He was around Hooligan and the collar both times. But that doesn't matter because we know Mr. Bryant didn't do it."

"How do we know?" Nate said.

"Because he's Mr. Bryant!" Tessa said.

"I have an idea," said Nate. "The first diamond disappeared during the helicopter chase, right? Maybe we can review the videos.

"Hey!" I said. "I know someone who can help. I can ask her tomorrow at Canine Class."

At bedtime, Mom had barely opened our door when Tessa pounced. "Who are those guys in the gray suits, anyway?"

Mom frowned. "I missed you, too, Muffin."

Tessa said, "Sorry, Mama. I love you. Who are those guys in the gray suits?"

Mom sighed and sat down on the edge of my bed. "I need to tell you both something, but I don't want you to worry. Canine Class is going to go on tomorrow as usual, but starting tonight, the White House is on heightened security alert. The two men are part of my national security team."

Tessa looked at me. "Translation?"

"She means they're part of the government, and they're being extra careful because bad guys might try to do something. Right?"

"More or less," Mom said.

Tessa squealed. *"Bad guys?!"*

"Shhh!" Mom put her fingers to Tessa's lips. "It's only a precaution. For a few days, the Secret Service will have a little extra help here in the White House. And you girls and your cousin will have to stick around, too. But there's a silver lining. Dad had been planning to work in California this week, and now he's going to stay here with us."

Sometimes when you're thinking hard about something, it seems like everything's connected. "Mom—does the security alert have anything to do with what Tessa and I are investigating?"

Mom's expression didn't change, but she stood up. "What you and Tessa are investigating?" she said. "Well, I should say."

I looked over at Tessa. "Was that a yes?"

"No idea," said Tessa. "Mom, was that a—" but the question turned into a giggle because Mom was tickling her. "*Mama-a-a-a!*" She was still giggling. "Sto-o-op!"

Mom's tickling became a snuggle and a kiss. Then it was my turn, and then—before we could ask more questions—Mom was heading out the door. "Good night, muffins," she said. "I love you."

CHAPTER TWENTY-TWO

WAS Mr. Bryant a thief?

Or Mr. Ng?

And what about the guys in the gray suits?

Was Mom investigating the missing diamonds?

And who was giving Hooligan fattening treats?

All those questions were on my mind when I woke up. But in the kitchen, Granny reminded me about something *way* more important—my turn to name the canary.

"How about Singalong?" I tried.

Before Granny could even express an opinion, Tessa was shaking her head. "No way! That's the same as Paul Song's dog. It would be confusing!"

"Confusing, how? It's not like the canary will ever even meet Paul Song's dog."

"And besides—" Tessa totally ignored my excellent point—"you stole that idea, Cammie. I think the name-less canary needs an original name, one that's all his own."

Granny sighed. "It should be a name we can agree on at least. Your turn tomorrow, Tessa."

The Canine Class topic of the day was "heel," and Hooligan got it right away. I didn't want to jinx it by talking about it, but at this rate he for sure was going to be Top Dog.

With the security alert, all the CBs and CITs had to be double-checked when they entered the White House grounds. Because of that, there was no time before class to arrange help with the videos. It was only when Mr. Mormora practiced with the other dogs that I got my chance.

Ms. Major and her cockapoo, Pickles, were next to me as usual. Pickles was trying to untie Ms. Major's shoelaces with his teeth. "Ms. Major," I said, "did I get it right that you keep track of news stories about us and Hooligan?"

Ms. Major tried to bump Pickles away without actually kicking him. It looked like she was tap dancing. "Indeed I do," she said.

"Then can I ask a favor? Is there a chance my sister, my cousin and I could look at some TV stories from Thursday afternoon?"

"Sure—there are plenty, and I'd be happy to help." Ms. Major stopped dancing to check the calendar on her phone. Pickles went back to chewing her laces. "How about one o'clock—right after lunch?"

"We'll be there," I said. "Thanks."

* * *

Ms. Major's office is in the West Wing. My mom's office, the Oval Office, is there, too. Mom's is really nice, but a lot of the West Wing is so crowded it's crazy. Almost everyone works in a cubicle, which is a room with no door and thin pretend walls.

Malik was on duty again, so Tessa, Nate and I had come downstairs with him. Trying to find Ms. Major was like being trapped in a maze. Finally, Malik called out: "Hello-o-o? Ms. Ann Major, are you there?"

When an answering voice called, "Hello-o-o-o!," we followed it and found her.

"Welcome to my world," Ms. Major said. It was a tiny space with bare walls except for a calendar turned to last January. The picture on it was a German shepherd. There was no place for four people to sit down, so we crowded around her desk. On it were an old, boxy computer, binders, papers and photos of Pickles.

"As you know, several stations covered the events on Thursday," she said. "So I pulled up four examples—Fox, CNN, CBS and the local news with Jan and Larry. We could probably find more if you need them."

It took us about half an hour to watch the four clips. A lot was the same, of course, but there were differences. Like three of the announcers treated the story mostly like a joke, and one treated it like the whole country had spun out of control. Also there were different views, depending on where the camera guys were standing.

The longest report was Jan and Larry's.

It started with a close-up of Hooligan before he

broke his leash, and Jan's voice saying, "With his diamond dog collar, the presidential pooch sported a glamorous new look this afternoon. But soon thereafter, chaos erupted on the South Lawn!"

"Ms. Major," Nate interrupted. "Could you go back over that part, please?"

"Sure." She restarted it.

"Look at that," Nate said. "When Hooligan turns, you can see all the diamonds—twelve of 'em."

What happened next on the video wasn't a picture, it was noise—the yakking birds. After that, Hooligan took off running with Tessa after him, her hair blowing everywhere, her eyes tearing in the wind.

"Well, *that's* not very flattering," she said.

The clip went on to show the parade of pursuers—with a close-up of the vice president—and even a view of flowers being crushed by stomping feet. Jan and Larry took turns narrating. At one point Jan said, "Look at that, Larry. For a time, when he was near the tennis courts, Hooligan eluded his pursuers altogether!"

"Bingo," said Nate.

"Is that what you were after?" Ms. Major asked.

"Partly," said Nate, "but keep going."

Now the view pulled back to a bunch of confused-looking people searching for Hooligan by the bushes near the garden plot. Among them were Tessa and the vice president, but you couldn't see Mr. Bryant. Maybe he was there, but he wasn't in the shot.

The final few seconds showed Dad's helicopter

landing and then Ms. Kootoor—cameraman catnip—
with Hooligan licking her face.

"I guess all's well that ends well," said the voice of
Larry.

"Bow wow to that," said Jan. "In other news..."

Ms. Major stopped the video on the last frame. Nate
pointed to the screen. "See that?" It was another view
of Hooligan's collar, and guess what? A diamond was
missing.

Ms. Major looked at her watch. Like everyone who
works for my mom, she must've been super busy. "Did
you get what you need?"

"I think so," I said. "It was really nice of you to help
us. Thanks."

"No problem," she said. "Would you like me to e-mail
you the links? Then you can watch the stories on your
own if you want to."

"E-mail them to me," Nate said. "I'm the only one
with a computer in my room."

Tessa said, "Must be *nice*," and stuck out her tongue
when he wasn't looking.

Nobody talked as we left the West Wing. Malik
was concentrating on finding a route out of the maze.
Nate, Tessa and I were putting together what the video
had told us. We now knew for sure that Hooligan himself had disappeared for a few minutes. And so had
Mr. Bryant. Did the diamond just fall off the collar? Or
did somebody take it?

Tessa said we should flat out ask Mr. Bryant.

Nate said that was crazy. "If he took it, he'll lie and say he didn't. If he didn't, he'll be mad we accused him."

"He might confess," Tessa said.

"Lame," Nate said.

"Maybe we need a break," I said.

Nate said fine. He was going to find Jeremy and shoot some hoops.

Tessa said, "I know—how 'bout if we dress Hooligan up in outfits and take pictures?"

This was not my first-choice idea. But I knew if I said no, she'd want to play Barbies—and that's worse.

We found Mr. Bryant and Hooligan in the West Sitting Hall.

"Be my guest," Mr. Bryant told us. "But you must promise to keep him under control. I'll just get myself a cup of coffee and check back."

Hooligan absolutely refused to step into Tessa's flamingo rain boots. But he didn't seem to mind the pink kimono, or the plastic pearls.

"Pretty puppy!" said Tessa, clicking the camera in his face.

"He's totally embarrassed," I said.

"He likes it!" Tessa said. "Hey, we can send these pictures to the Empress Pu-Chi! She of all dogs would appreciate them."

"We can put them in with the thank-you note," I said.

Tessa shook her head. "I'm pretty sure—and Aunt Jen will back me up—that when the gift's been stolen, you don't have to write a thank-you note."

"Really? High five!" I guess it's true there's always a bright side.

CHAPTER TWENTY-THREE

MOM had to eat dinner with her advisers in the Oval Office. At bedtime, Dad came in to give us our kisses. Nothing against Dad, but I was really missing my mom.

The next morning, I woke up even before Granny came in. So did Tessa. "I've got a really good name for the canary," she announced.

Oh, fine. My mom's gone AWOL. Bad guys are threatening. Diamonds are missing. And my sister's all happy because she's got a name for the canary! Was this supposed to brighten my day?

When we got to the kitchen, Nate was already there. And so was Ms. Kootoor. I guess one thing about getting up early is you get used to getting up early.

"This is your moment, Tessa," I said. "What's the 'really good' name?"

"Ghanamamma!" she cried.

I had been expecting to hate it, but instead I cracked up—Nate, too. Then we heard a thump. Ms. Kootoor had been standing by the breakfast table. When I turned, I saw she had dropped her Blueberry Bag—*thump*—to the floor. Her face looked whiter than usual, too.

"Are you okay?" Granny asked.

Ms. Kootoor smiled weakly. "Got out of bed too fast, I guess. Uh...what was that name, Tessa?"

"Ghanamamma. It's the name of somebody—" Tessa didn't finish her sentence. I guess she suddenly remembered how we weren't going to advertise that we'd phoned a certain nearby nation.

"Somebody?" Ms. Kootoor prompted.

"A singer my dad used to like," said Tessa.

Before Ms. Kootoor could ask for details, Mr. Bryant came in with Hooligan.

"How's everyone this morning?" he asked, then he turned to the canary. "Have these kids come up with a name for you yet?"

"How do you know we're naming the canary?" Tessa asked.

"It was my idea," said Mr. Bryant.

Tessa looked at Granny. "Is that true?"

Granny gave Mr. Bryant a look. I don't know what there was about it, but all of a sudden I got a funny feeling.

"Yes, it's true," Granny said. "And they haven't named him yet. Some of their ideas are real humdingers, though."

Mr. Bryant stroked his chin. "Hmm. What's the matter with that name for a canary? Humdinger?"

"I like it!" said Tessa.

"Cammie? Nate?" Granny asked.

"I'm down," I said.

Nate sighed. "If you all prefer Humdinger to Serinus..."

"Then it's settled," said Granny. And what she did next almost knocked me over. She kissed Mr. Bryant on the cheek!

"I think I'm still in shock," said Nate a few minutes later. Along with Hooligan, we were heading to the South Lawn for Canine Class.

Mr. Bryant had gone down already to get Cottonball. Ms. Kootoor had gone back to her room to lie down.

I shook my head. "So the way it turns out, Mr. Bryant gave her the canary."

"And that date Mr. Bryant went out on...?" Tessa said.

"And when Granny went to church with 'a friend'...?" I said.

"Not to mention the tennis date," Tessa said.

"And all the coffee they've both been drinking!" Nate said.

Talking about it, we walked slower and slower. Now, in the hall outside the Dip Room, we stopped altogether. "I'm not sure how I feel about Granny dating Mr. Bryant," Tessa said. "But there is one good thing. For sure Mr. Bryant has to be innocent. Granny would never date a diamond thief."

Canine Class that day was review—sit, stay and heel. I remembered how Mr. Mormora had predicted that by graduation all the dogs would be "models of canine class." Mostly he was right. Pickles still got distracted, and the Chihuahua forever wanted his belly scratched. But most of the dogs were getting the hang of good behavior.

And Hooligan was on track to be Top Dog!

When class was almost over, Mr. Mormora made an announcement: "Tomorrow is our graduation ceremony. We have planned some surprises, so please be sure your canines look their best. Also, if any of you wishes to say good-bye to me, may I ask you to stay after class today? Because after class tomorrow, I have a plane to catch. I have been asked by an old friend to go with him on safari!"

CHAPTER TWENTY-FOUR

YOU might have noticed, if you're paying attention, that for all the detecting Tessa, I and Nate had done, we still had not

- found the first diamond
- found the other 11 diamonds
- figured out who stole them
- figured out if their disappearance was connected to El Brillante, the missing diamond in a certain nearby nation.

In fact, the only mystery we'd solved was one we weren't trying to solve: where Granny's canary came from.

As detectives we were totally lame.

After lunch, Tessa, Nate, Jeremy and I went outside to play Frisbee with Hooligan on the lawn. This lasted about fifteen minutes. The wind had picked up after Canine Class, and by now it was gray and freezing outside!

I've lived in Washington ever since Mom first was

elected to the Senate. For Tessa, that's her whole life. But Nate just moved from San Diego in January. He was shivering. "I thought winter was over!" he said.

"March is always like this," I told him. "Sometimes it even snows."

"What if we go bowling?" Nate asked. The White House has a bowling alley on the ground floor. We had only been there a couple of times. Usually we were too busy.

"Bad news on bowling," said Jeremy. "I understand they're refinishing the lane. It should be dry by the end of the week, though."

In the end, we were so desperate we decided to watch TV in the Solarium. Of course, the second we got there, Nate grabbed the remote. And what did he turn on? News!

Tessa said, "*Ewwww!*," and I tackled him, but he held the remote away so I couldn't get it, then Tessa jumped and almost had it, but he said, "Hey, wait— look!" which I thought was a trick, but it turned out not to be. The picture on the screen was a dog with a red bow in her hair, the Empress Pu-Chi!

I don't mean the actual empress. I mean a photo of her on a sign outside a palace in the capital city of the nearby nation. There was writing in a foreign language on the sign, too. The news guy translated: "People are more important than dogs!"

According to the news guys, protesters in the nearby nation believed Empress Pu-Chi was treated better than poor people, and they wanted a new government.

"You mean they want to fire President Alfredo-Chin?" said Tessa. "But I like him! He forgave Hooligan, and Mom says he's a friend of the American people."

"Mr. Mormora doesn't like him," I remembered. "Do you think Mr. Mormora is on the side of the protesters?"

The news guy was still talking. "Opposition forces say their major stumbling block is raising the financial means necessary to effect change...."

"What is he talking about now?" Tessa looked at Nate.

"The people who want a different government need money to get one," Nate said.

"Is Mr. Ghanamamma one of those people?" asked Tessa.

Nate shook his head no. "He works for President Alfredo-Chin."

"But Mr. Mormora said he used to sing about poor people and beautiful women," said Tessa. "That makes him sound like more of a protester."

"And now he's gone to the jungle," I said.

Then I thought of something—don't safaris happen in jungles?

"You guys?" I said. "I just thought of something...."

"So did I," said Nate. "The protesters need money to change the government, right? Well, one way to get money is to work for it. But another is...."

"Steal it," said Tessa.

"Or steal something valuable—like a diamond," said Nate.

Sometimes thoughts are like rolling snowballs—they

grow and grow, out of control. All of a sudden we couldn't think—or talk—fast enough. "You mean El Brillante," I said. "But it's famous like the Hope Diamond, worth everything and nothing."

"Do you have your notebook, Cammie?" Tessa asked. "I want to see something."

The television was still talking, but we had stopped watching. We were huddled together on the floor, reading over pages of notes.

"There!" Tessa pointed. "That's what I remembered. Mr. Rubio said sometimes diamonds are cut up into smaller diamonds. So if you needed to get money from a famous diamond, couldn't you cut it up? And sell the pieces?"

Nate was nodding. "If that's true, it could be there's not just a connection between Hooligan's diamonds and El Brillante—Hooligan's diamonds *are* El Brillante."

Now it was like our snowball had become an avalanche. "Are you saying the protesters stole the diamond, cut it up, put the pieces on a collar and mailed it to Hooligan?" I asked.

"Bingo," said Tessa.

"But there's a million problems with that!" I said. "I mean, how do you get money from Hooligan? And besides, the collar came from the Empress Pu-Chi—with a letter from Mr. Ghanamamma. Like Nate just said, he's not a protester."

Nate the know-it-all rolled his eyes like I was the dumbest cousin ever. "Pay attention, Cameron. Let's say Tessa's got it right about Mr. Ghanamamma. Let's say he's secretly on the side of the protesters. When he sent the collar here, he wasn't really sending it to Hooligan. He was sending it to a confederate."

"What's confederate?" said Tessa.

"Someone he knew he could trust," said Nate, "someone who would sell the diamonds then send back the money."

Tessa was nodding. "But before that person could sell the diamonds," she said, "they would have to steal the diamonds. So if we find the confederate, then we've found the thief."

CHAPTER TWENTY-FIVE

NATE and Tessa's theories were giving me a headache.

But I had to admit they made a weird kind of sense. And my own puzzle piece fit, too. "Guys?" I said. "There's something else. Mr. Ghanamamma's in the jungle, right? And Mr. Mormora says he's going on safari? So that might mean—"

"Mr. Mormora is going to meet up with Mr. Ghanamamma!" Tessa finished my sentence. "He's the confederate. He's the thief."

"Too easy," said Nate. "If Mr. Mormora was the confederate, he wouldn't have told us he knew Empress Pu-Chi and spent time in the nearby nation. He would have tried to keep all that a secret."

"Maybe he thought we'd find out anyway," I said.

Nate shook his head. "I'm betting it's Mr. Bryant."

"But Granny—" Tessa began.

"That's part of his plot, Tessa," Nate said. "He's

pretending to like Granny, just like Mr. Ghanamamma pretended he was working for President Alfredo-Chin. If Mr. Bryant's the thief, he probably thinks his friendship with Granny will protect him. Except for you guys, he's the one who's closest to Hooligan. If the protesters in the nearby nation wanted to recruit someone to help them, that's who they'd go to."

"But Mr. Bryant doesn't care about a nearby nation," Tessa said. "Does he?"

"I bet they're paying him a bundle of money," Nate said.

"Unless it's Mr. Ng," I said.

Tessa and Nate looked at me.

"Where did that come from?" Nate asked.

"Mr. Bryant's worked in the White House forever," I said, "but Mr. Ng came to work right before the collar arrived and right after El Brillante was stolen. That was—" I looked at my notes—"sometime in the last month, according to Jan and Larry."

Nate and Tessa were listening like this made sense. But the truth is I was making it up as I went along. I just didn't want the thief to be Mr. Bryant.

"Uh...," I said, "and...well, Mr. Mormora thinks Mr. Ng is feeding Hooligan unhealthy treats. So maybe he is, and he's doing it, uh...so Hooligan will be his special friend and come whenever he calls. Like maybe on Thursday, he called Hooligan when he was down in the trees by the tennis court hiding."

Tessa nodded. "Good thinking, Cammie."

"You're kidding," I said.

"No, seriously," said Tessa. "I am officially completely confused. If you ask me, they all did it. But there's still something I can't figure out. Where are the diamonds now?"

CHAPTER TWENTY-SIX

IN Nate's room we looked up El Brillante on the computer and learned it weighed sixty karats. Divided by twelve, it would break up into new diamonds that were about five karats each. When we found a picture of a five karat diamond, it looked like the ones on the collar. In other words, it was big and fat for a diamond but small for anything else, about the size of a jelly bean.

Finding twelve jelly beans in the White House would be impossible! In case you don't know, the White House is huge—132 rooms in the main part, plus work rooms and storage areas—not to mention the grounds outside.

Besides, the diamonds might already be gone.

Or maybe not? With the security alert, people going in and out were being checked super carefully—even the staff. It could be that whoever had the diamonds was waiting till it was safer to take them away.

"I have one last idea," said Tessa dramatically. "And if it doesn't work, I am officially giving up."

*   *   *

On our way down to the second floor, we ran into Mr. Bryant and Hooligan in the elevator. It was a little strange seeing Mr. Bryant. We not only thought he might be a diamond thief; we also thought he might be lying to our very own Granny about how much he liked her.

And then he said, "Just the people I was looking for! Would you kids mind watching the star pupil for a while? I thought I might get a cup of coffee."

"With Granny?" Tessa asked suspiciously.

"Why, yes, as a matter of fact," said Mr. Bryant. "Uh...do you have a problem with that?"

Tessa sighed and looked at me, then Nate. "I guess not," she said. "Come on, puppy."

Tessa's idea was to interview Mrs. Hedges. We found her coming out of the Lincoln Bedroom. She had a vacuum cleaner in one hand and a rag in the other. Of course, Hooligan was delighted to see his old pal, and lunged—causing Mrs. Hedges to drop everything and duck behind a sofa.

"Hooligan, *heel!*" I said.

Hooligan stopped and looked back, like, Do I have to? But then he circled around and dropped to his haunches beside me the way he'd been taught. "Good dog!"

Now Mrs. Hedges peeked over the sofa and narrowed her eyes. "That dog doesn't fool me. As soon as these classes are over, he'll be back to his old tricks."

"Mrs. Hedges," Tessa crossed her arms over her chest. "We have a few questions for you."

Keeping an eye on Hooligan, Mrs. Hedges came

around to our side of the sofa, sat and made herself comfortable. "Go ahead. I don't mind getting off my feet. That woman Ms. Kootoor is more trouble than half a dozen normal—"

"Mrs. Hedges—" Tessa tried to interrupt.

"—it took a whiskbroom, the vacuum cleaner, and furniture oil to get the dried mud off her closet floor. And there's that cooler she keeps. The ice needs replacing twice a day! What's she need a cooler for? The White House food isn't good enough? Anyway, I've only got one more day of putting up with her. She's packing to leave tomorrow. Now that Mr. Mormora, on the other hand, I'll be sorry—"

"Mrs. Hedges?" Tessa tried again.

"Yes?" Mrs. Hedges said.

"While you've been cleaning and stuff, have you noticed twelve mysterious diamonds lying around?"

"Subtle," Nate said.

Mrs. Hedges looked shocked. "Now, you children know I can't go talking about what I see. There is such a thing as privacy."

"We know," I said quickly. "And we would never even ask. Only it's really important."

"To the future of a nearby nation," Nate said.

"Not to mention Granny's happiness," I said.

"And Hooligan's," Tessa said.

"All that?" said Mrs. Hedges. "Well, let me think." Approximately two seconds passed, then, "Nope." She shrugged. "No diamonds. Sorry."

* * *

True to her word, Tessa gave up.

And after I had finished writing down my notes, I did, too.

At dinnertime, Dad and Granny ate with us, but Aunt Jen and Mom were too busy. Later, we watched a movie called *That Darn Cat* in the White House theater. It was Mr. Mormora's suggestion. It turns out he doesn't even have a dog of his own. In his off hours, he prefers cats.

Dad came in to kiss us good night.

"*Again?*" Tessa said. "We haven't seen Mom all day."

"If it's any consolation, I've barely seen her myself," Dad said. "And that brings me to some news. Good or bad first?"

"Bad!" I said.

"Good!" Tessa said.

Dad had a quarter in his pocket. When he flipped it, Tessa called tails and won. "The crisis your mom's been working on? It should blow over tomorrow. And then she'll have some time. If it warms back up, maybe a picnic."

Tessa pumped her fist—"*Yes!*"—but I was too worried about the bad news.

"And?" I said.

"Well...okay. The thing is, I don't want to upset you...."

"Uh oh," said Tessa.

"But perhaps you've heard there's some trouble in a certain nearby nation—"

"Protesters!" Tessa interrupted.

Dad nodded. "And quite unexpectedly those troubles have spilled over into the United States. In fact, tomorrow morning after Canine Class, there's going to be an arrest made here at the White House. The timing is unfortunate, but necessary. I'm telling you because I don't want you to be alarmed. At the same time, just in case there's an emergency, it's important that you stay out of the way."

Of course we had a million questions. Like who was going to be arrested? And what had they done? And was it because of the diamond dog collar?

But Dad just shook his head. "I can't say anymore, I'm sorry." After that, he gave us our kisses and said, "Sweet dreams."

After the door closed, the dark in our room seemed especially dark. Then Tessa asked, "Did Dad say emergency?"

"He said *maybe* emergency."

"Same difference," said Tessa. "So I know just what we need to take to Canine Class—our emergency whistles! That's why Granny gave them to us, right?"

CHAPTER TWENTY-SEVEN

SWEET dreams?

Ha!

Falling asleep was worse than on Christmas Eve, and instead of presents, my dreams were full of hand-cuffs and escaping canines, not to mention diamonds, diamonds everywhere.

It felt like I hadn't slept at all when someone shook my shoulder. Granny never does that. "Wha—hello, who?" I opened my eyes, and I couldn't believe it. Cousin Nathan!? He had never gotten up this early in his life!

"Shhh!" he whispered. "I'm sorry. But what I found out...you'll never believe it. I had to come and tell you. I think it's important."

"Okay," I said. "Tessa, wake up!"

Tessa and I made Nate look the other way while we put on our bathrobes. Then the three of us sat together on the sofa. It turned out Nate's mom had told him the same thing Dad told us. After that, he couldn't sleep either. So he decided to do some research online. "And," he said, "I learned something very interesting about Eb Ghanamamma's most famous folk song, 'Lina.'"

"The two of them? Really?" I said after he told us. "So that means the confederate has to be—?"

Nate nodded. "I think so."

"Let's look at the notes again," I said.

The sun still wasn't up, so we sat in the lamplight and read like we were studying for a test. It took a while, but then I spotted it, a clue we had missed all along: mud.

Piece by piece, the case came together—finally. But there was one more thing we could do to be sure. It was still dark when we tiptoed down the hall and up the stairs to the third floor.

In Nate's bedroom, the computer was the only light. He opened his e-mail and got the link Ms. Major had sent, put the volume on mute so he wouldn't wake his mom, and clicked through the Jan and Larry video till he stopped at the very last frame.

I shook my head. "I can't believe we missed that the first time."

"But what do we do now?" Tessa said. "Tell Mom? Tell Dad? What if they're going to arrest the wrong person?"

"No way," said Nate. "The grown-ups have it figured out—same as we do."

Remember how Mr. Mormora said to expect a surprise at the last Canine Class?

What he meant was Sports TV Network—STVN!

It turned out Mr. Mormora and Aunt Jen had seen a great opportunity for a story that would make the first family, the first dog and Canine Class all look good. And with Hooligan so popular, STVN loved the idea.

So that day instead of only the usual press guys watching, there were tons more cameras plus play-by-play and color commentary from two veteran sports-casters, Vin and Myron.

Having been up half the night, Tessa, Nate and I moved slowly that morning. By the time we got outside, the rest of the dogs were ready to go. With Mr. Mormora smiling and the sun shining again—it was hard to believe that after class, a diamond thief was going to be arrested.

Mr. Mormora welcomed us and also the audience watching on TV at home. Then he said, "For graduation day at Canine Class, I like to give the canines and their buddies a reward for all their work. For that reason, we are going to play a game."

The rules were easy. Each CB told his CIT to stay, then ran about fifty feet across the lawn and stopped. On the way, the CB dropped Canine Cookies. If the CIT stayed like he was supposed to, the team got a point. If he didn't—like if he tried to steal a cookie—the team lost a point. After that, the CB called, "Come!" and the CIT was supposed to run to him or her without stop-ping. If the CIT did it, the team got more points—one for every cookie the dog ran past.

We divided into four teams. Team One, my team, had

Ms. Major and Pickles, Mr. Bryant and Cottonball, the labradoodle and his CB, plus one of the I-don't-know-whats. Because everybody had so much confidence in Hooligan, he and I were chosen to go last.

Tessa, Nate, Granny and Dad were watching from the spectators' area as usual. Mom was in the Oval Office, as usual. Malik was over by the spectators, and Charlotte was near the STVN crew, including Myron and Vin.

"A-a-a-a-and—*go!*" said Mr. Mormora.

Mr. Bryant was first up. He told Cottonball to stay, then he started running.

Mr. Bryant is not a fast runner. But Cottonball did great. He only ate one cookie, and then it was Ms. Major's turn.

Sadly, Pickles ate every cookie! Now we were way behind—and Ms. Major was really embarrassed.

Lucky for us, the Chihuahua on Team Four was so excited he chased his tail, got dizzy and ran the wrong way. And a golden retriever on Team Three staged a sit-down strike. Finally, his CB had to carry him to the finish line.

Meanwhile, Vin and Myron narrated and kept score. When finally it was our turn, I heard: "Going into the final lap, Team One, anchored by presidential pooch Hooligan Parks, is in second place, just five points behind Team Two. Will the First Dog choke? Or will he run to victory?"

The thing about a race is—it's fun. And with the STVN excitement and the crowd, I forgot all about diamonds and bad guys and protesters. I just wanted to win!

"Go Team One!" hollered Nate from the sidelines.

"*Woo-hoo-hoo!*" hollered my drama queen sister.

I was sprinting across the South Lawn, dropping Canine Cookies as I went—and that's when I saw her: Ms. Kootoor! She had her Blueberry Bag over her shoulder, a matching sun hat on her head. She was pulling a rolling suitcase. And she was almost to the White House East Gate!

But where were the marines, the Secret Service, the D.C. police to arrest her? Didn't they know she was a diamond thief escaping?

"Hurry, Cameron! Hurry—what's the matter?" Ms. Major hollered.

I didn't know what to do. I looked over at Tessa and Nate. Couldn't they stop her? But from where they were standing, they couldn't even see her.

"What's Cameron Parks doing, Vin?" I heard Myron ask.

"Can't tell, Myron. She appears to have stopped dead in her tracks."

"Could it be a strategic move, Vin?"

"Well, she'd better move fast. The newfie-cross on Team Four is trying hard to stage a comeback!"

I dropped a cookie, ran and dropped another. Then things got worse. Ms. Kootoor was only a few yards from the East Gate, and no one seemed to care. Instead, Charlotte, Malik, a couple more Secret Service agents and three marines were all walking toward Mr. Mormora.

I got a bad feeling.

Had the grown-ups gotten it wrong? Did they think Mr. Mormora was the thief?

At the finish line, I turned back toward Hooligan, who was sitting and staying like a Top Dog to be.

"Go ahead, Cameron. Call him! Hurry up!" said Mr. Bryant.

Mr. Mormora, by now, was looking right to left as marines and officers approached. Meanwhile, Ms. Kootoor got closer and closer to the gate. The guards might stop her, but only for a moment. Everybody loved Ms. Kootoor, and she'd been going in and out for days.

If I didn't do something fast, she'd escape.

And an innocent man would be arrested!

Hooligan cocked his head. He couldn't figure out what was wrong with me either. And that's when I knew what I had to do. The whistle! It was for emergencies, wasn't it? And this was an emergency.

CHAPTER TWENTY-EIGHT

"THE girl had a powerful whistle in her pocket, don't you think so, Vin?"

"My ears are ringing, Myron. What do you suppose she's up to?"

My whistle's shriek had been followed by an echo—Tessa's. She hadn't seen Ms. Kootoor. But she knew if I had an emergency, she had an emergency, too.

Then the strangest thing happened. Every bird in every tree on the South Lawn went crazy all at once—shrieking, trilling and singing. I even heard Humdinger up in his cage: *Twee! Twee! Twee!*

A second after that, the canines started in, either howling or trying to dig down under the sound—all but Hooligan. He looked up, spotted Ms. Kootoor and forgot Canine Class altogether. So much for Top Dog—he bounded toward her at top speed. She must have known she'd never outrun him, but she dropped her suitcase and tried.

No way.

Hooligan was on her in a flash, while all the time Myron and Vin kept talking.

"What's that going on by the East Gate, Vin? Oops and ow! *That's* gotta hurt. Looks like the presidential pooch knocked down the thin lady with the big plaid purse."

"Mmm hmm, knocked the purse clean out of her hands, Myron. Did you see that?"

The shrieking whistles distracted the officers closing in on Mr. Mormora, but only for a moment. Then, when they had him surrounded, a funny thing happened. The CITs—the dogs—all looked in his direction. And next thing you know, they forgot everything they learned in Canine Class and sprang to the rescue.

Have I mentioned dogs love Mr. Mormora?

Meanwhile, I was chasing Hooligan. Even though Ms. Kootoor was a diamond thief, I couldn't let him hurt her.

Would he hurt her?

My mind was going as fast as my feet. Why had the birds gone crazy? Why had Hooligan acted different than the other dogs?

Meanwhile, a couple of Secret Service agents had peeled off to chase me, and I could hear them on their radios. "Fussbudget in jeopardy, Fussbudget in jeopardy."

Oh, *fine*. Remember how I didn't want to tell you my Secret Service code name? Tessa's is Fireball. Mine is...Fussbudget. It's what Granny calls me when I'm having a bad day.

Ms. Kootoor was on the ground when I reached her. But Hooligan didn't want to hurt her. He didn't even want to sniff her. He was all about the Blueberry Bag—trying to get his nose inside. I could see right away Ms. Kootoor wasn't dead or anything, but her stockings were torn and her jacket was dirty. I bent down, but before I could ask if she was okay, I heard Myron again.

"Vin—what do you suppose is going on there? It appears the Secret Service agents are attempting to arrest Mr. Julius Mormora."

"But the loyal canines have formed a wall of protection, Myron. They're snapping and snarling! They won't let the officers through!"

At the same time, Hooligan's head emerged from Ms. Kootoor's Blueberry Bag—and there was something familiar-looking in his mouth: a bright red diamond dog collar!

CHAPTER TWENTY-NINE

HOOLIGAN was not the Top Dog. In fact, Mr. Mormora announced that just this once, there wasn't going to be a Top Dog.

Instead, he wagged his finger at the CITs. "While all of you have made excellent progress, canines that truly have class always stay in place until their CBs release them."

I was disappointed, but Hooligan thumped his tail and smiled his doggie smile. You would have thought he got a trophy! I don't know why, but I had a funny feeling Mrs. Hedges was right. Now that Canine Class was over, he would forget all about being perfect and go back to having too much energy.

When commencement was over, Mr. Mormora waved good-bye and got into his limousine. He had a plane to catch. Oh—and it turned out his safari wasn't in the jungle at all. It was at a wild animal park in Ohio.

Myron and Vin were packing up, and the last dogs

were leaving when Tessa and Nate came over from the spectator area. Nate looked like I felt—dazed—but Tessa had a huge grin on her face. "We did it, Cammie! We solved the case, found the diamonds, and saved President Alfredo-Chin from protesters!"

I held up my hand. "High five."

"You don't seem excited," said Tessa.

"Ms. Kootoor looked awfully sad when Malik put the handcuffs on her," I said.

"Did she say anything?" Tessa asked.

"*Oh*, yeah," I said. "She wanted to know how we figured it out. I told her about Nate going online and finding out about her and Mr. Ghanamamma—that they used to be sweethearts long ago, and he wrote his song 'Lina' about her. And I told her how we saw the mud on her shoes in the clip from Jan and Larry, so we knew she'd been out on the South Lawn when the diamond disappeared."

"But how did she call Hooligan from so far away?" Tessa asked.

"It was the diamond whistle," I said. "The whole thing about her dad giving it to her? She made that up. The truth is the whistle's that special kind that only dogs can hear. Dogs and birds, that is. While she was staying in the White House, she trained Hooligan to come whenever he heard it. For a reward, she used cut-up hot dogs!"

"So that's what was in the cooler," Nate said.

"Oh!" said Tessa. "And when Hooligan went crazy?

And knocked over Mrs. Hedges? Ms. Kootoor must have blown the whistle. We couldn't hear it, but Humdinger and Hooligan did."

"That's what I figured, too," I said. "Then today when I blew the whistle, Hooligan ran for Ms. Kootoor—just the way she'd trained him. He must've expected there'd be hot dogs in the Blueberry Bag. But instead, he found this." The collar had been in my pocket for safe-keeping. Now I pulled it out. With all twelve diamonds, it sparkled in the sunlight. Pretty soon either Charlotte or Malik or the guys in gray suits would take it. But for now? I bent down and buckled it on Hooligan's neck.

He raised his nose in the air. He knew he looked handsome.

"Ms. Kootoor told me one more thing," I said. "She didn't do it for the money. She did it for love."

"*Awwww*," said Tessa.

"*Ewwww*," said Nate.

"But there are still some things I don't understand," said Tessa. "Like—"

Surrounded by aides and Secret Service agents, here came Mom striding toward us through the Rose Garden. "*Mama-a-a-a!*" Tessa called, and the two of us ran to meet her.

"Good news, girls. The security alert has been lifted," Mom said. "So things will be getting back to normal around here."

"What's normal?" I asked.

"Madam President?" said one of her aides. "Excuse

me, Madam President?" said another. "It's very important that we—" "You have a meeting in five minutes, do you realize—" "There's an urgent call from—"

Mom squinched her eyes shut, took a deep breath and held up her hand. Instantly, her aides stopped talking. "Muffins?" she said. "If the weather holds, I am planning a family picnic for noon today on the Oval Office patio. How does that sound?"

Her aides started to protest. Three mayors and an admiral were waiting! And what about the walnut blight in Michigan? Mom raised her hand again. "After lunch," she said.

"Is Granny invited?" Tessa asked.

"Of course," Mom said.

"Then you'd better invite Mr. Bryant," Tessa said.

"Mr. Bryant?" Mom said.

"We'll catch you up," I said.

It stayed sunny, so we got to eat on the patio—sandwiches, cole slaw, drinks, fruit salad and cookies.

Dad raised a glass of cider. "To Cammie and Tessa and Nate!" he said. "Without their hard work and detecting, the wrong person would now be in jail."

We all raised our glasses, but—like me—Mom didn't look that happy. "Are you sad because Ms. Kootoor was your friend?" I asked her.

"You get knocked around a lot when you're in politics," Mom said, "even by your friends. I'm getting pretty tough, but yes, it makes me sad."

"Do you think Ms. Kootoor and Eb Ghanamamma really wanted to help the people?" I asked.

"Possibly," Mom said. "But they sure went about it the wrong way."

"A few more things are bugging me," I said. "Like was the 'heightened security' because of the missing diamonds?"

"And is that what you were spending all your time on, Mama?" Tessa asked.

"I can't tell you everything yet," said Mom. "But generally? Yes and yes. Just like you girls and Granny, my security team realized pretty quickly that there was a connection between El Brillante and the diamonds on Hooligan's collar. So they started looking into it. All the evidence seemed to point to Mr. Mormora, and we knew he was leaving today. With time running out, they decided to arrest him, but they had to keep it quiet. And of course we wanted to wait till after Canine Class."

"What everybody missed was the old romance between Ms. Kootoor and Eb Ghanamamma," Dad explained. "And I, for one, can't believe I didn't put that together. When he sang 'Lina,' there were rumors it was about a famous American model. But I never thought how Lina could be a nickname for Madeline."

"There's more things I don't get," Tessa said. "Like how come only one diamond was missing, and then the whole collar?"

"My guess," Mom said, "is that the thief had to prove to her buyer that the diamonds were what she said they were. She took one, hoping it wouldn't be missed."

"And what about the Canine Cookies Hooligan found?" I asked.

Granny answered that one. "I think Ms. Kootoor took that box from the outdoor shed, then dropped cookies here and there. She was in the kitchen and heard you talking Saturday morning, remember? She must have thought if she dropped the cookies, you'd suspect Mr. Mormora instead of her."

"Ahem?" One of Mom's aides had come across the lawn. He was holding a phone. You could tell he was embarrassed to interrupt.

Mom reached for the phone. "What is it?"

"Oh—it's not for you, ma'am. It's for the children." He held the phone out. "It's on speaker."

A voice said, "Hello? Am I speaking to the children of the president of the United States?"

"Hey, President Alfredo-Chin!" said Tessa. "How ya doin'?"

"Very well, thank you," answered the voice. "Although, we have had a difficult time here in our nation. Now, I am confident things will be better. So I call to thank you for your efforts."

"You're welcome!" said Tessa, Nate and I.

"And when the time is right," President Alfredo-Chin went on, "I am planning to bring my dog, Empress Pu-Chi, to your country for a visit. I know how very much she would enjoy meeting your handsome dog, Hooligan."

Nate, Tessa and I looked at each other. After what

Mr. Mormora had said, we didn't expect we'd like the empress very much. But then we shrugged and said in a chorus *"Sure!"* It didn't really matter, did it? What were the chances the president of a nearby nation would ever bring his dog to Washington, D.C.?

AFTERWORD

THE South Lawn of the White House is the backyard for the president's family.

And what a great backyard!

Together with the smaller North Lawn in front, it takes up eighteen acres—the size of a dozen football fields.

The South Lawn includes plenty of beautiful trees, some of them dedicated by presidents long ago. The oldest still standing are two southern magnolias next to the South Portico (the White House backdoor), planted in 1830 by President Andrew Jackson in memory of his wife, Rachel. They usually flower in June.

And speaking of flowers, thousands bloom on the grounds every year. In the spring, more than forty thousand grape hyacinths and oxford tulips bloom around the two fountains alone. John Quincy Adams, president from 1825 to 1829, planted the first gardens and wrote in his diary about two acres covered with at least a thousand "forest and fruit-trees, shrubs, hedges, esculent (edible) vegetables, kitchen and medicinal herbs, hot-house plants, flowers, and weeds."

Today, a twenty-person National Park Service crew takes care of the White House grounds, and it's a lot of work. Just mowing the lawn takes eight hours in warm weather, and has to be done twice a week. In charge of it all is the superintendent, who has an office on the ground floor of the White House. Most days he gets to work at six a.m.

And while fictional White House pooch Hooligan has Mr. Bryant to watch over him, real White House pets are often looked after by the White House gardeners and groundskeepers.

Of course, the South Lawn isn't just for pets and plants. Like any backyard, it's also for fun!

In the 1920s President Herbert Hoover often invited his advisers to have breakfast and play a game of "Hoover Ball" on the lawn for exercise. Many presidents have enjoyed golf, and near the president's office in the West Wing is a putting green. The first one was installed in 1954, and the squirrels liked it as much as President Dwight Eisenhower did. He blamed the critters on the president before him, Harry Truman, who enjoyed feeding them by hand.

Along with the putting green, there is a swimming pool, tennis courts and horseshoe pitch—all put in by different presidents to suit their favorite pastimes. In 2009, for example, President Barack Obama had the lines on one tennis court repainted so it could also be used for full-court basketball.

Of course it's not just grown-ups who get to play in the big backyard. President Franklin D. Roosevelt's grandchildren, Sistie and Buzz, had a slide, jungle gym and swing on the east side of the lawn. The Kennedy children had playground sets, as do Sasha and Malia Obama. President Jimmy Carter's daughter, Amy, had her own treehouse.

Also for children is a special garden installed in 1968 by President Lyndon Johnson and his wife. Tucked away near the tennis courts, it features a goldfish pond, child-size outdoor furniture and an apple tree for climbing. Bronze castings of the footprints and handprints of presidents' children and grandchildren are embedded in the paving stones of the garden's path.

The Children's Garden is one of three on the South Lawn. The other two—the Rose Garden and the Jacqueline Kennedy Garden, which is sometimes called the First Ladies Garden—are larger. Where today's Rose Garden is located, stables and greenhouses once stood. You can see this garden on TV quite a lot because it's used for news conferences and other events like the president's annual pardoning of the turkey at Thanksgiving. Visitors on White House tours get to see Mrs. Kennedy's garden through the windows as they walk along the East Wing colonnade.

The White House is often called "the people's house," and presidents say it belongs to all Americans. Still, the president would have a hard time getting any work done if all Americans felt free to drop by anytime. When President Jackson was sworn into office in 1829, he had an open house to celebrate—and twenty thousand guests showed up! They made such a mess that no one knew what to do, until the president ordered orange punch to be served from washtubs on the lawn. When the guests went out to get a drink, the staff closed the doors on them.

To visit the president's backyard today, you have to make special arrangements or else have an invitation. One tradition that brings a lot of visitors is the annual Easter Egg Roll on the Monday after the holiday. Another tradition was started by President George W. Bush, who once owned a baseball team. Every year, he invited Little League T-ball players for a game on the lawn. When First Lady Michelle Obama oversaw the planting of a kitchen garden in 2009, she invited Washington, D.C., schoolchildren to help her.

If you'd like to see the White House grounds for yourself, visit www.WhiteHouse.gov. There you will find information about garden tours, entering the lottery for tickets to the Easter Egg Roll. Even if you're not lucky enough to get an invitation to the president's backyard, you can get a view from E Street in Washington, D.C.